REO

Writer: Warren Ellis
Artist: Cully Hamner
Colors: David Self
Letters: John Costanza

Covers by Cully Hamner

Ben Abernathy	Editors–Original Series
John Layman	
Kristy Quinn	Assistant Editor–Original Series
Kristy Quinn	Editor
Ed Roeder	Art Director
Diane Nelson	President
Dan DiDio and Jim Lee	Co-Publishers
Geoff Johns	Chief Creative Officer
John Rood	Executive Vice President–Sales, Marketing and Business Development
Patrick Caldon	Executive Vice President–Finance and Administration
Amy Genkins	Senior VP–Business and Legal Affairs
Steve Rotterdam	Senior VP–Sales and Marketing
John Cunningham	VP–Marketing
Terri Cunningham	VP–Managing Editor
Alison Gill	VP–Manufacturing
David Hyde	VP–Publicity
Hank Kanalz	VP–General Manager, WildStorm
Sue Pohja	VP–Book Trade Sales
Alysse Soll	VP–Advertising and Custom Publishing
Bob Wayne	VP–Sales
Mark Chiarello	Art Director

RED published by WildStorm Productions. 888 Prospect St. #240, La Jolla, CA 92037. Cover, scriptbook, sketches and compilation © 2009 Warren Ellis and Cully Hamner. All Rights Reserved. RED is ™ Warren Ellis and Cully Hamner. WildStorm and logo are trademarks of DC Comics. Originally published in single magazine form as RED #1-3, © 2003 Warren Ellis and Cully Hamner. The stories, characters, and incidents mentioned in this magazine are entirely fictional. Printed on recyclable paper. WildStorm does not read or accept unsolicited submissions of ideas, stories or artwork. Printed by Quad/Graphics, Dubuque, IA, USA. 10/13/10. Third printing.

ISBN: 978-1-4012-2346-5   DC Comics, a Warner Bros. Entertainment Company.

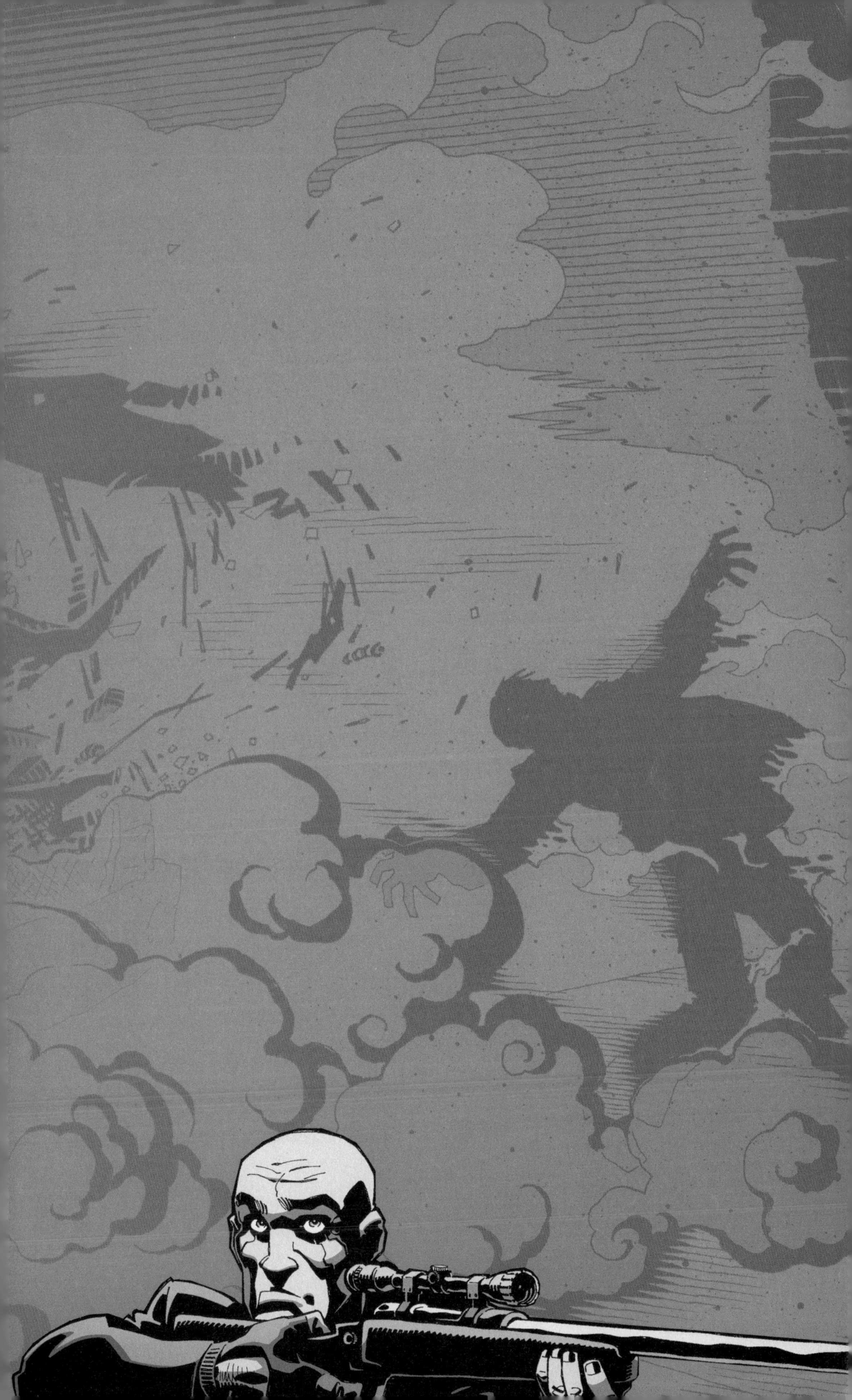

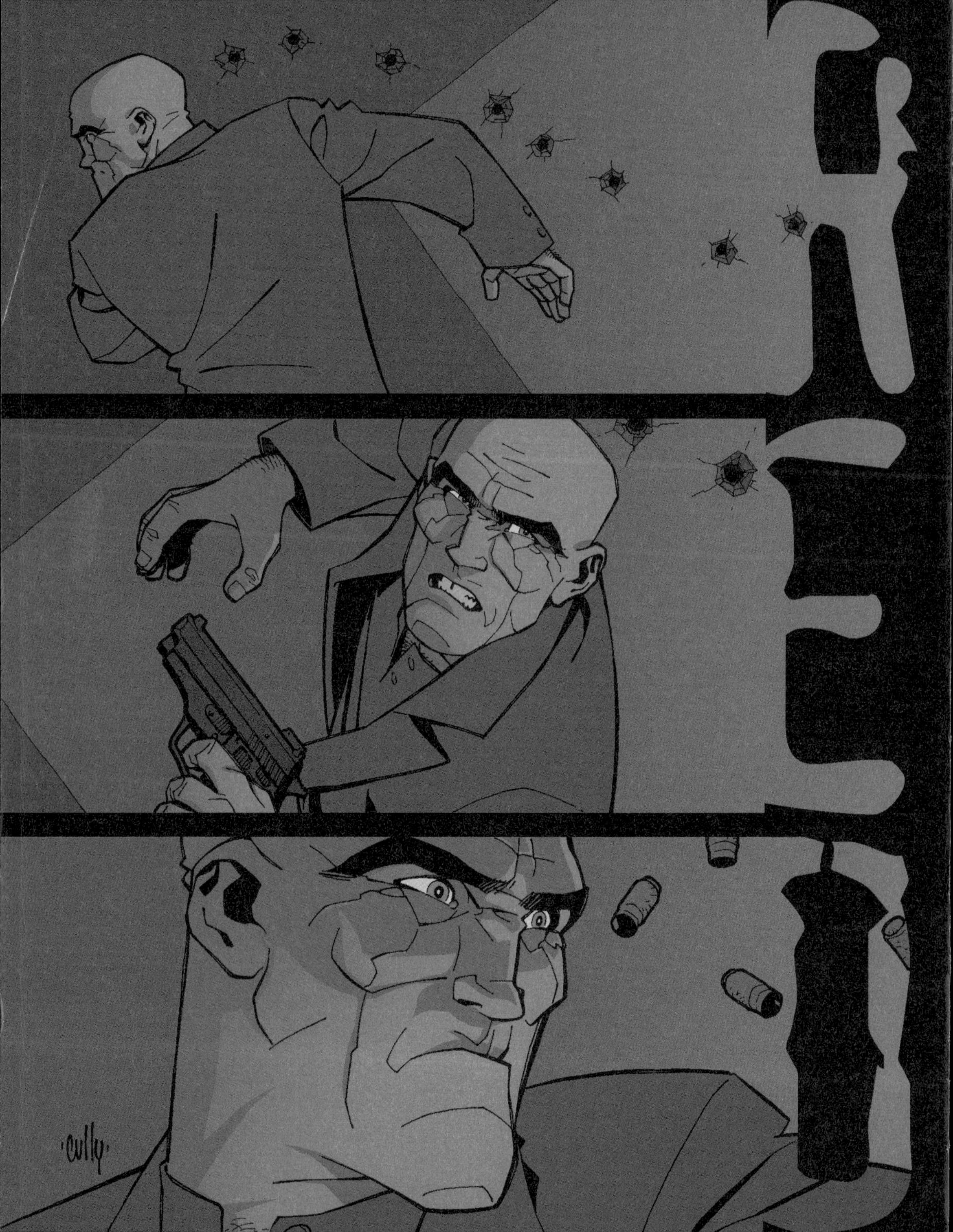
RED

Chapter One

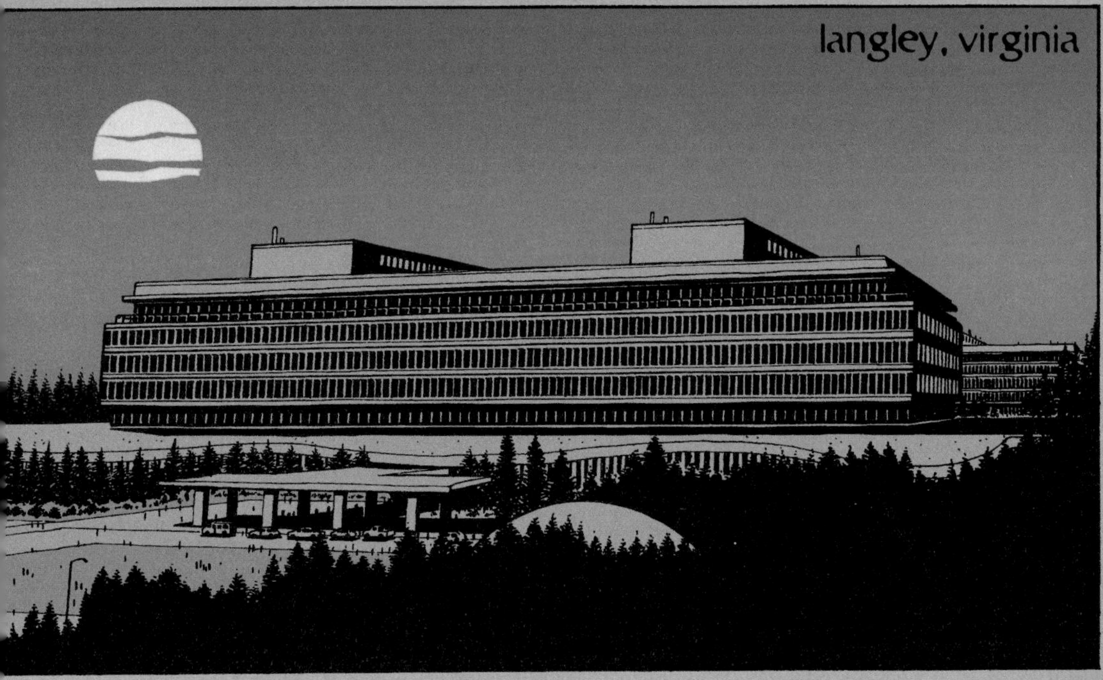
langley, virginia

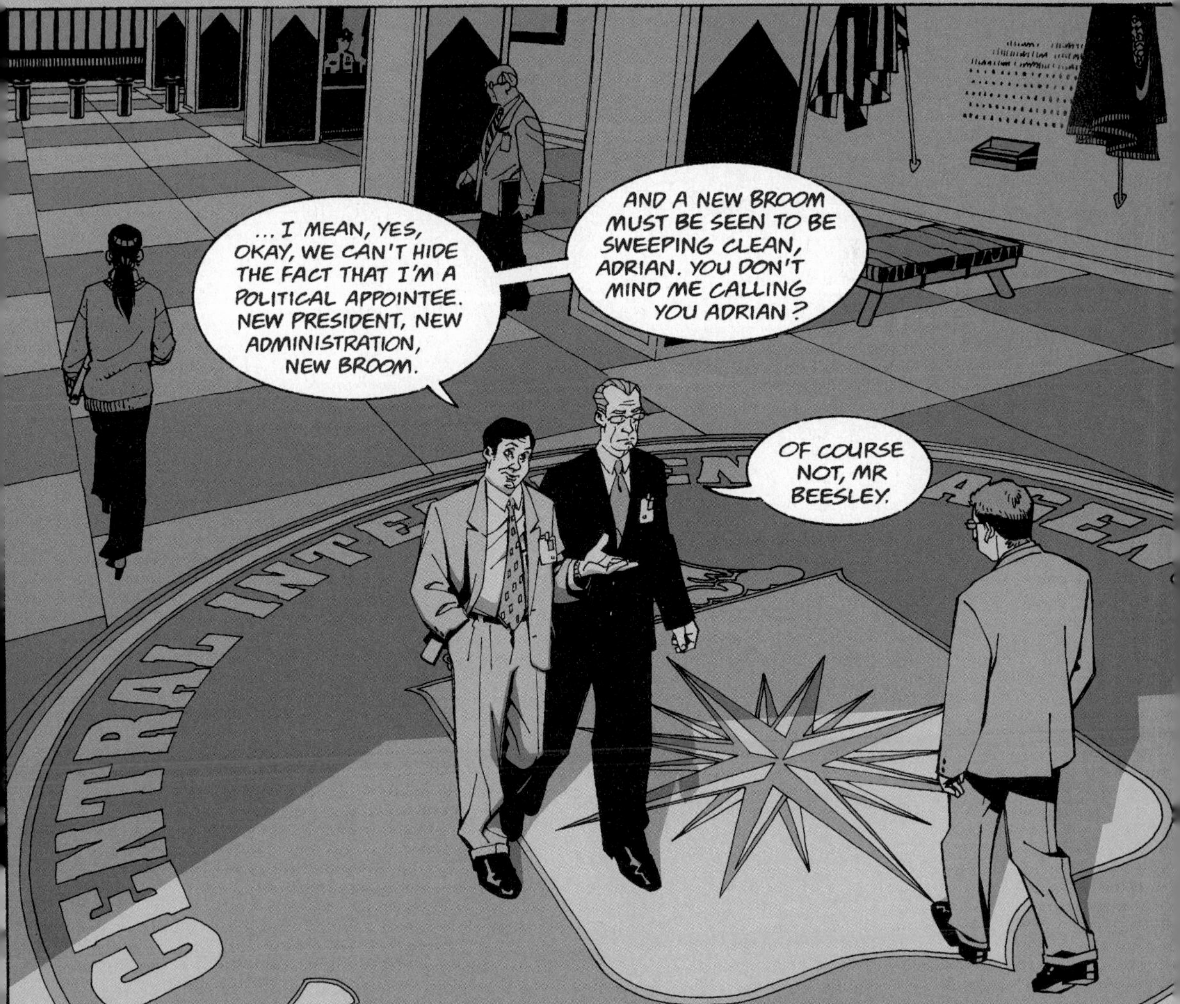
... I MEAN, YES, OKAY, WE CAN'T HIDE THE FACT THAT I'M A POLITICAL APPOINTEE. NEW PRESIDENT, NEW ADMINISTRATION, NEW BROOM.
AND A NEW BROOM MUST BE SEEN TO BE SWEEPING CLEAN, ADRIAN. YOU DON'T MIND ME CALLING YOU ADRIAN?
OF COURSE NOT, MR BEESLEY.
CENTRAL INTELLIGENCE AGENCY

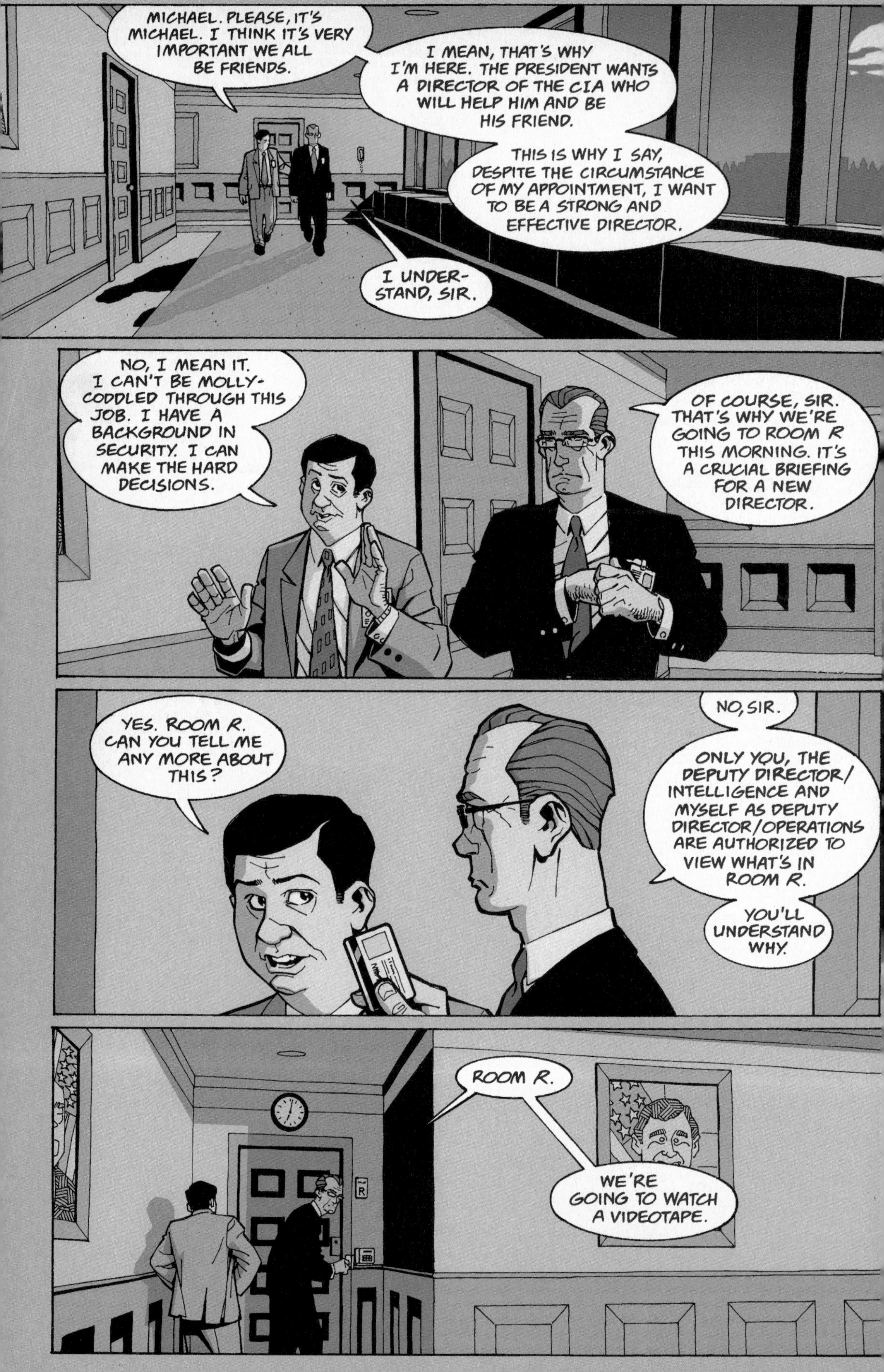
MICHAEL. PLEASE, IT'S MICHAEL. I THINK IT'S VERY IMPORTANT WE ALL BE FRIENDS.
I MEAN, THAT'S WHY I'M HERE. THE PRESIDENT WANTS A DIRECTOR OF THE CIA WHO WILL HELP HIM AND BE HIS FRIEND.
THIS IS WHY I SAY, DESPITE THE CIRCUMSTANCE OF MY APPOINTMENT, I WANT TO BE A STRONG AND EFFECTIVE DIRECTOR.
I UNDER-STAND, SIR.
NO, I MEAN IT. I CAN'T BE MOLLY-CODDLED THROUGH THIS JOB. I HAVE A BACKGROUND IN SECURITY. I CAN MAKE THE HARD DECISIONS.
OF COURSE, SIR. THAT'S WHY WE'RE GOING TO ROOM R THIS MORNING. IT'S A CRUCIAL BRIEFING FOR A NEW DIRECTOR.
YES. ROOM R. CAN YOU TELL ME ANY MORE ABOUT THIS?
NO, SIR.
ONLY YOU, THE DEPUTY DIRECTOR/INTELLIGENCE AND MYSELF AS DEPUTY DIRECTOR/OPERATIONS ARE AUTHORIZED TO VIEW WHAT'S IN ROOM R.
YOU'LL UNDERSTAND WHY.
ROOM R.
WE'RE GOING TO WATCH A VIDEOTAPE.
R

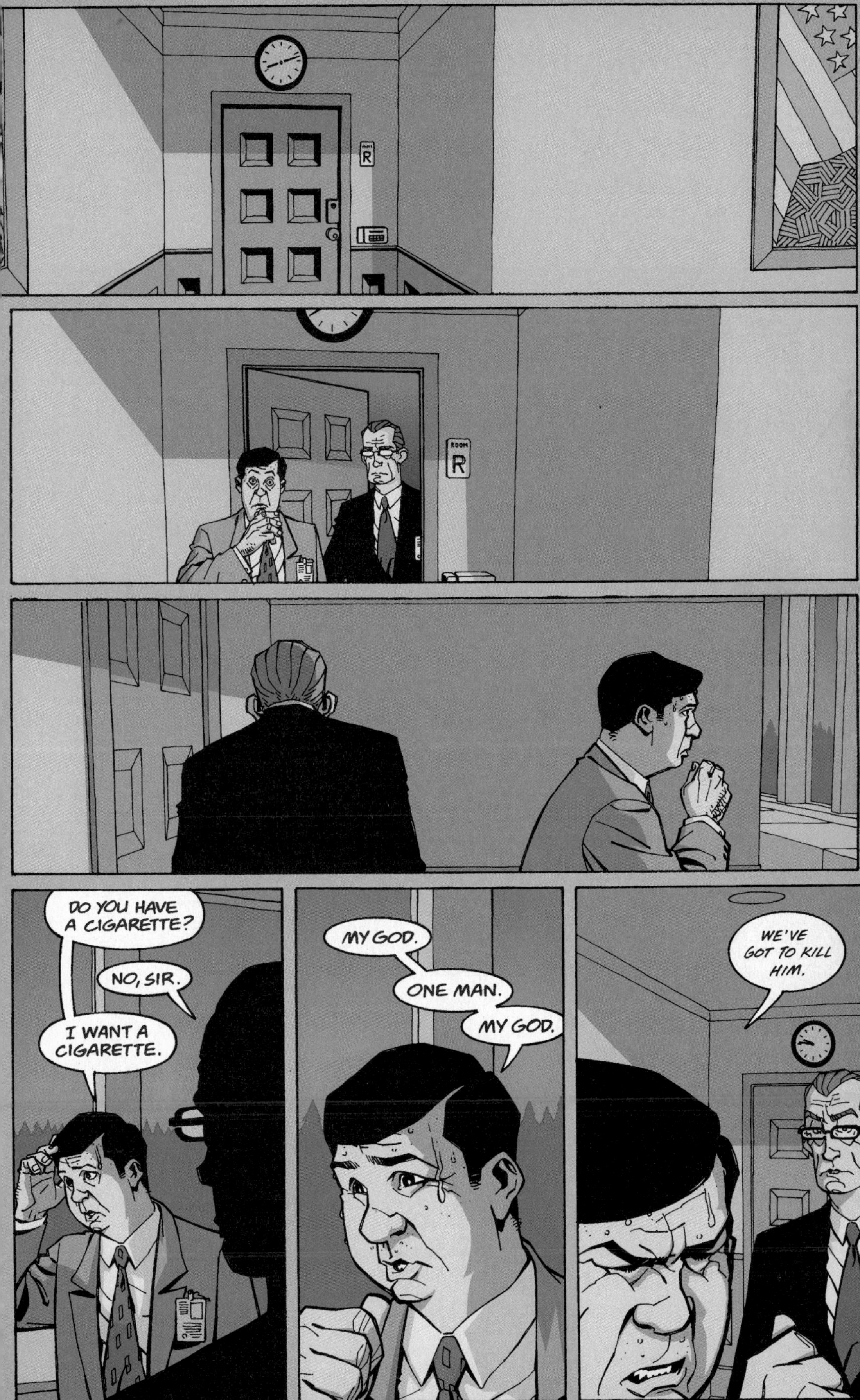

DO YOU HAVE A CIGARETTE?
NO, SIR.
I WANT A CIGARETTE.
MY GOD.
ONE MAN.
MY GOD.
WE'VE GOT TO KILL HIM.

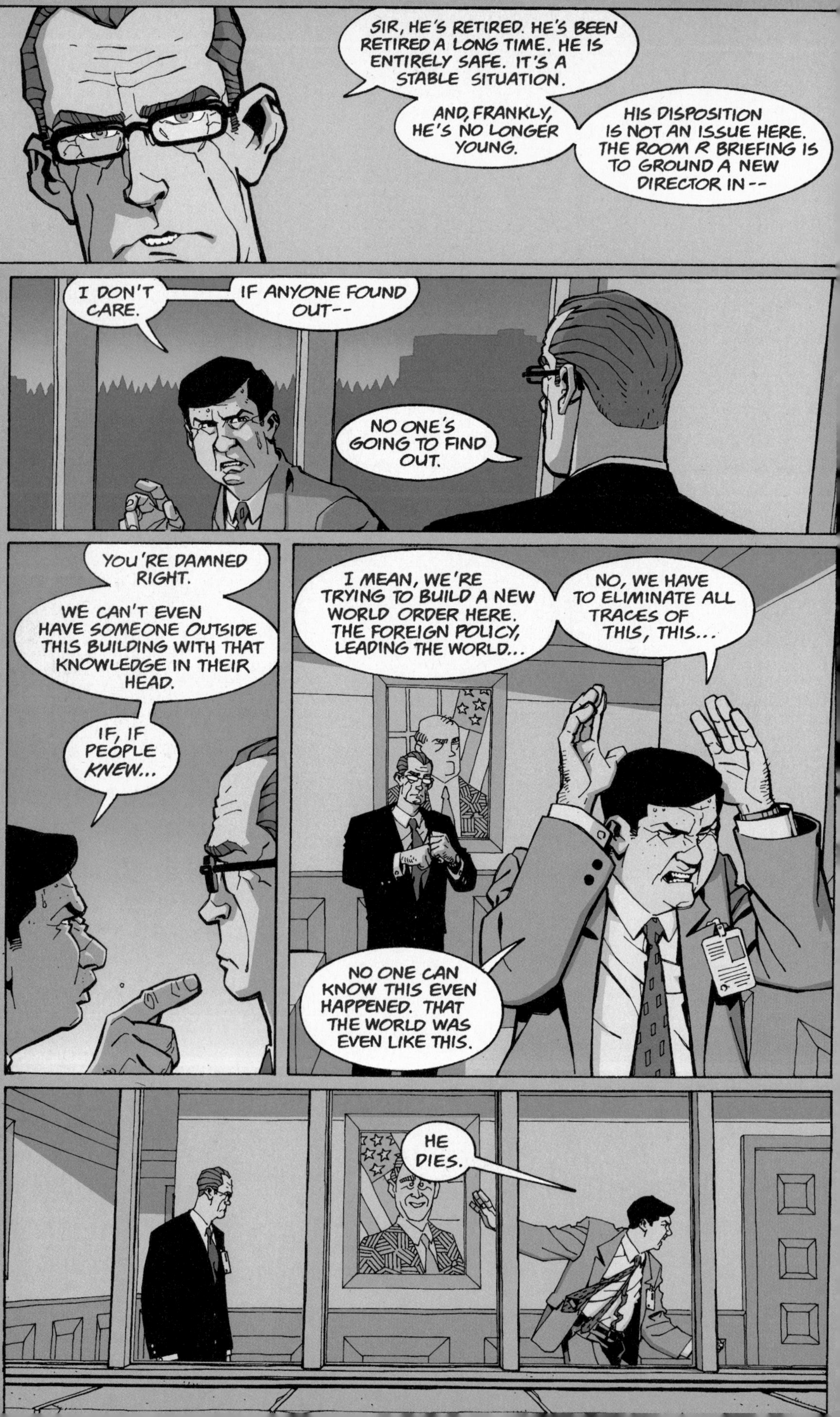
SIR, HE'S RETIRED. HE'S BEEN RETIRED A LONG TIME. HE IS ENTIRELY SAFE. IT'S A STABLE SITUATION.
AND, FRANKLY, HE'S NO LONGER YOUNG.
HIS DISPOSITION IS NOT AN ISSUE HERE. THE ROOM R BRIEFING IS TO GROUND A NEW DIRECTOR IN--
I DON'T CARE.
IF ANYONE FOUND OUT--
NO ONE'S GOING TO FIND OUT.
YOU'RE DAMNED RIGHT.
WE CAN'T EVEN HAVE SOMEONE OUTSIDE THIS BUILDING WITH THAT KNOWLEDGE IN THEIR HEAD.
IF, IF PEOPLE KNEW...
I MEAN, WE'RE TRYING TO BUILD A NEW WORLD ORDER HERE. THE FOREIGN POLICY, LEADING THE WORLD...
NO, WE HAVE TO ELIMINATE ALL TRACES OF THIS, THIS...
NO ONE CAN KNOW THIS EVEN HAPPENED. THAT THE WORLD WAS EVEN LIKE THIS.
HE DIES.

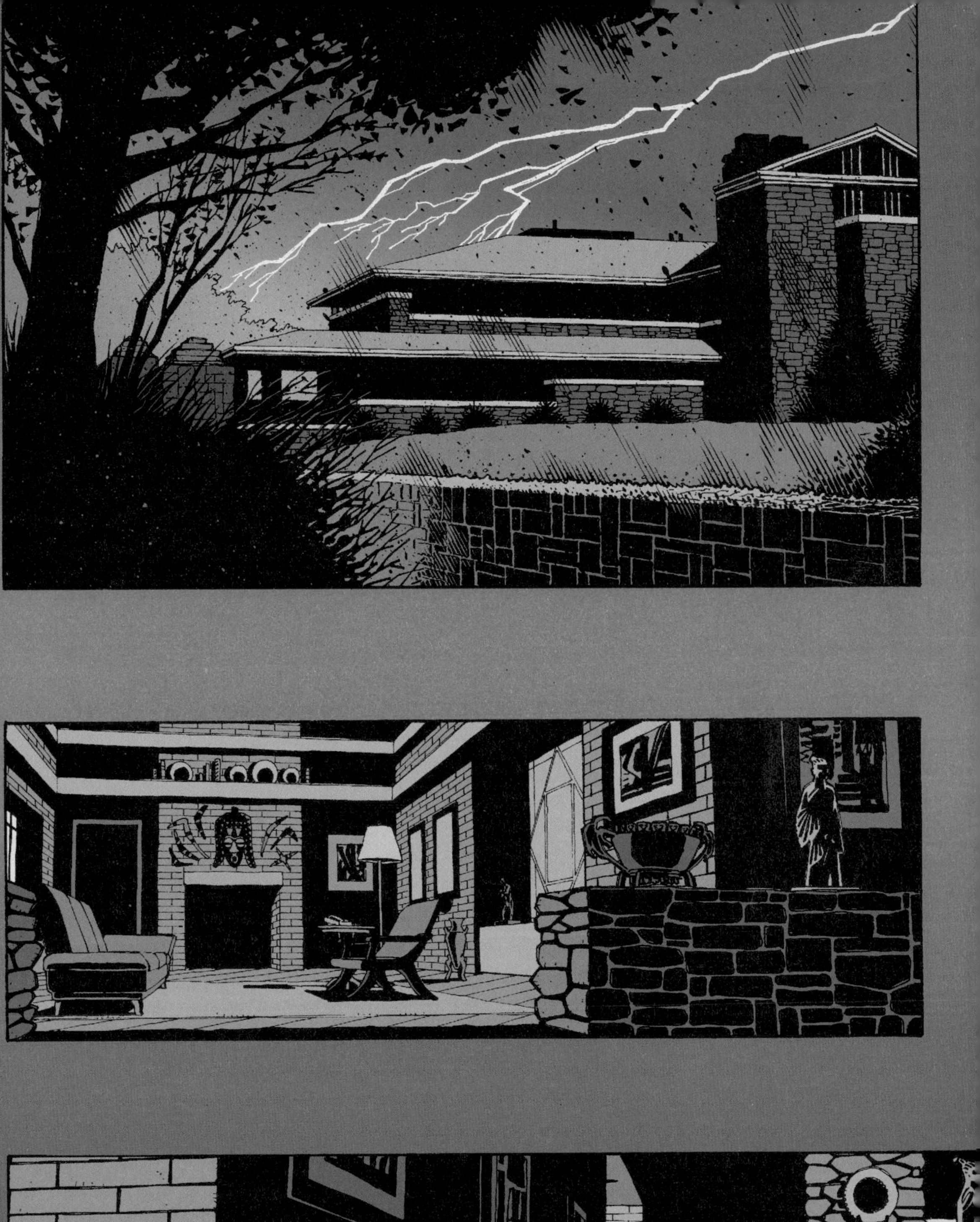

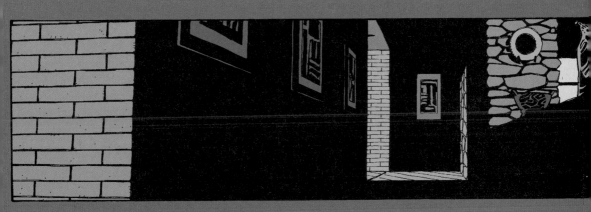

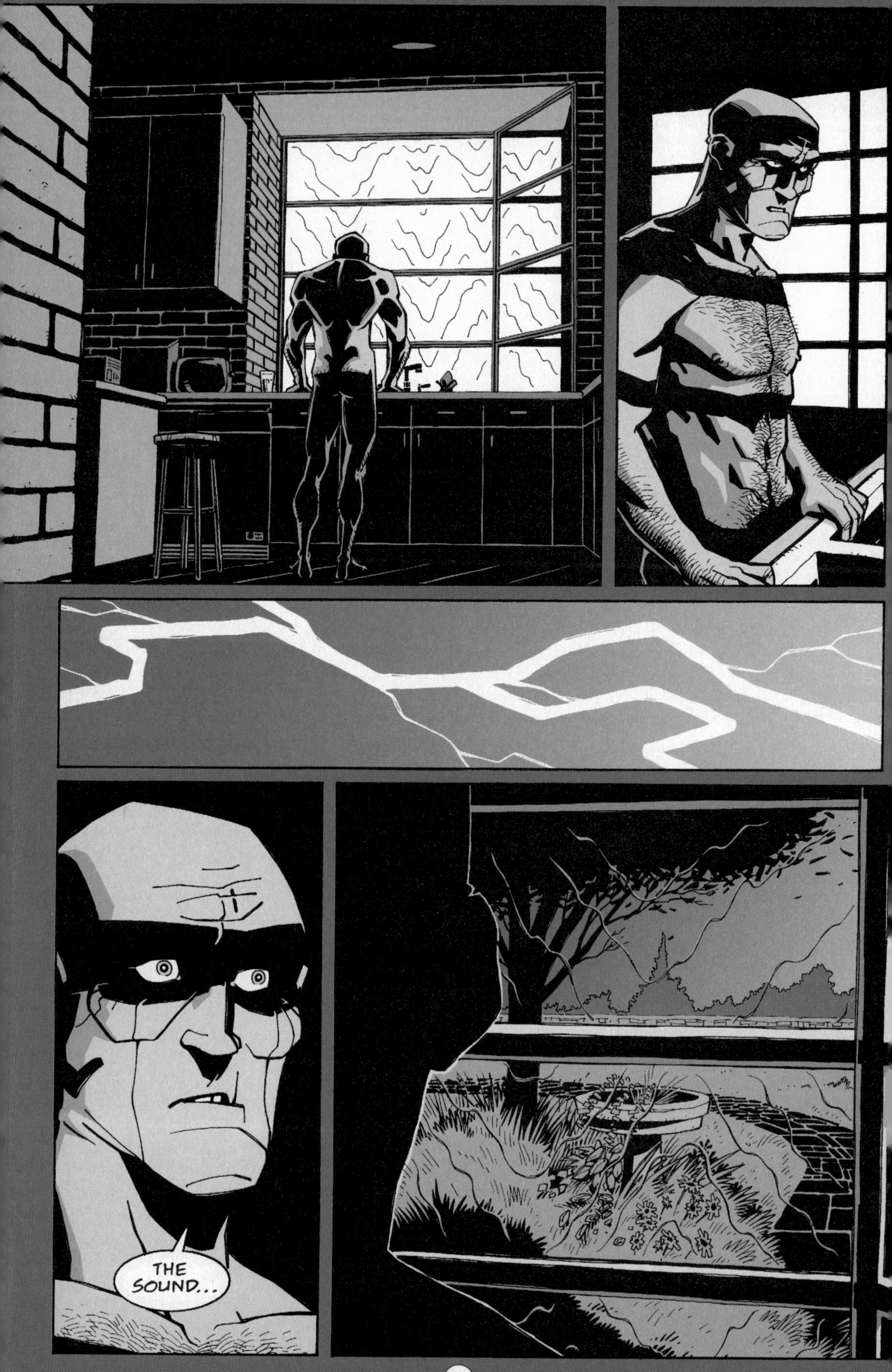
THE SOUND...

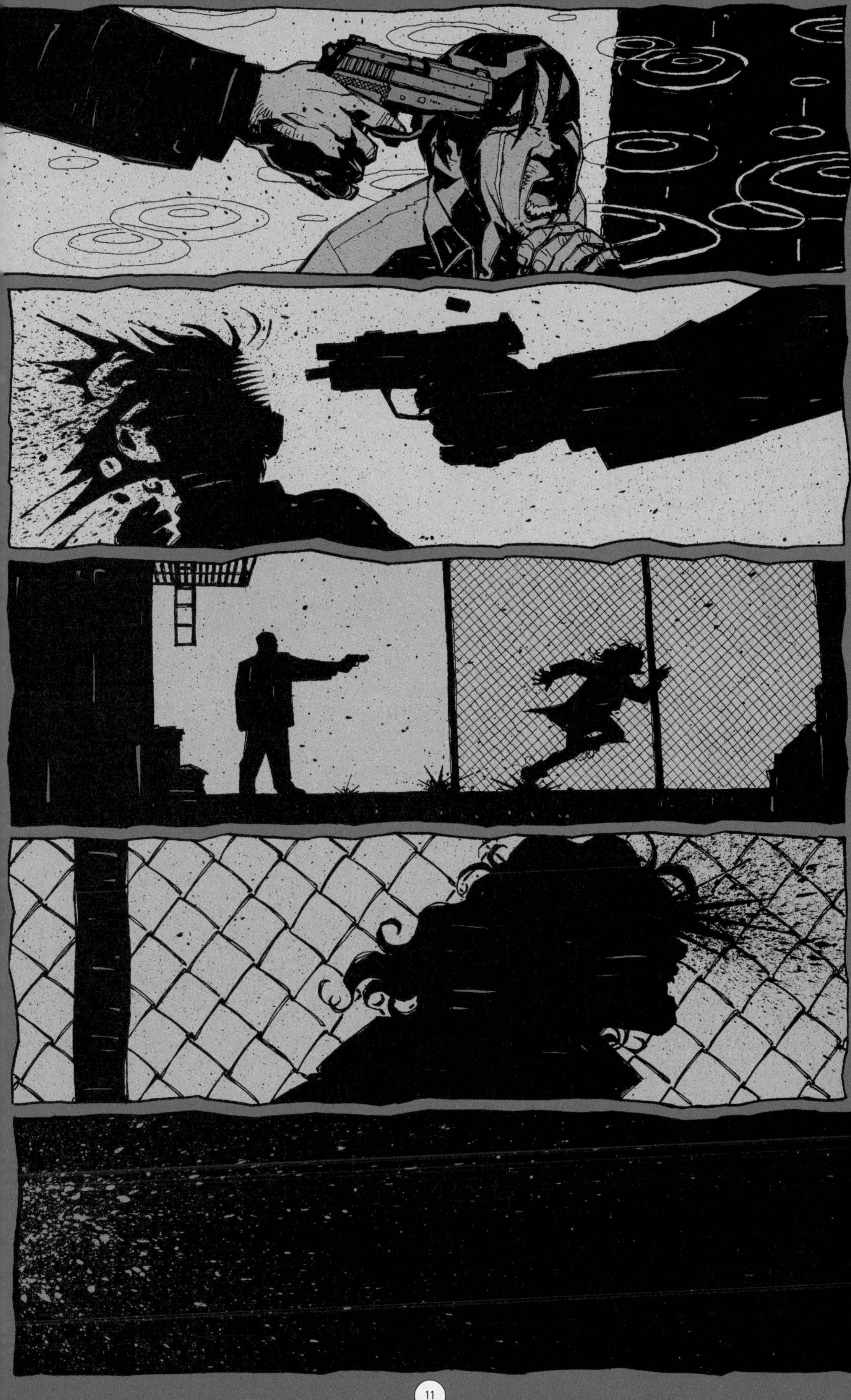

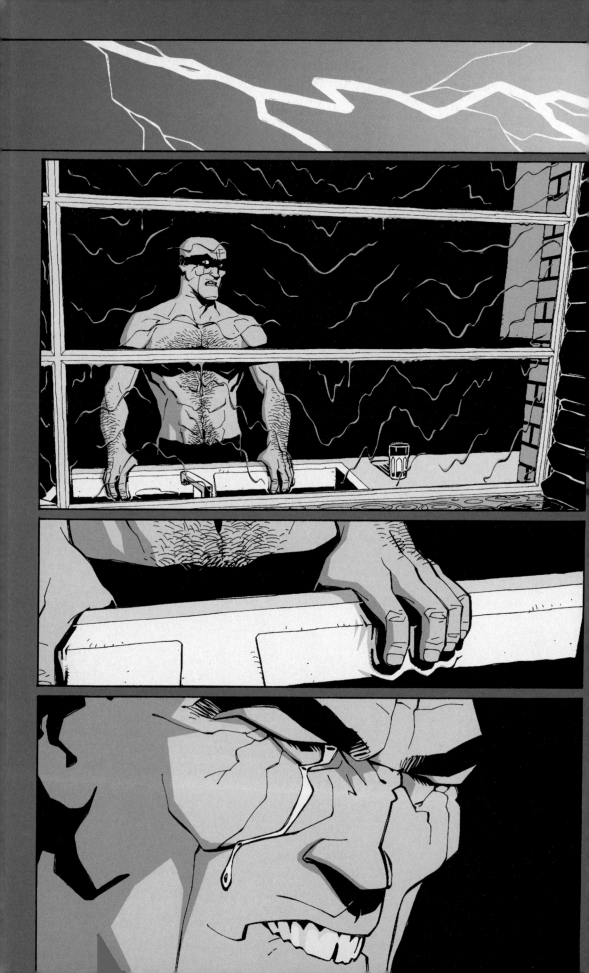

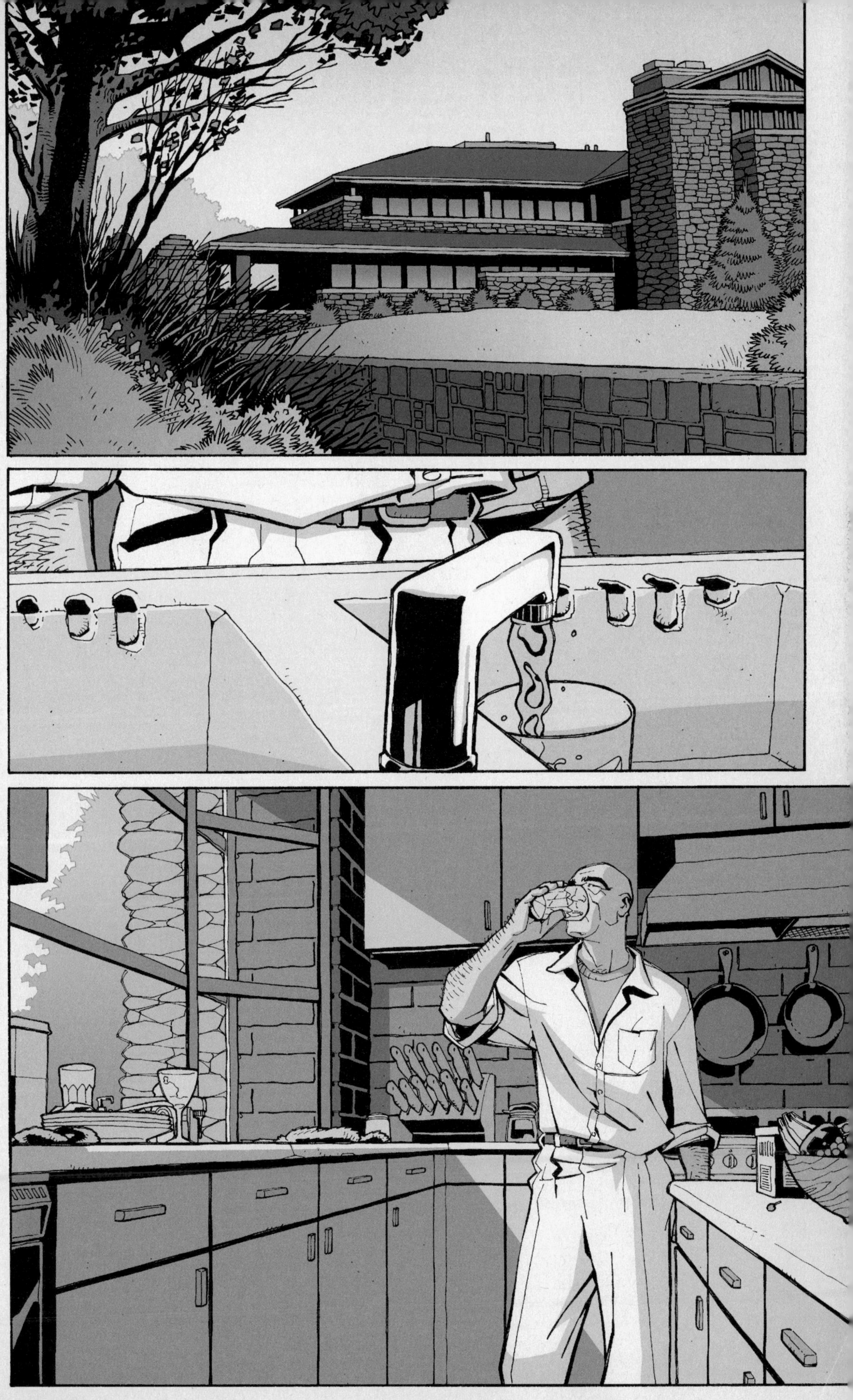

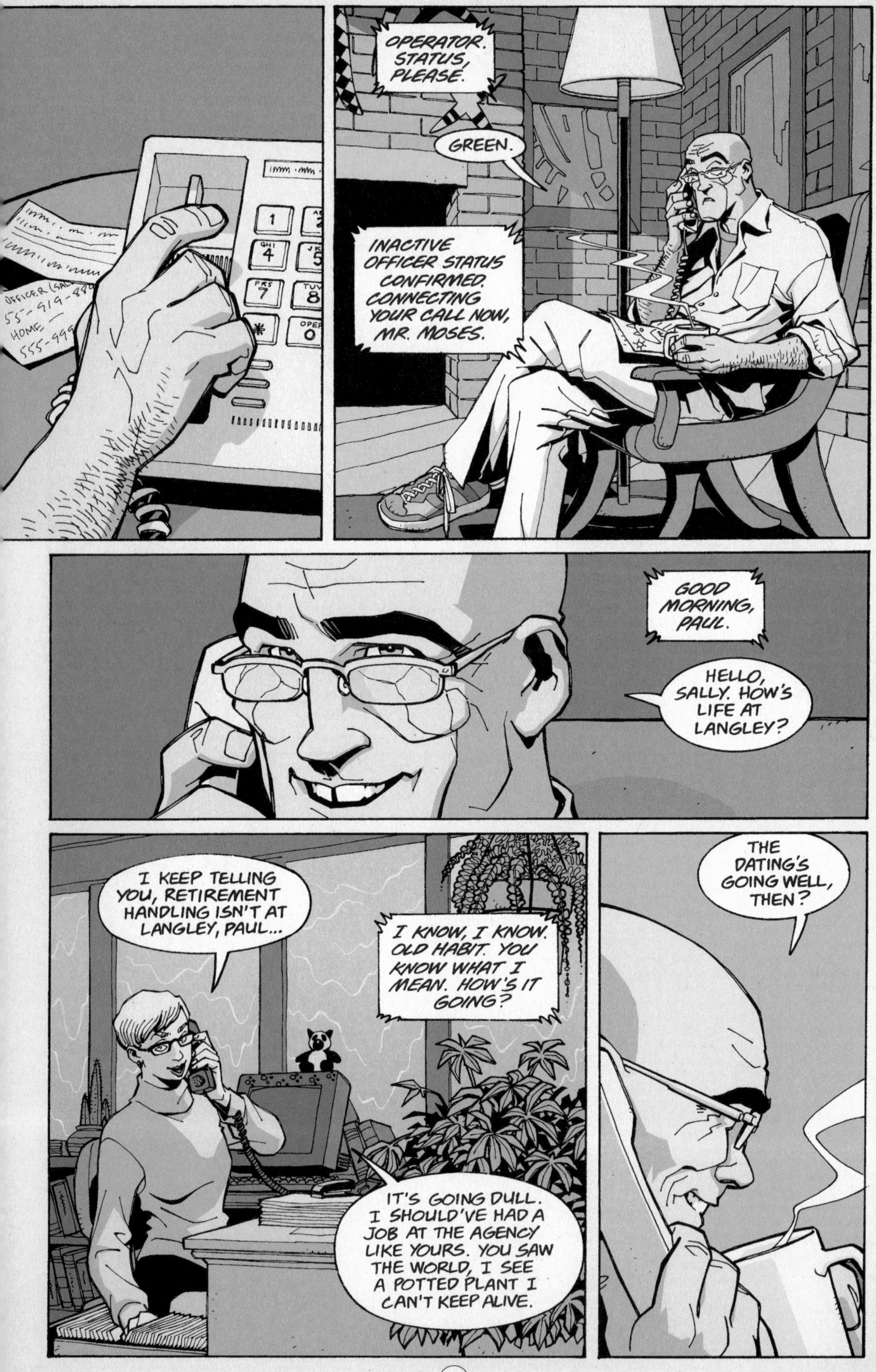
OFFICER (SAL
55-919-88
HOME —
555-999
OPERATOR. STATUS, PLEASE.
GREEN.
INACTIVE OFFICER STATUS CONFIRMED. CONNECTING YOUR CALL NOW, MR. MOSES.
GOOD MORNING, PAUL.
HELLO, SALLY. HOW'S LIFE AT LANGLEY?
I KEEP TELLING YOU, RETIREMENT HANDLING ISN'T AT LANGLEY, PAUL...
I KNOW, I KNOW. OLD HABIT. YOU KNOW WHAT I MEAN. HOW'S IT GOING?
IT'S GOING DULL. I SHOULD'VE HAD A JOB AT THE AGENCY LIKE YOURS. YOU SAW THE WORLD, I SEE A POTTED PLANT I CAN'T KEEP ALIVE.
THE DATING'S GOING WELL, THEN?

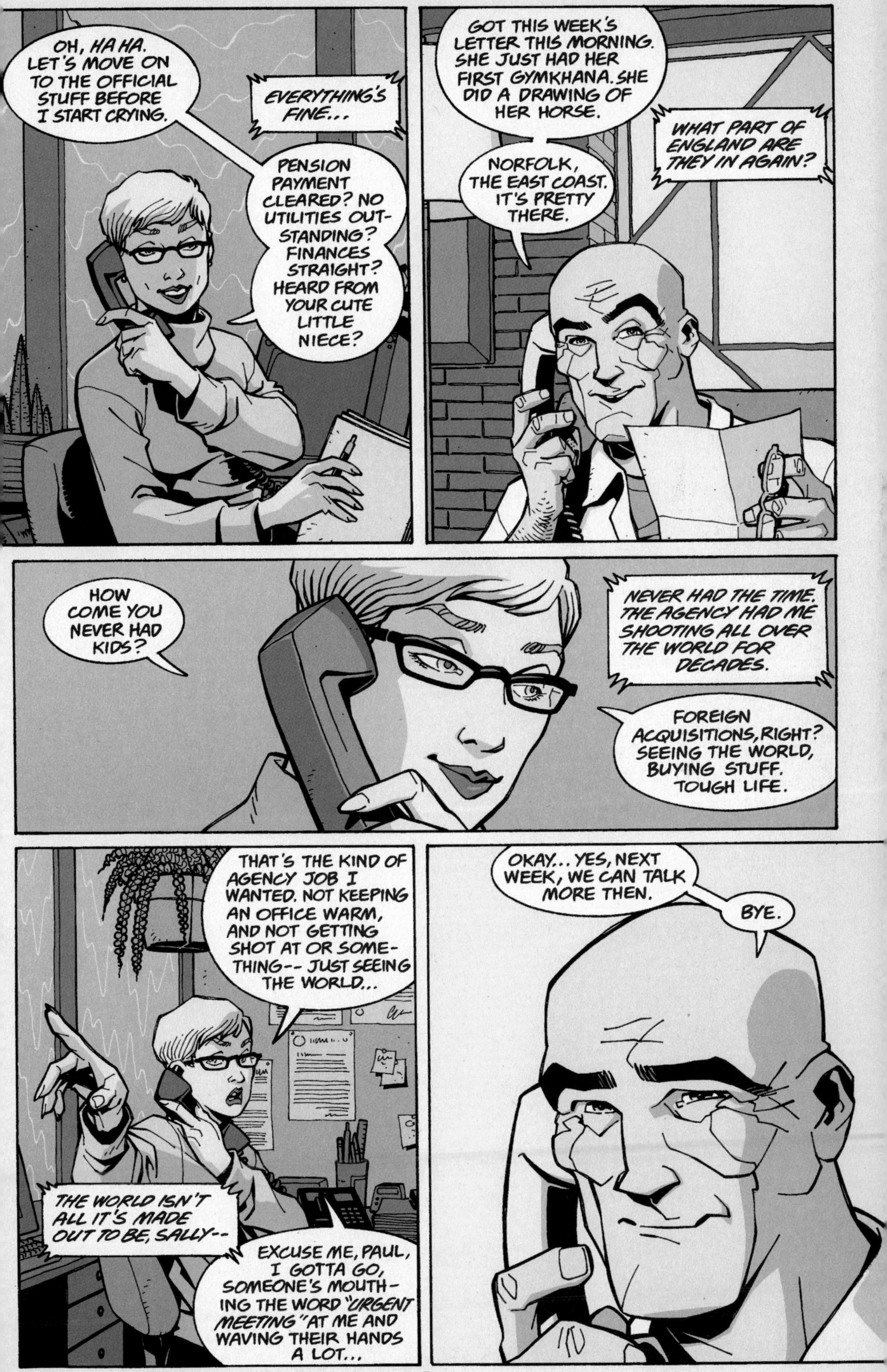
OH, HA HA. LET'S MOVE ON TO THE OFFICIAL STUFF BEFORE I START CRYING.
EVERYTHING'S FINE...
PENSION PAYMENT CLEARED? NO UTILITIES OUT-STANDING? FINANCES STRAIGHT? HEARD FROM YOUR CUTE LITTLE NIECE?
GOT THIS WEEK'S LETTER THIS MORNING. SHE JUST HAD HER FIRST GYMKHANA. SHE DID A DRAWING OF HER HORSE.
WHAT PART OF ENGLAND ARE THEY IN AGAIN?
NORFOLK, THE EAST COAST. IT'S PRETTY THERE.
HOW COME YOU NEVER HAD KIDS?
NEVER HAD THE TIME. THE AGENCY HAD ME SHOOTING ALL OVER THE WORLD FOR DECADES.
FOREIGN ACQUISITIONS, RIGHT? SEEING THE WORLD, BUYING STUFF. TOUGH LIFE.
THAT'S THE KIND OF AGENCY JOB I WANTED. NOT KEEPING AN OFFICE WARM, AND NOT GETTING SHOT AT OR SOME-THING-- JUST SEEING THE WORLD...
THE WORLD ISN'T ALL IT'S MADE OUT TO BE, SALLY--
EXCUSE ME, PAUL, I GOTTA GO, SOMEONE'S MOUTH-ING THE WORD "URGENT MEETING" AT ME AND WAVING THEIR HANDS A LOT...
OKAY... YES, NEXT WEEK, WE CAN TALK MORE THEN.
BYE.

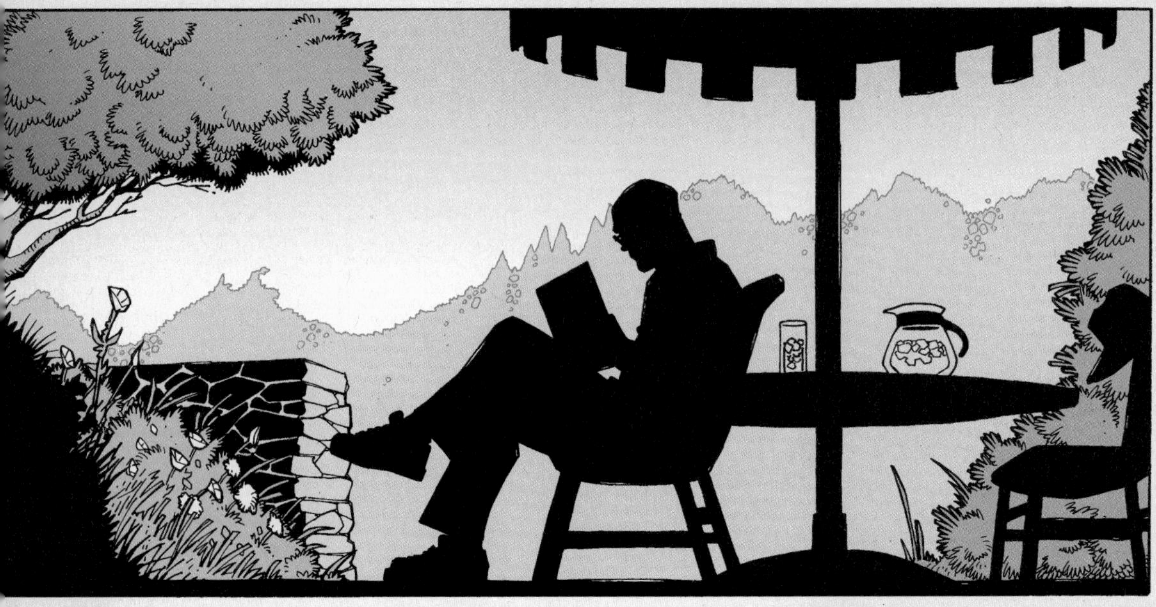

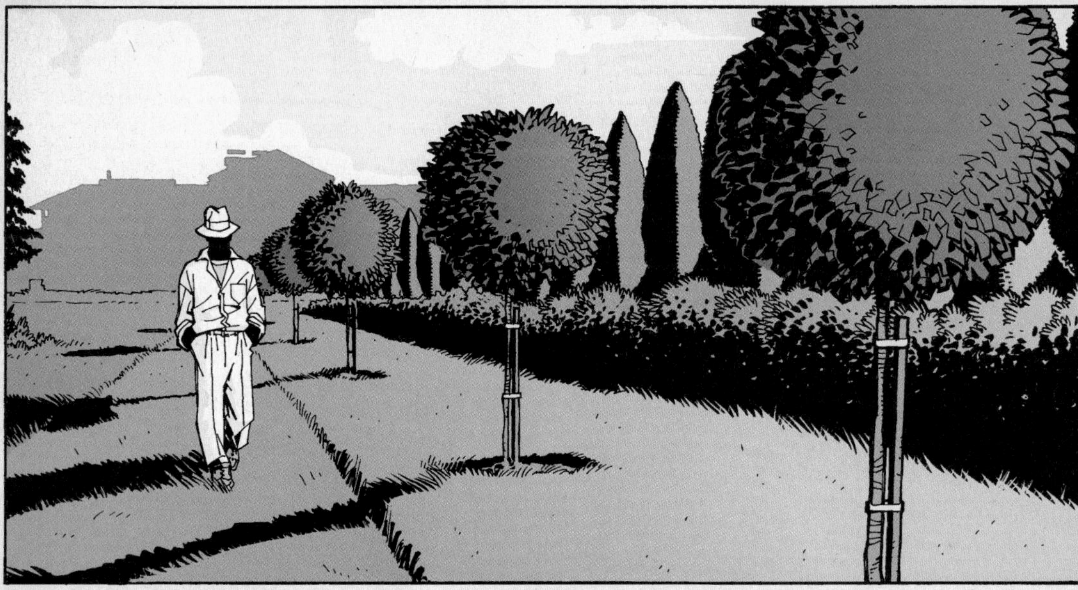

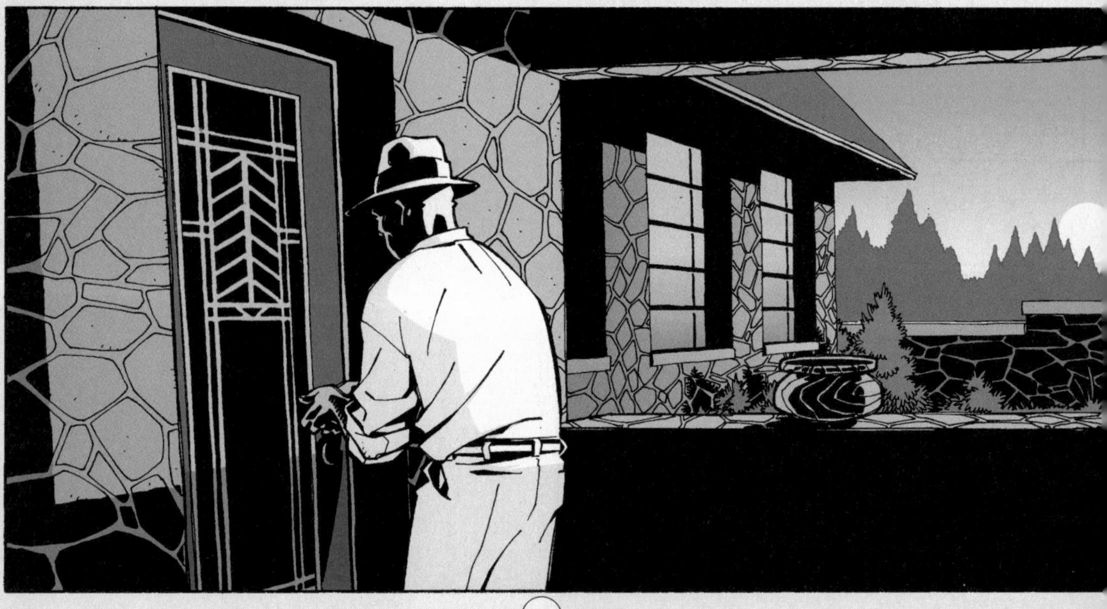

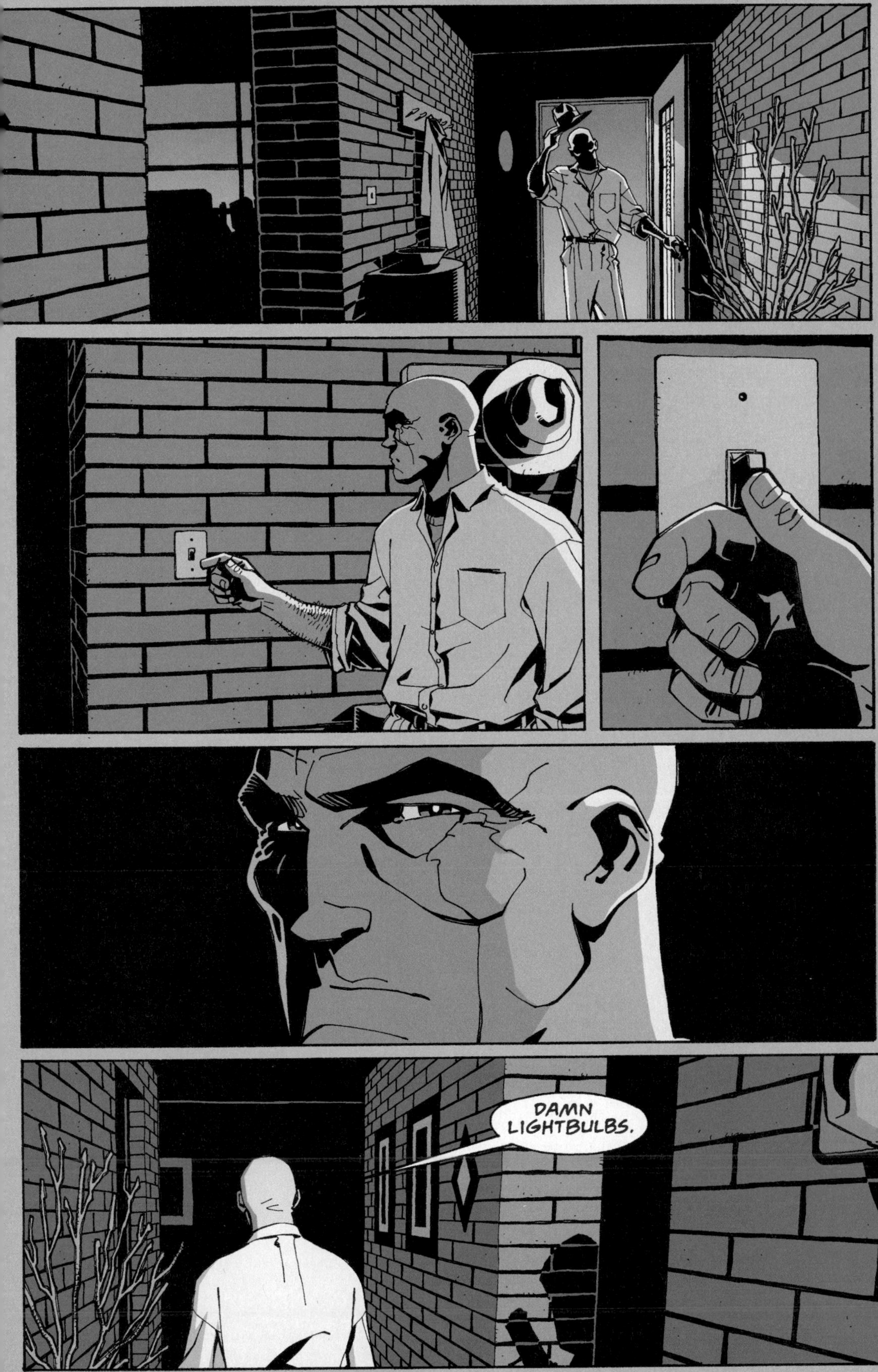
DAMN LIGHTBULBS.

GOT TO GET AN ELECTRICIAN IN HERE, CHECK OUT THE

WIRING.

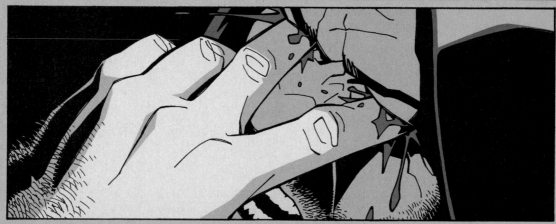

EEEEEEEEEEE

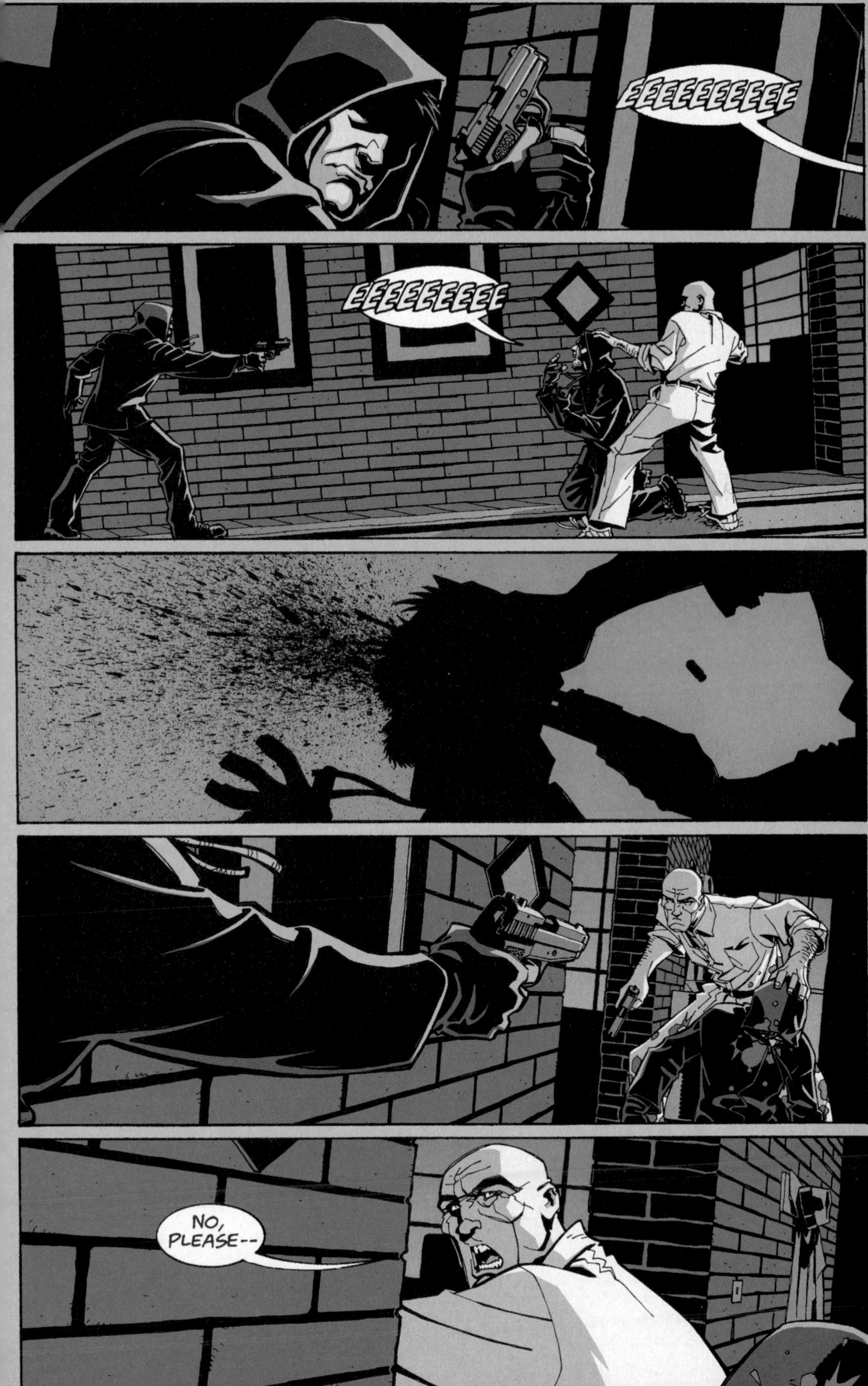
EEEEEEEEEEE
EEEEEEEEEE
NO, PLEASE--

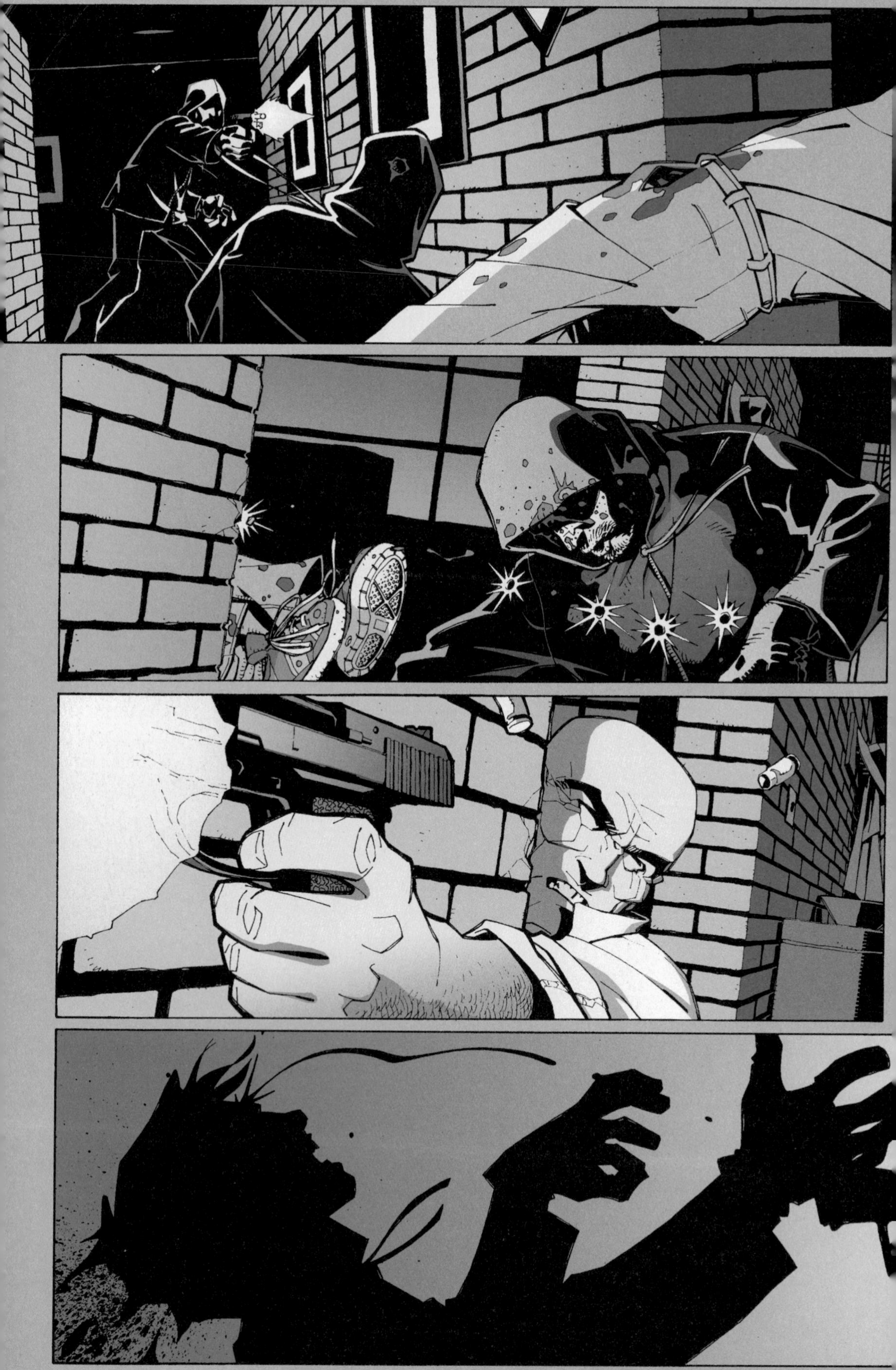

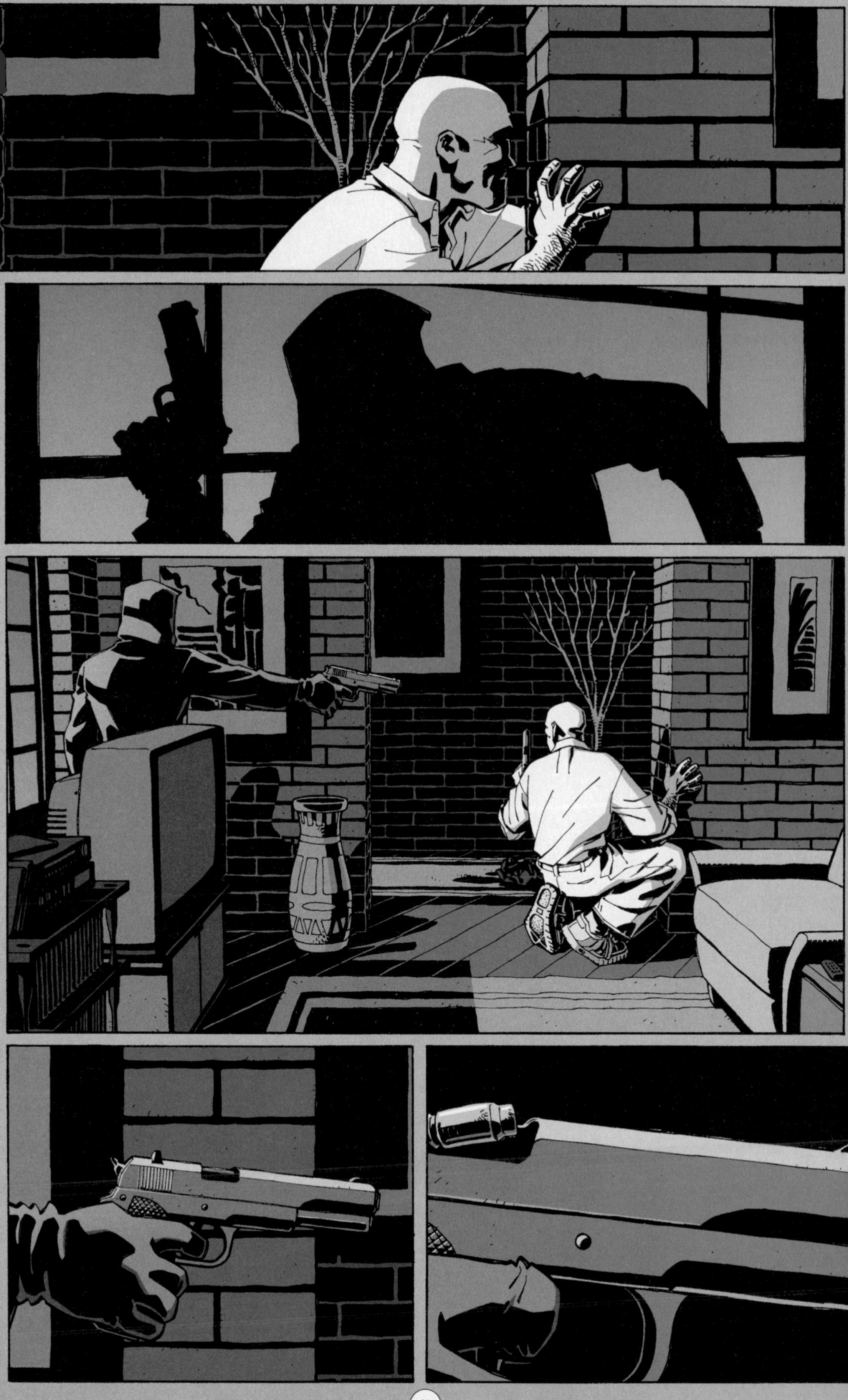

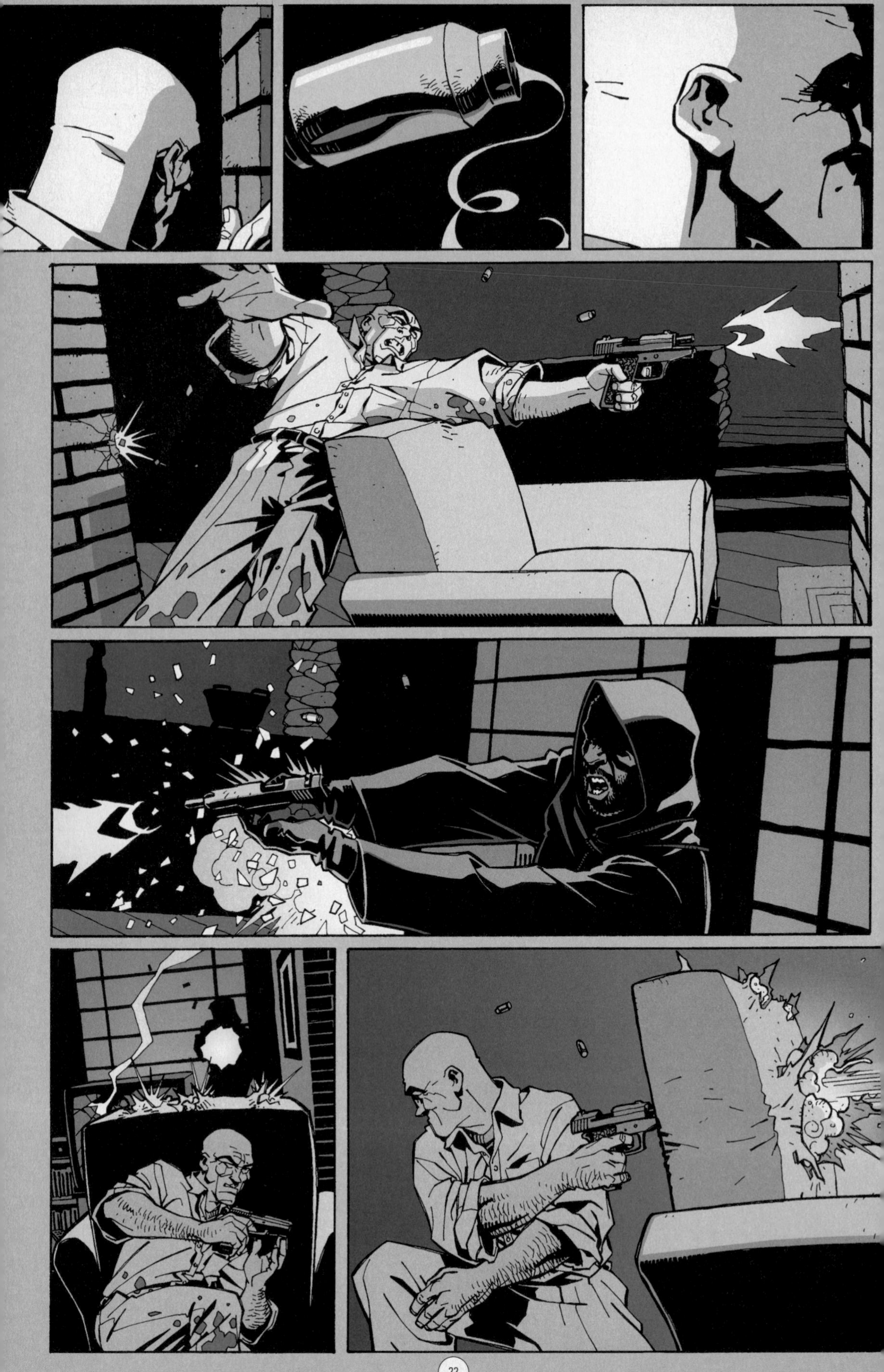

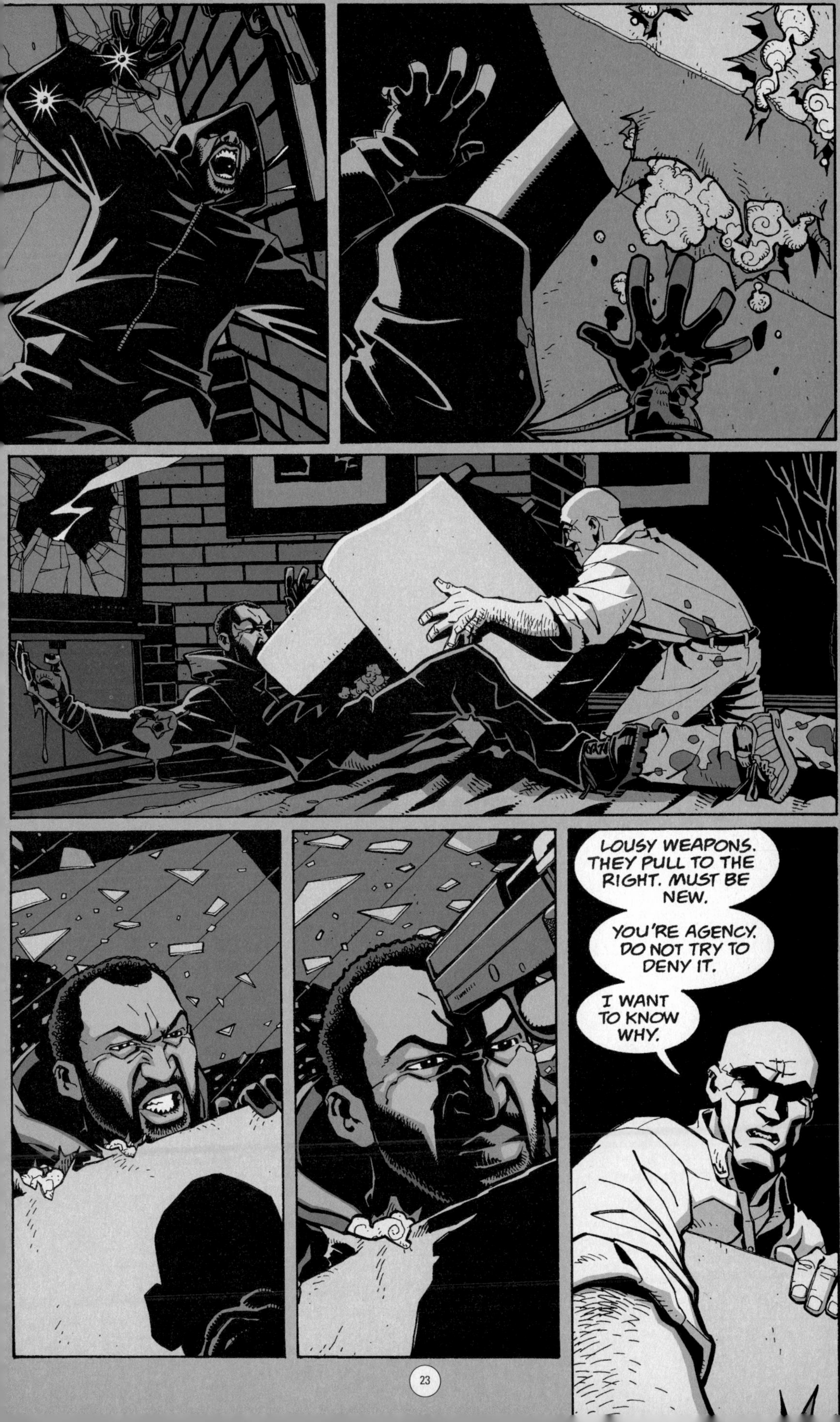
LOUSY WEAPONS. THEY PULL TO THE RIGHT. MUST BE NEW.
YOU'RE AGENCY. DO NOT TRY TO DENY IT.
I WANT TO KNOW WHY.

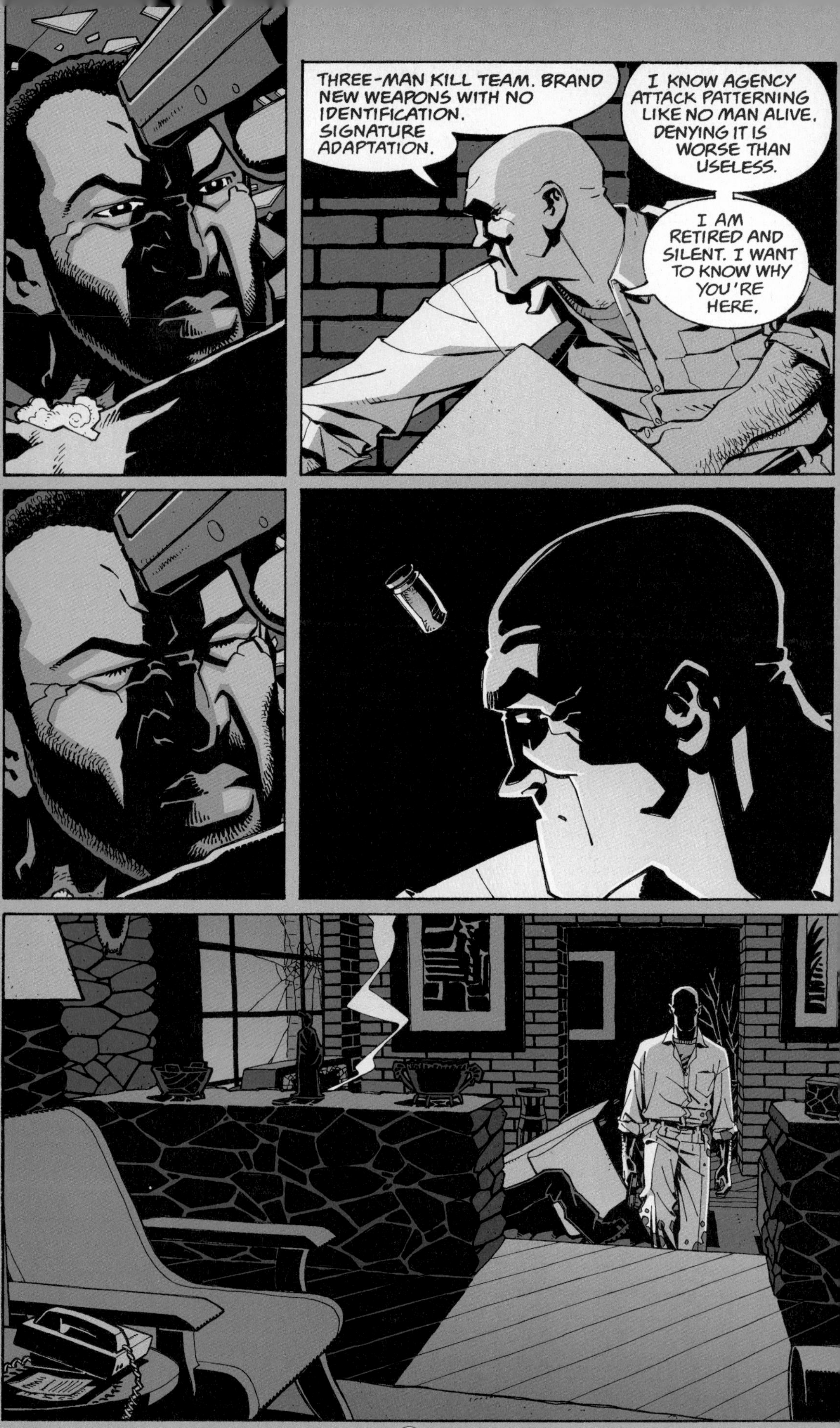
THREE-MAN KILL TEAM. BRAND NEW WEAPONS WITH NO IDENTIFICATION. SIGNATURE ADAPTATION.
I KNOW AGENCY ATTACK PATTERNING LIKE NO MAN ALIVE. DENYING IT IS WORSE THAN USELESS.
I AM RETIRED AND SILENT. I WANT TO KNOW WHY YOU'RE HERE.

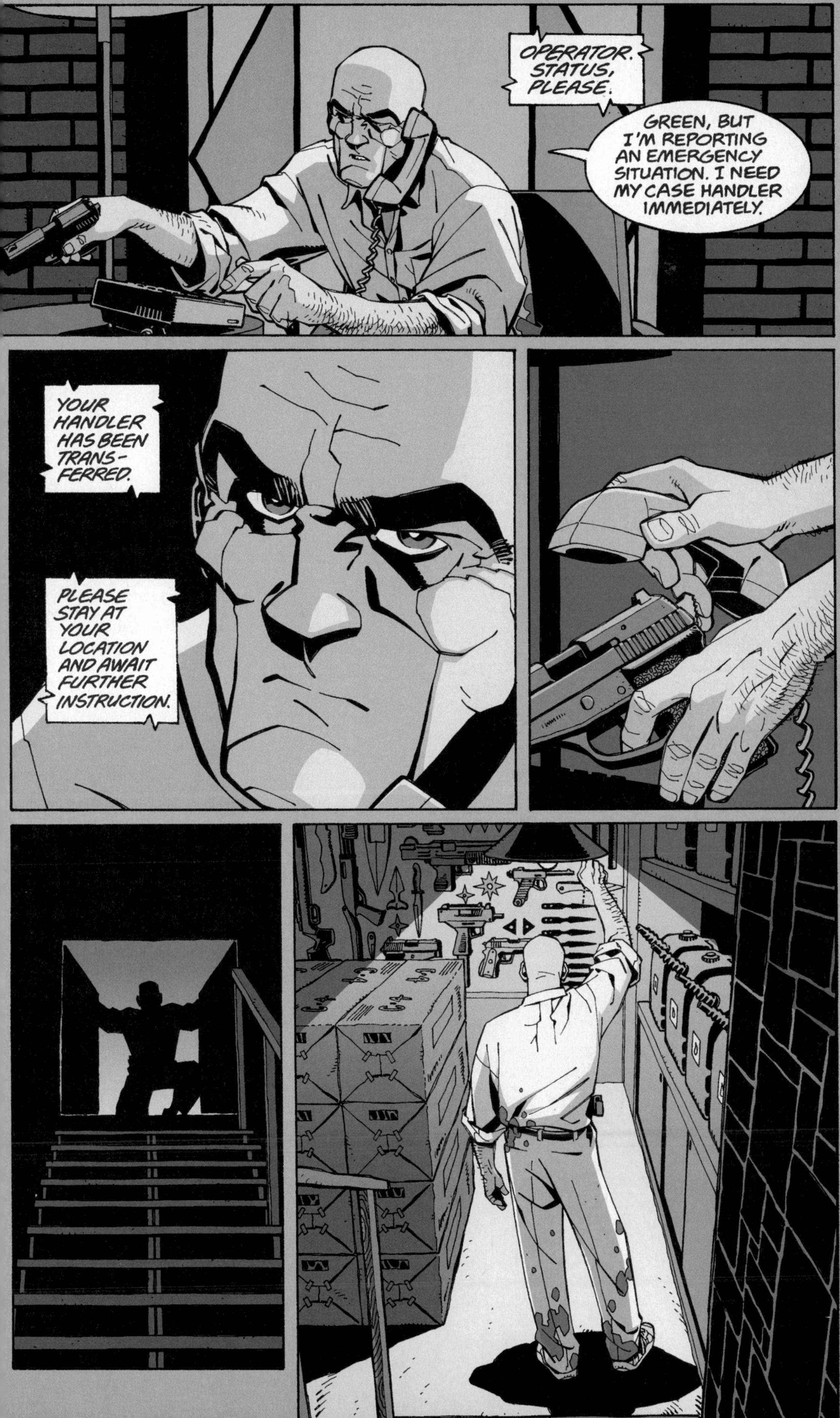
OPERATOR. STATUS, PLEASE.
GREEN, BUT I'M REPORTING AN EMERGENCY SITUATION. I NEED MY CASE HANDLER IMMEDIATELY.
YOUR HANDLER HAS BEEN TRANS-FERRED.
PLEASE STAY AT YOUR LOCATION AND AWAIT FURTHER INSTRUCTION.

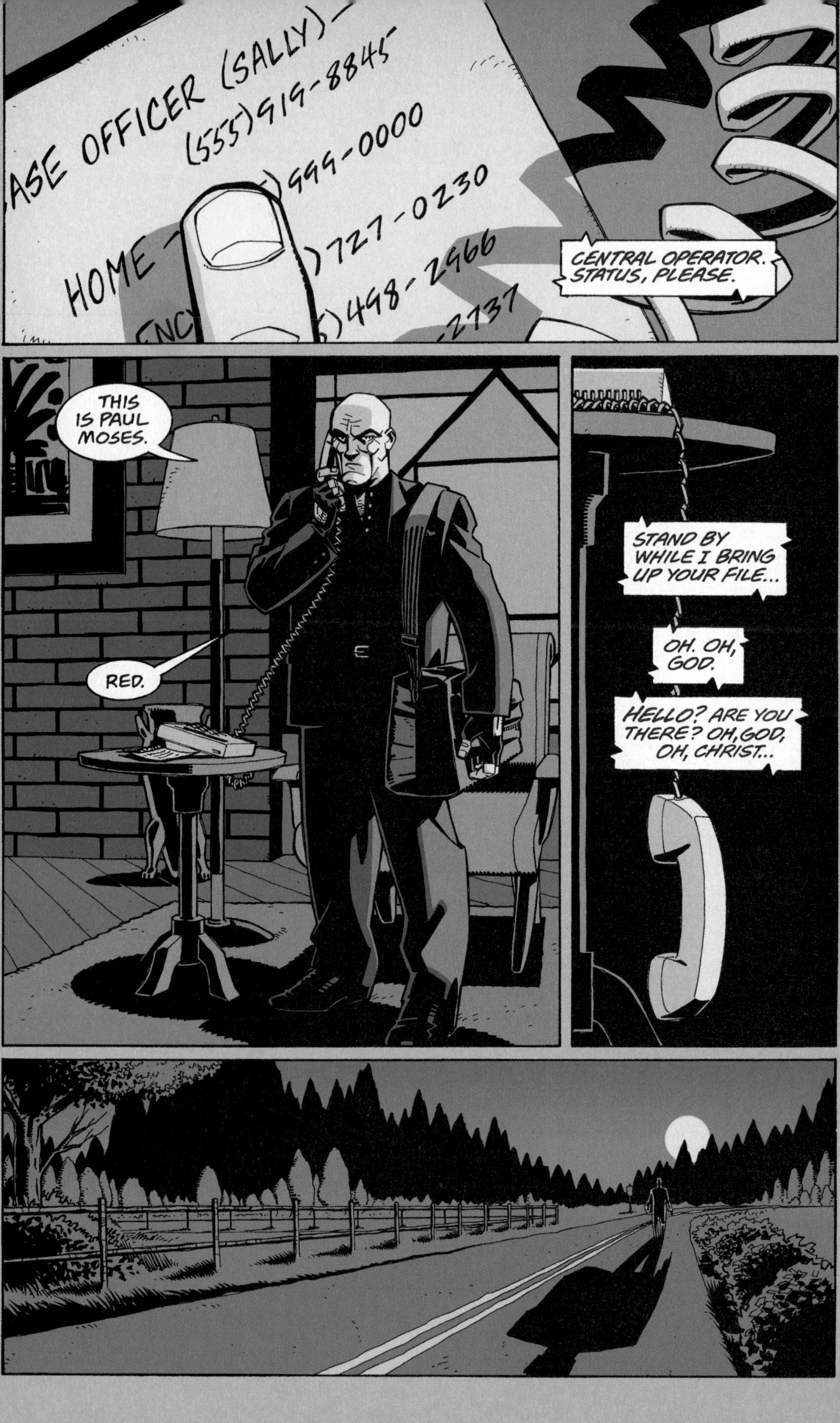
ASE OFFICER (SALLY)
(555)919-8845
999-0000
HOME
727-0230
498-2966
2737
CENTRAL OPERATOR. STATUS, PLEASE.
THIS IS PAUL MOSES.
RED.
STAND BY WHILE I BRING UP YOUR FILE...
OH. OH, GOD.
HELLO? ARE YOU THERE? OH, GOD, OH, CHRIST...

COVER 2 SKETCH

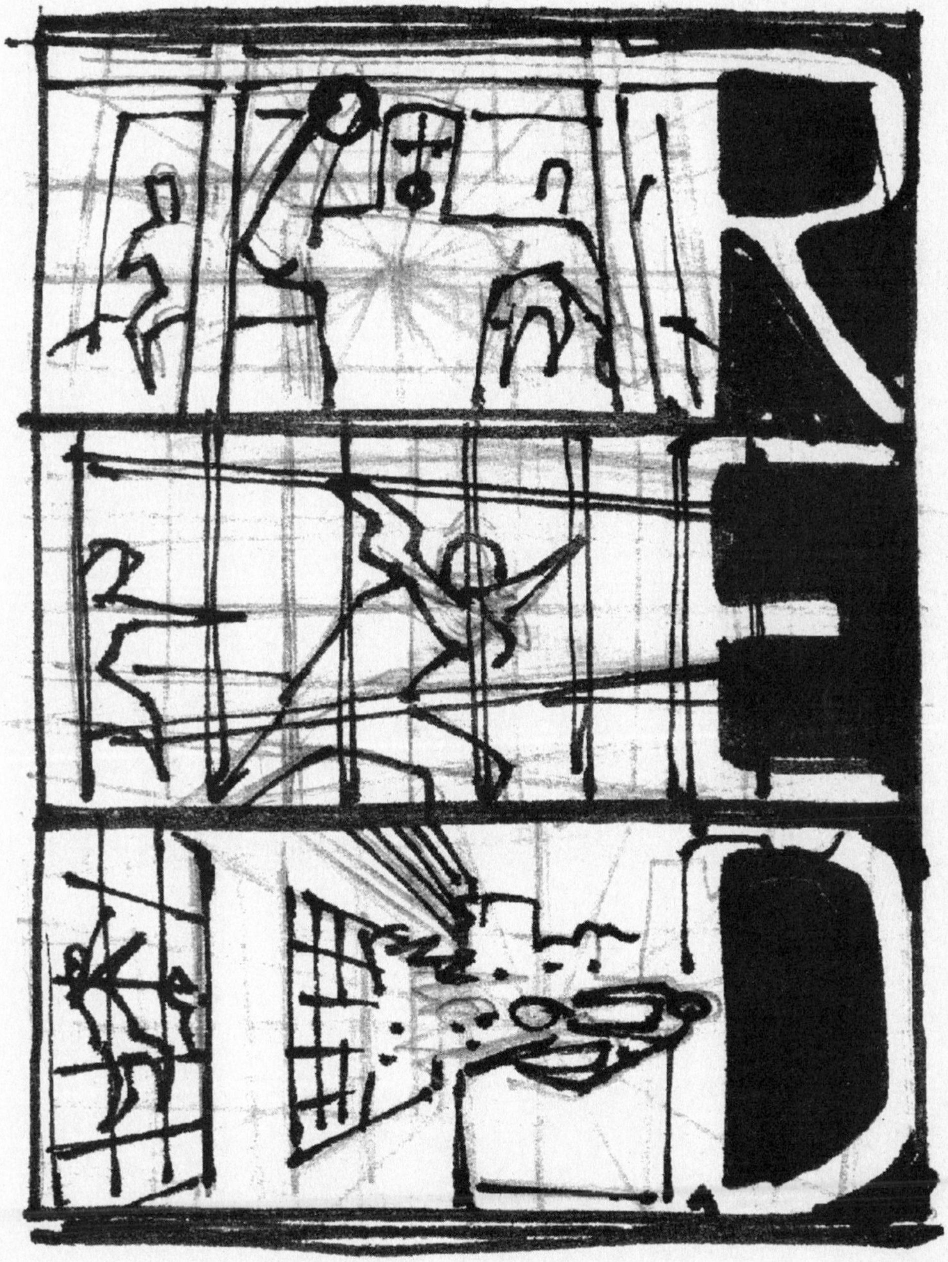

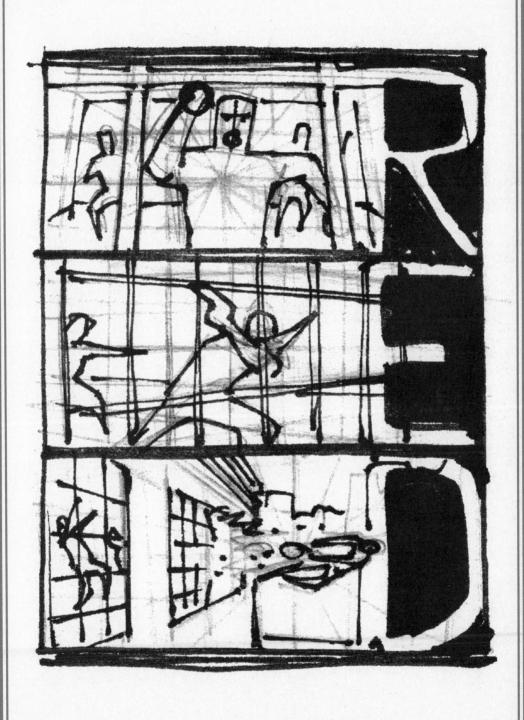

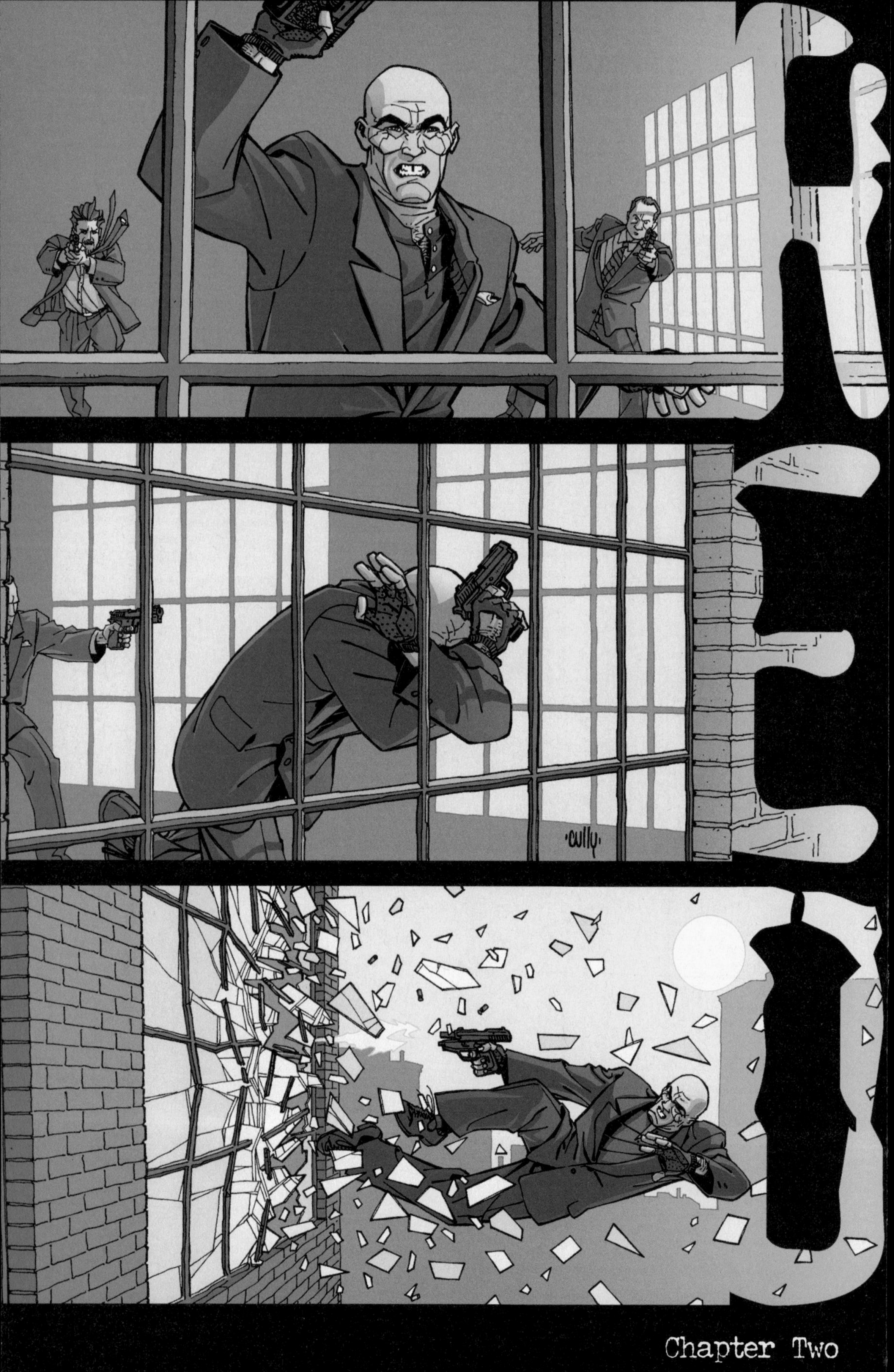

Chapter Two

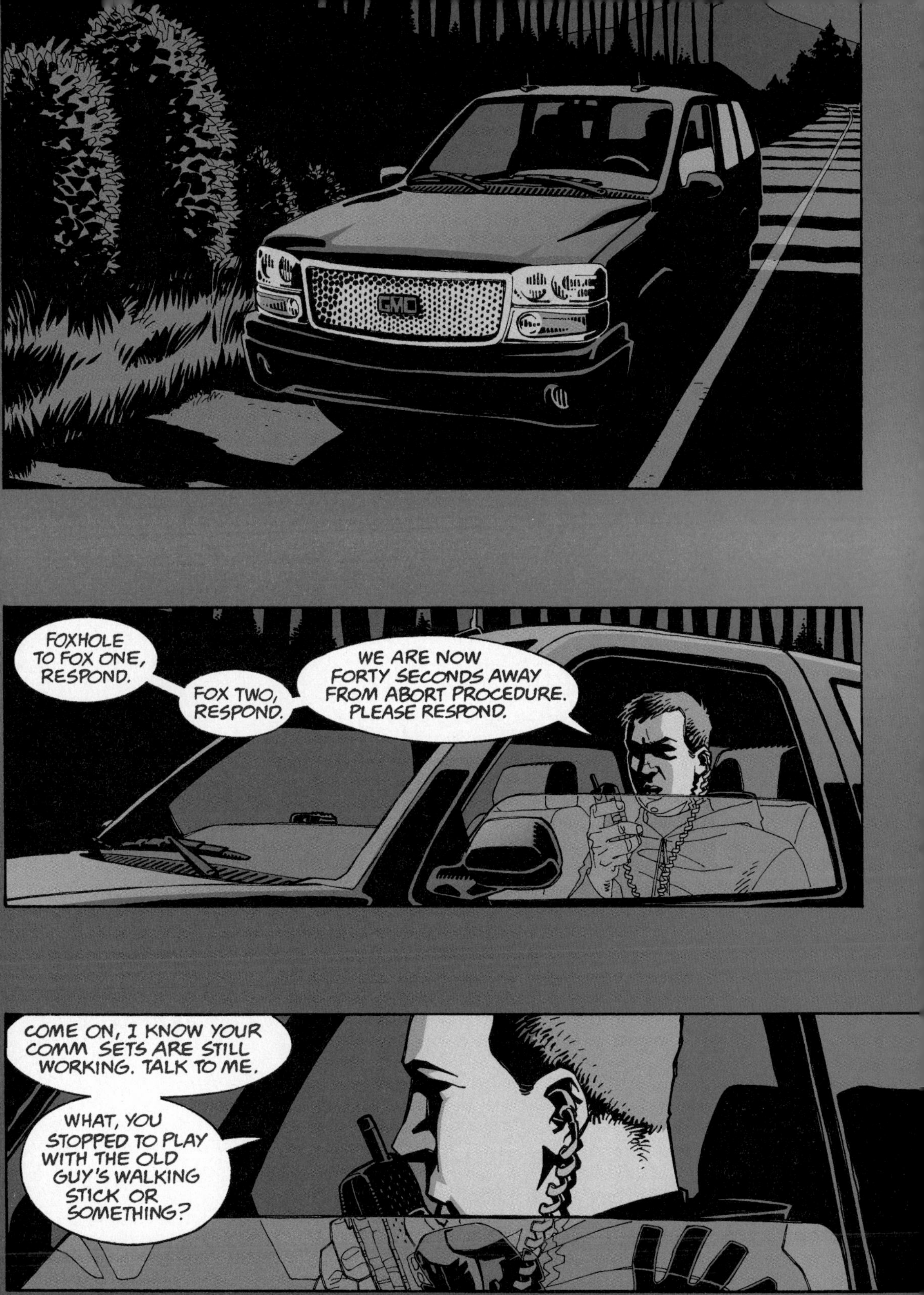
FOXHOLE TO FOX ONE, RESPOND.
FOX TWO, RESPOND.
WE ARE NOW FORTY SECONDS AWAY FROM ABORT PROCEDURE. PLEASE RESPOND.
COME ON, I KNOW YOUR COMM SETS ARE STILL WORKING. TALK TO ME.
WHAT, YOU STOPPED TO PLAY WITH THE OLD GUY'S WALKING STICK OR SOMETHING?

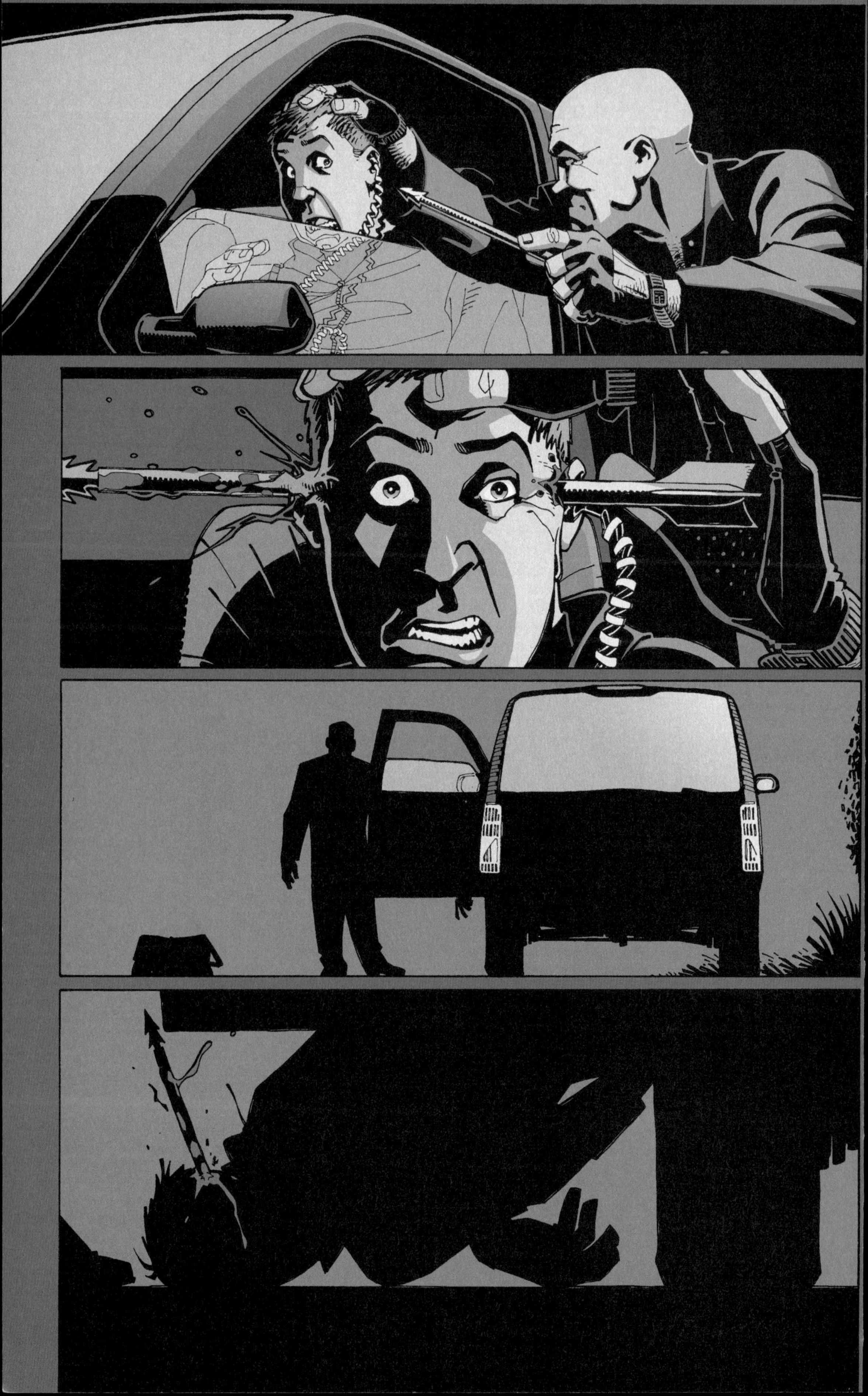

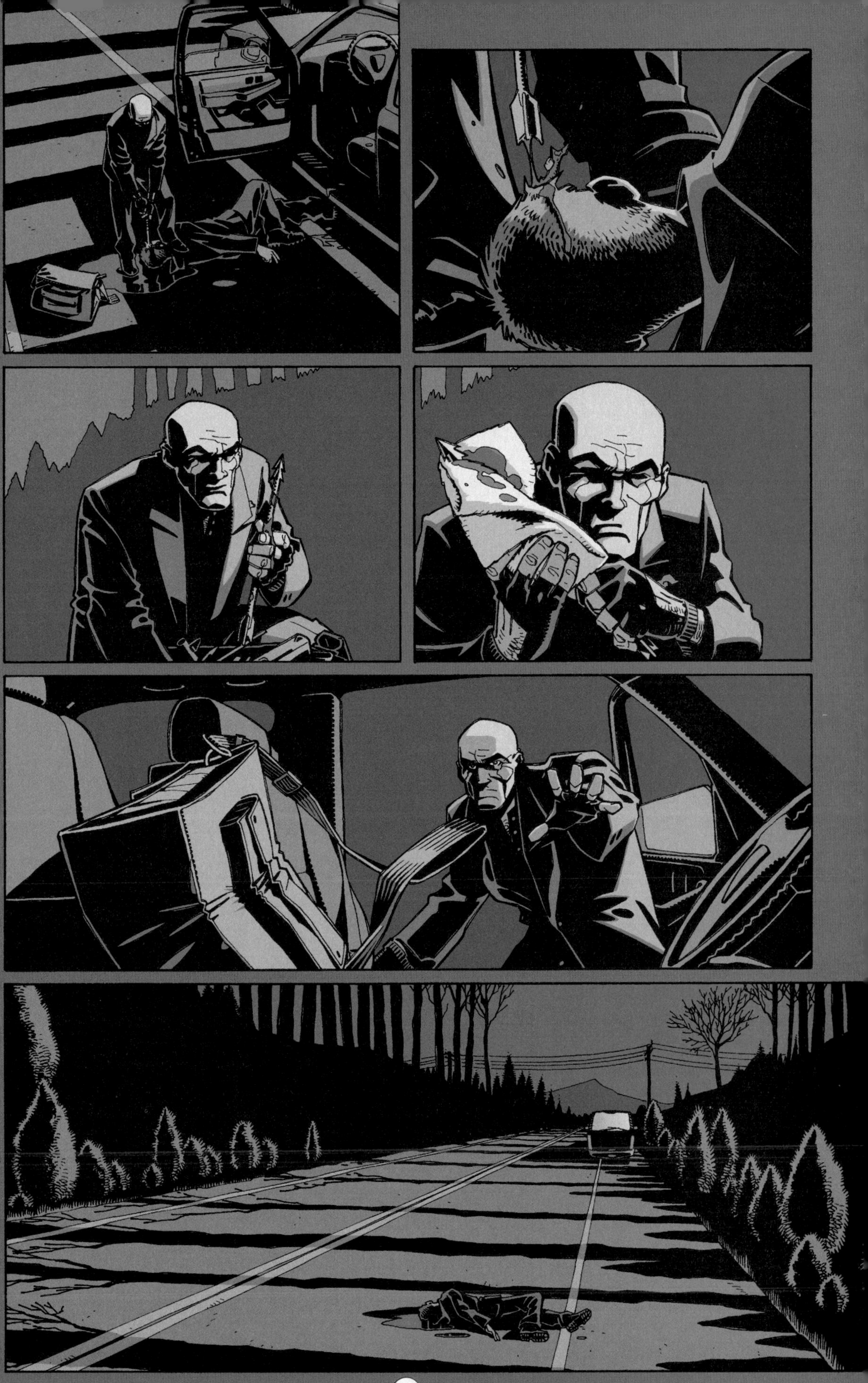

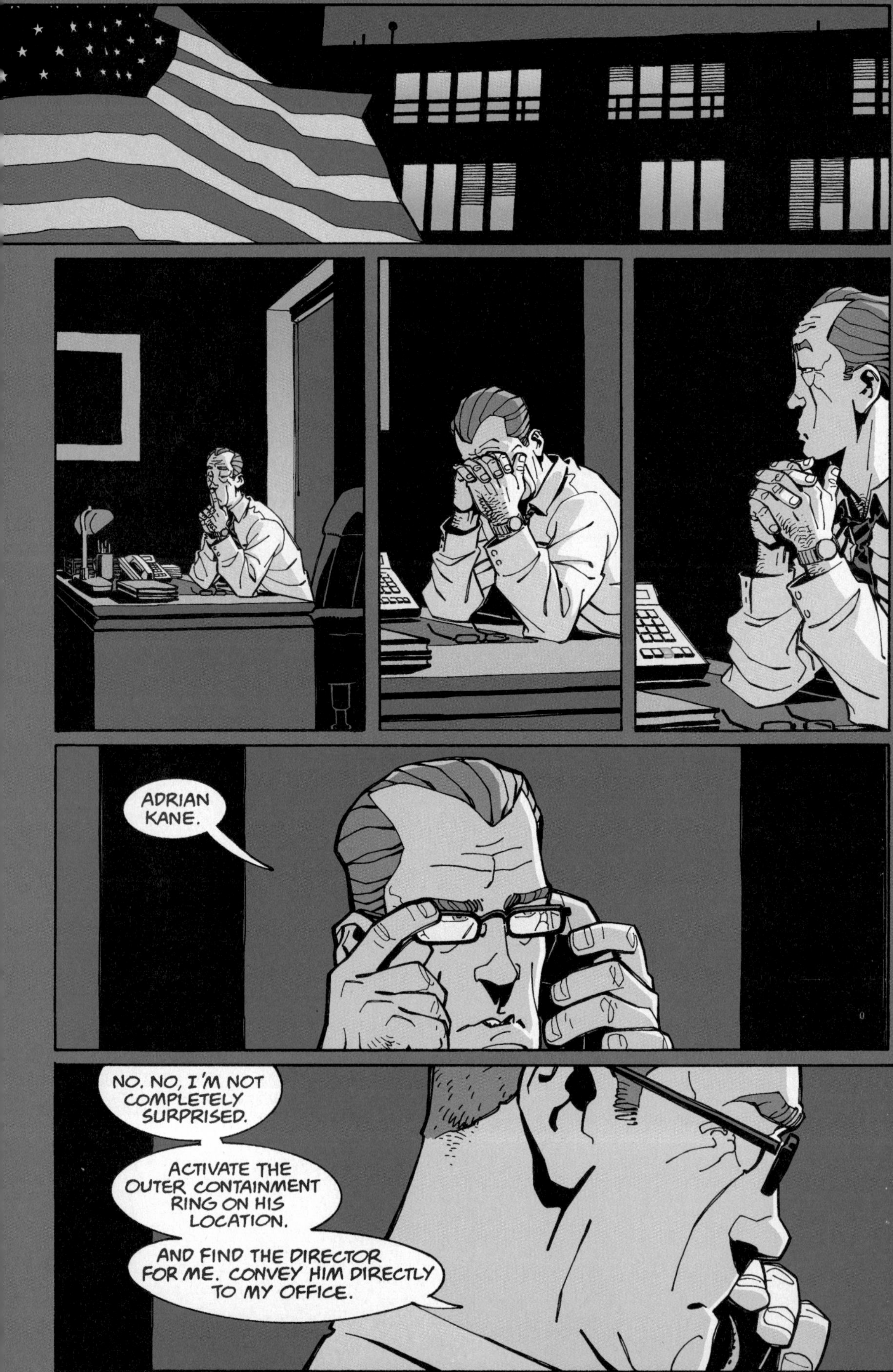
ADRIAN KANE.
NO. NO, I'M NOT COMPLETELY SURPRISED.
ACTIVATE THE OUTER CONTAINMENT RING ON HIS LOCATION.
AND FIND THE DIRECTOR FOR ME. CONVEY HIM DIRECTLY TO MY OFFICE.

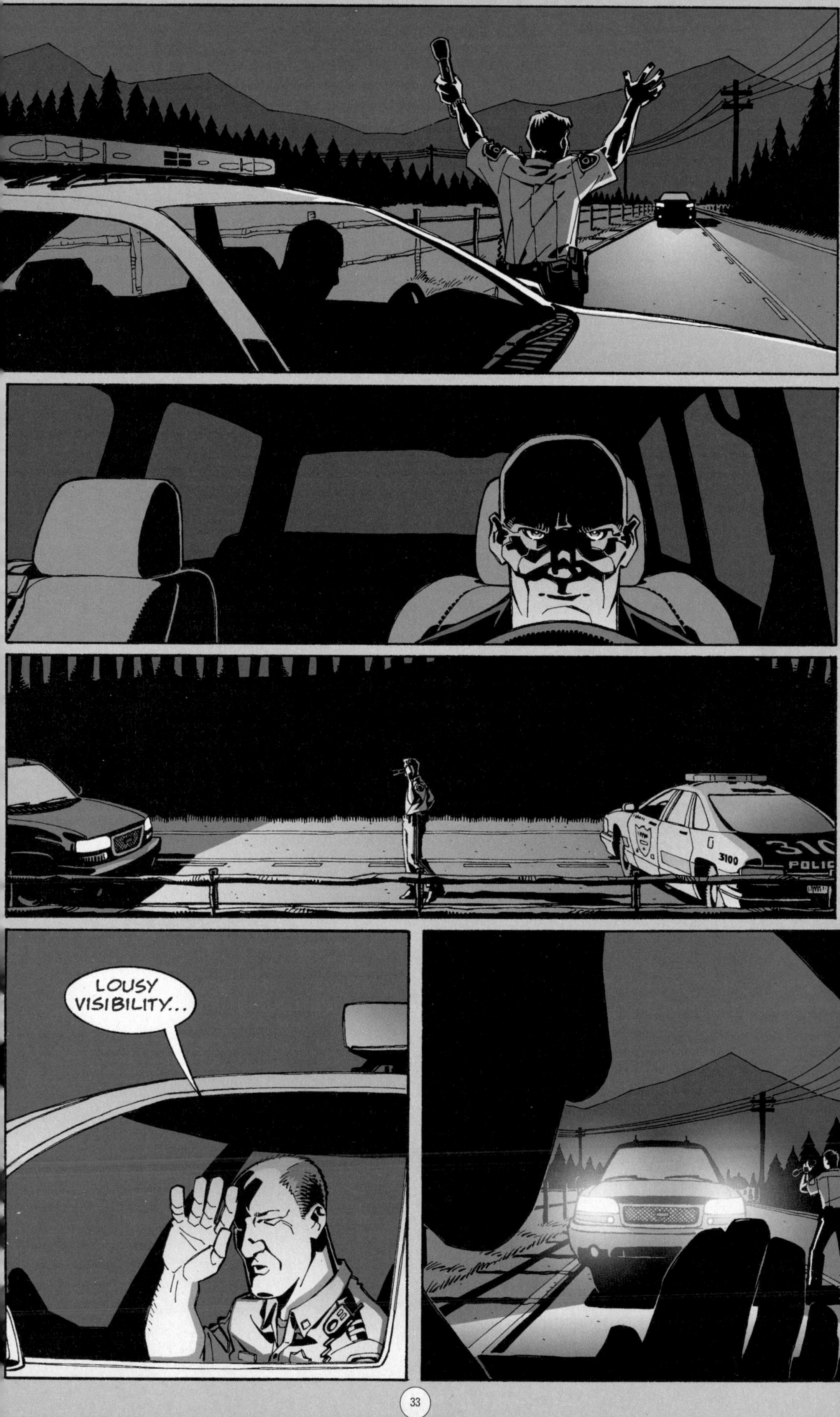
3100
POLIC
LOUSY VISIBILITY...

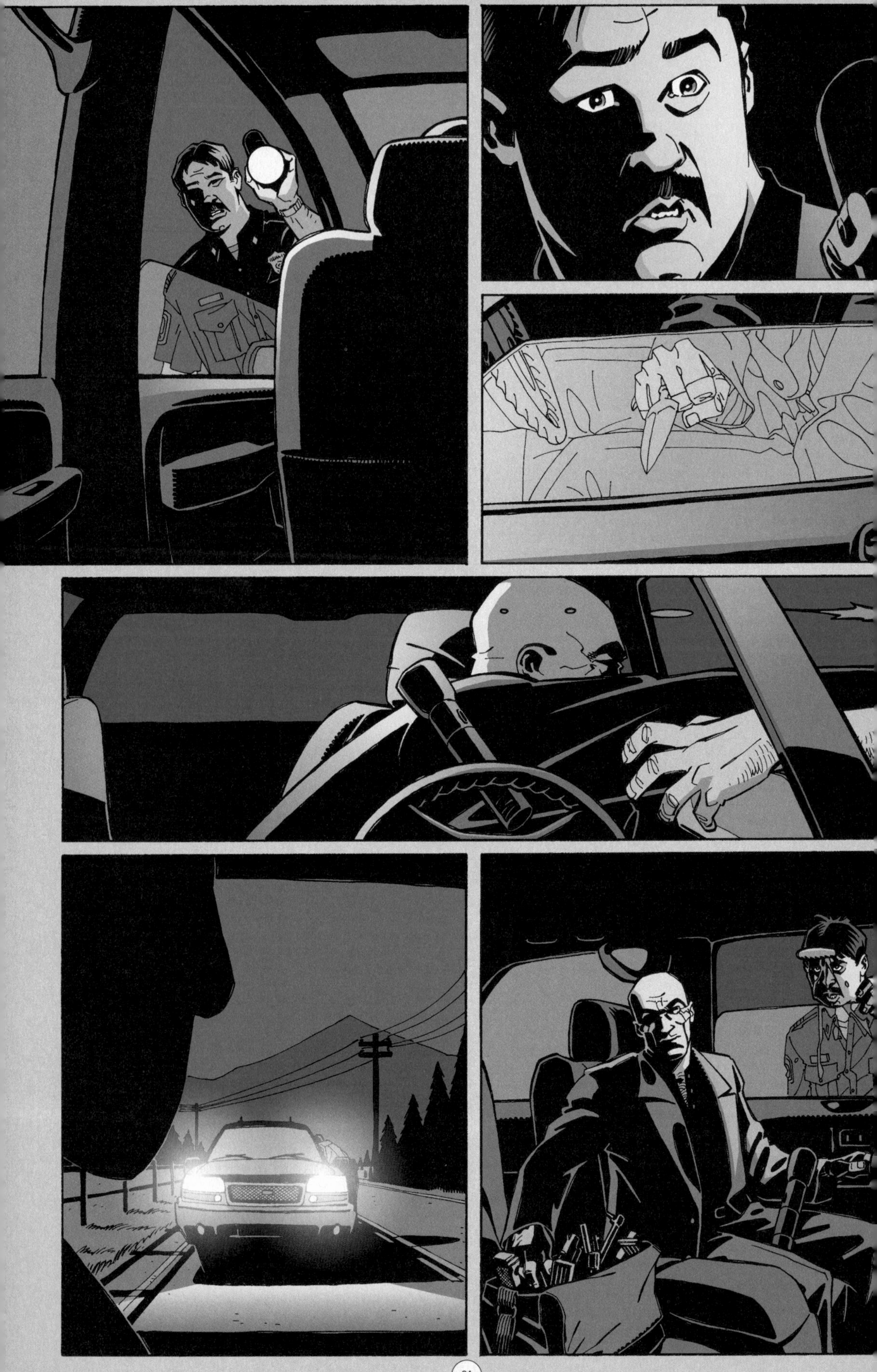

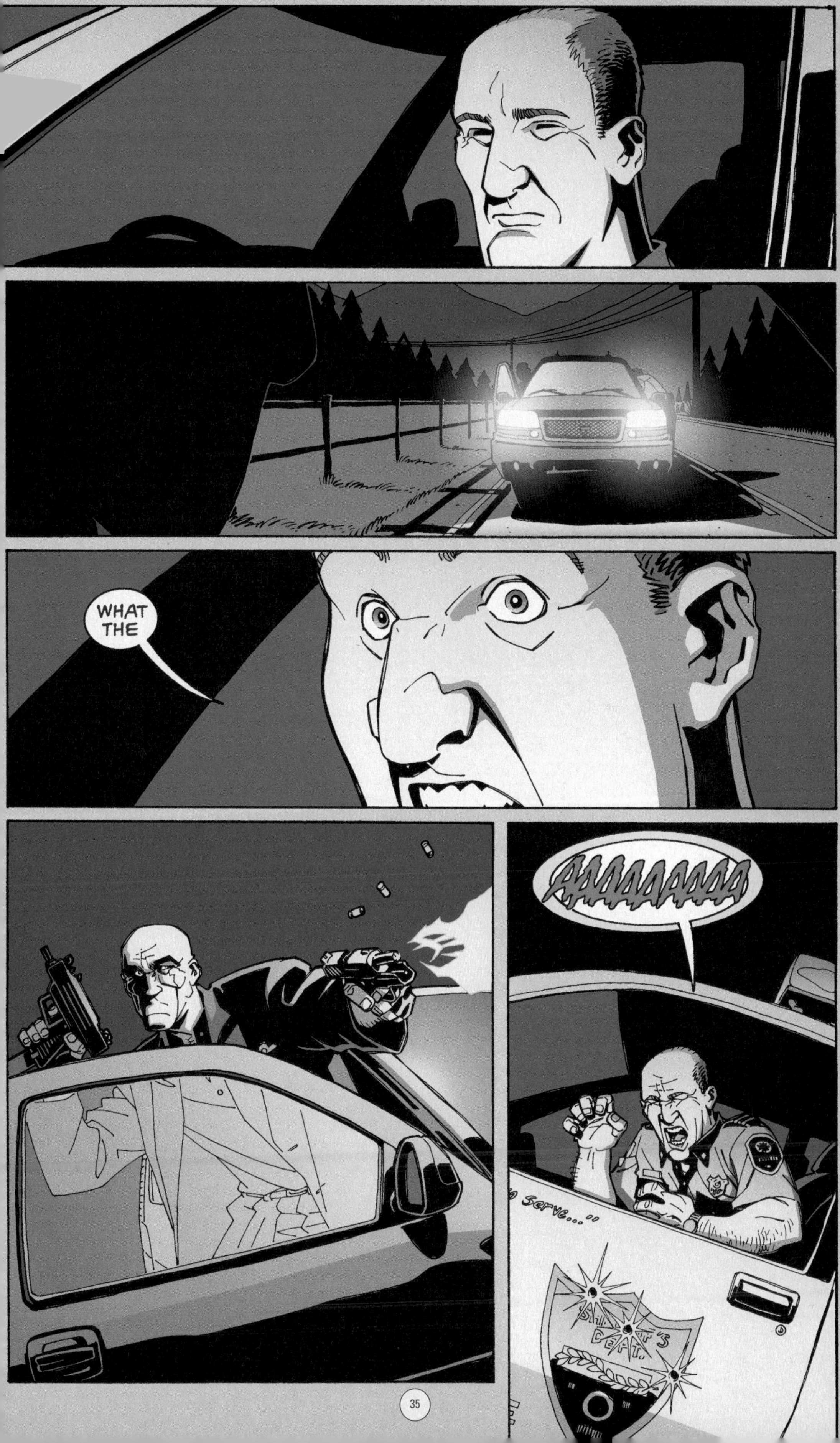
WHAT THE
AAAAAAAAA

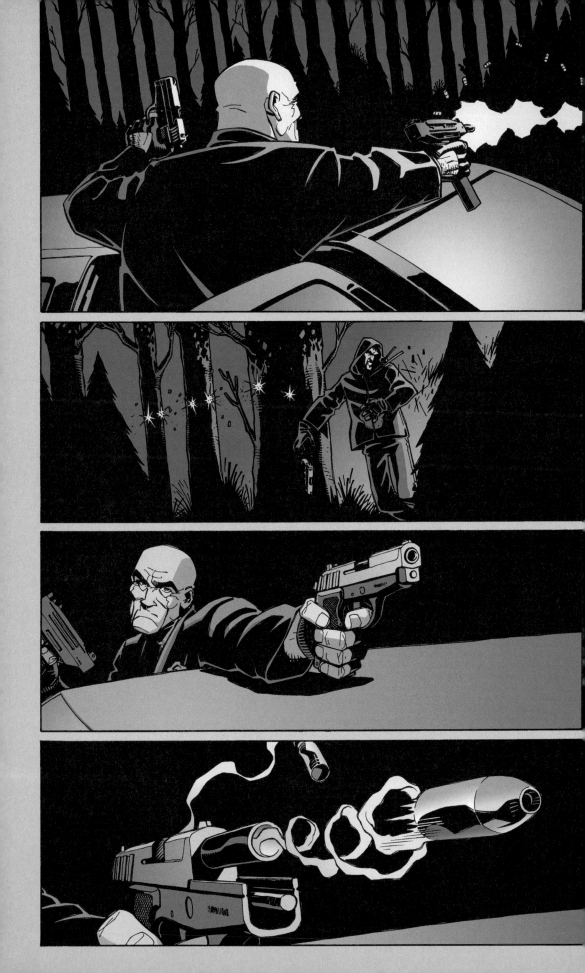

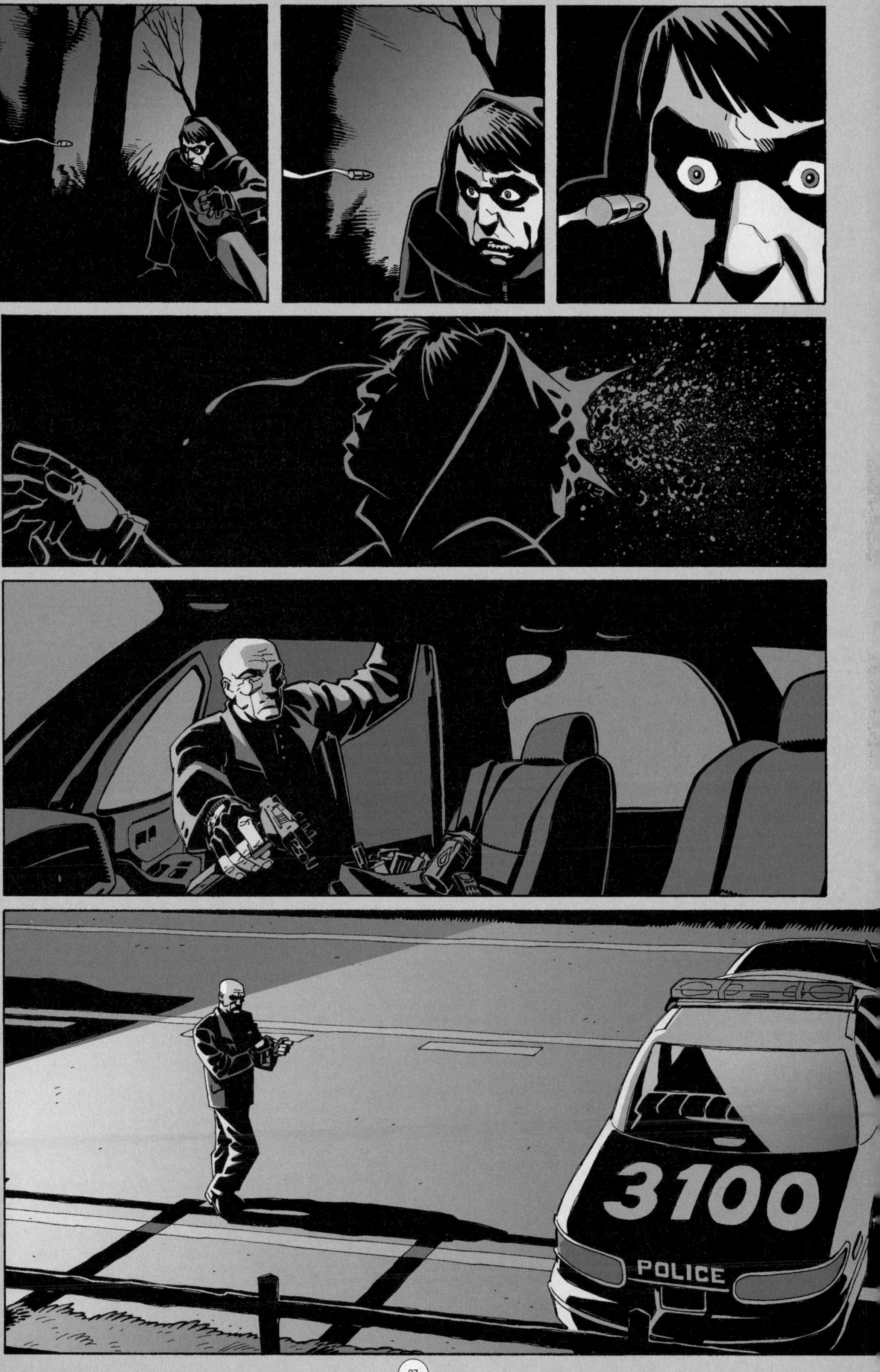
3100
POLICE

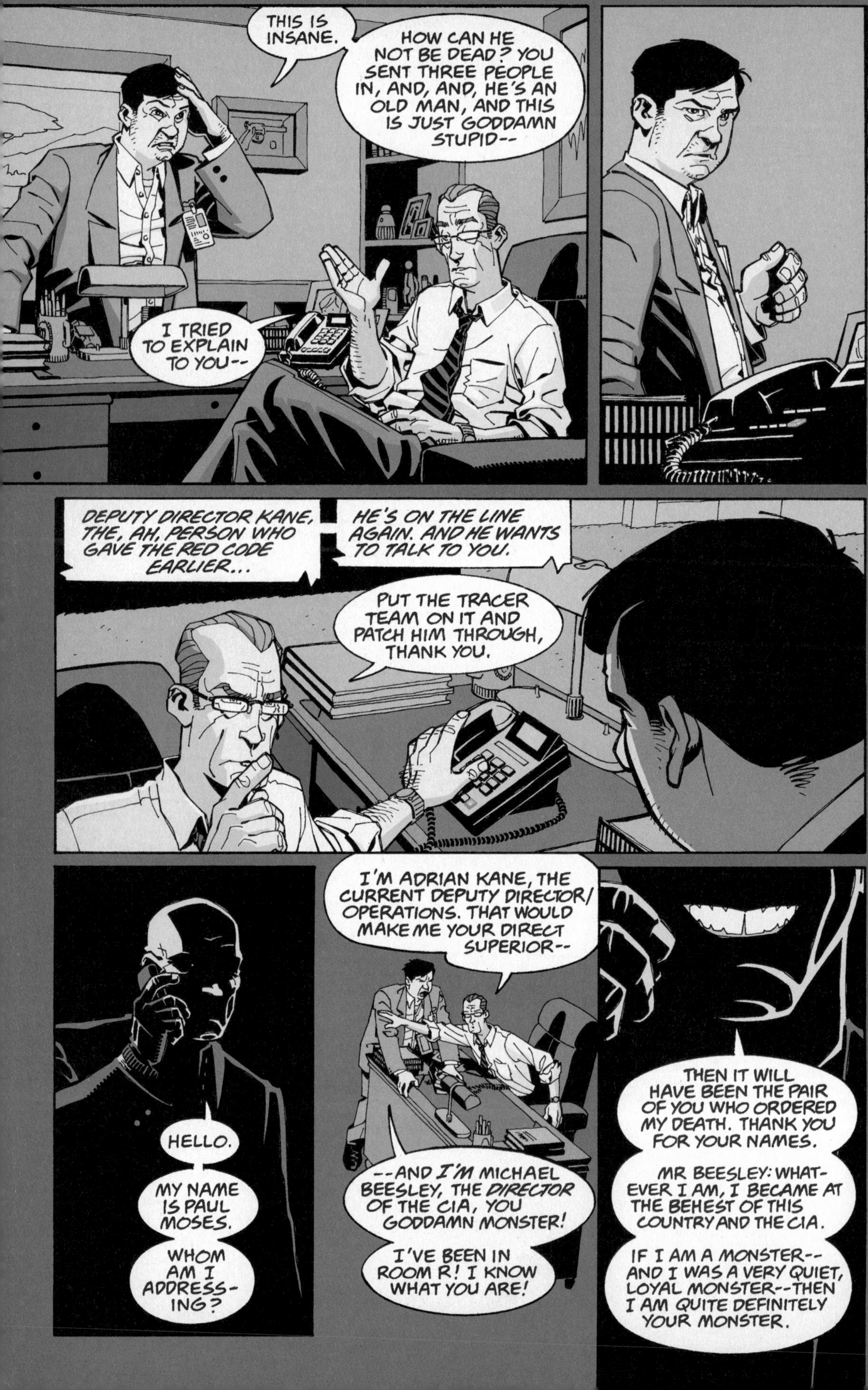

THIS IS INSANE.
HOW CAN HE NOT BE DEAD? YOU SENT THREE PEOPLE IN, AND, AND, HE'S AN OLD MAN, AND THIS IS JUST GODDAMN STUPID--
I TRIED TO EXPLAIN TO YOU--
DEPUTY DIRECTOR KANE, THE, AH, PERSON WHO GAVE THE RED CODE EARLIER...
HE'S ON THE LINE AGAIN. AND HE WANTS TO TALK TO YOU.
PUT THE TRACER TEAM ON IT AND PATCH HIM THROUGH, THANK YOU.
HELLO.
MY NAME IS PAUL MOSES.
WHOM AM I ADDRESSING?
I'M ADRIAN KANE, THE CURRENT DEPUTY DIRECTOR/ OPERATIONS. THAT WOULD MAKE ME YOUR DIRECT SUPERIOR--
--AND I'M MICHAEL BEESLEY, THE DIRECTOR OF THE CIA, YOU GODDAMN MONSTER!
I'VE BEEN IN ROOM R! I KNOW WHAT YOU ARE!
THEN IT WILL HAVE BEEN THE PAIR OF YOU WHO ORDERED MY DEATH. THANK YOU FOR YOUR NAMES.
MR BEESLEY: WHATEVER I AM, I BECAME AT THE BEHEST OF THIS COUNTRY AND THE CIA.
IF I AM A MONSTER-- AND I WAS A VERY QUIET, LOYAL MONSTER--THEN I AM QUITE DEFINITELY YOUR MONSTER.

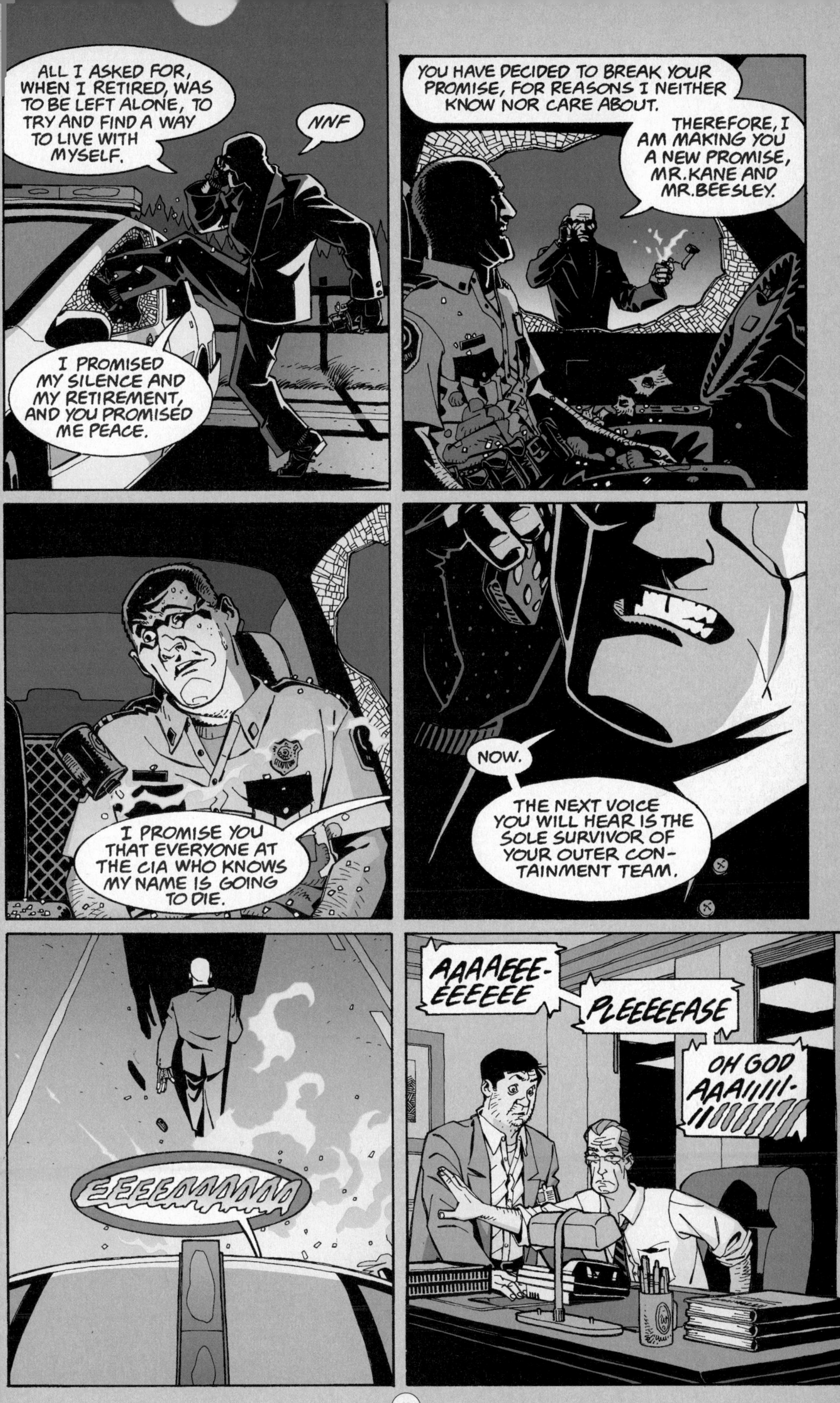
ALL I ASKED FOR, WHEN I RETIRED, WAS TO BE LEFT ALONE, TO TRY AND FIND A WAY TO LIVE WITH MYSELF.
NNF
I PROMISED MY SILENCE AND MY RETIREMENT, AND YOU PROMISED ME PEACE.
YOU HAVE DECIDED TO BREAK YOUR PROMISE, FOR REASONS I NEITHER KNOW NOR CARE ABOUT.
THEREFORE, I AM MAKING YOU A NEW PROMISE, MR. KANE AND MR. BEESLEY.
I PROMISE YOU THAT EVERYONE AT THE CIA WHO KNOWS MY NAME IS GOING TO DIE.
NOW.
THE NEXT VOICE YOU WILL HEAR IS THE SOLE SURVIVOR OF YOUR OUTER CONTAINMENT TEAM.
EEEEAAAAAA
AAAAEEE-EEEEEE
PLEEEEEASE
OH GOD AAAIIIII-IIIIIIIIII

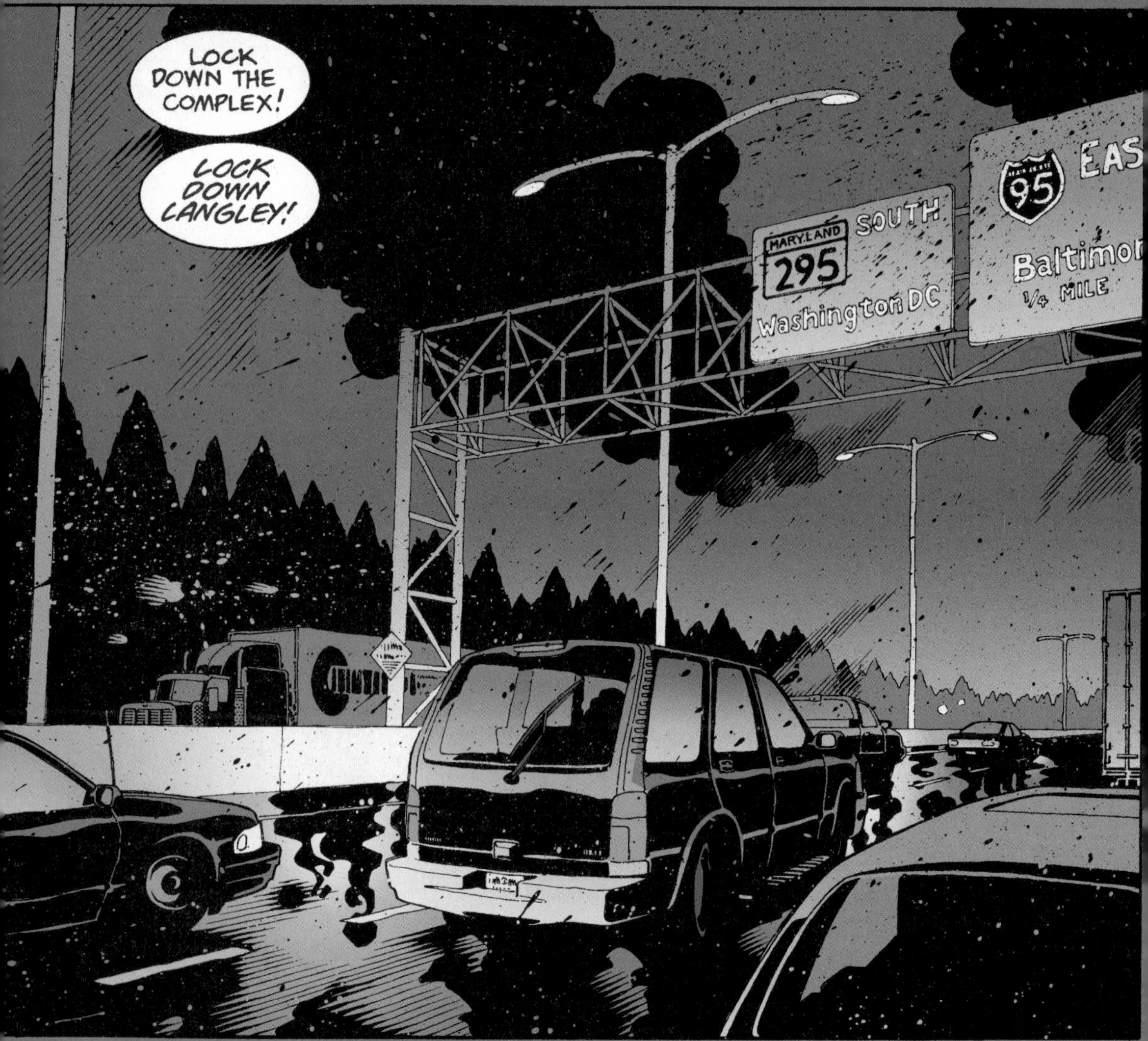
LOCK DOWN THE COMPLEX!
LOCK DOWN LANGLEY!
MARYLAND
295
SOUTH
Washington DC
95
EAS
Baltimor
1/4 MILE

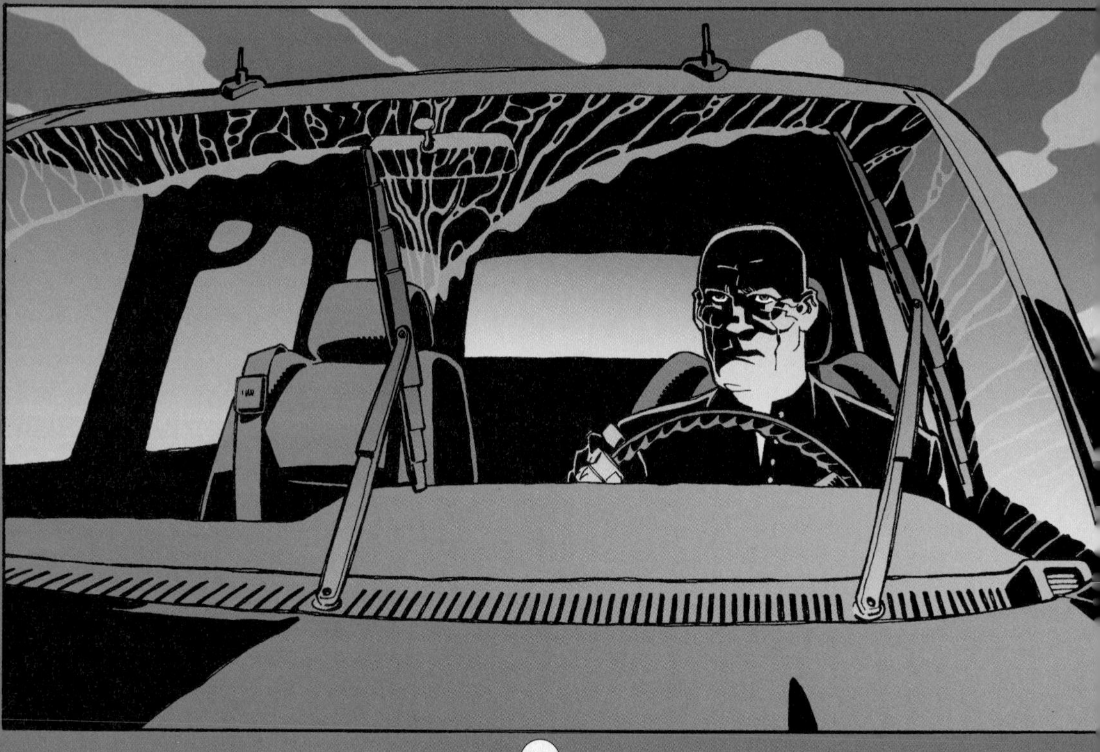

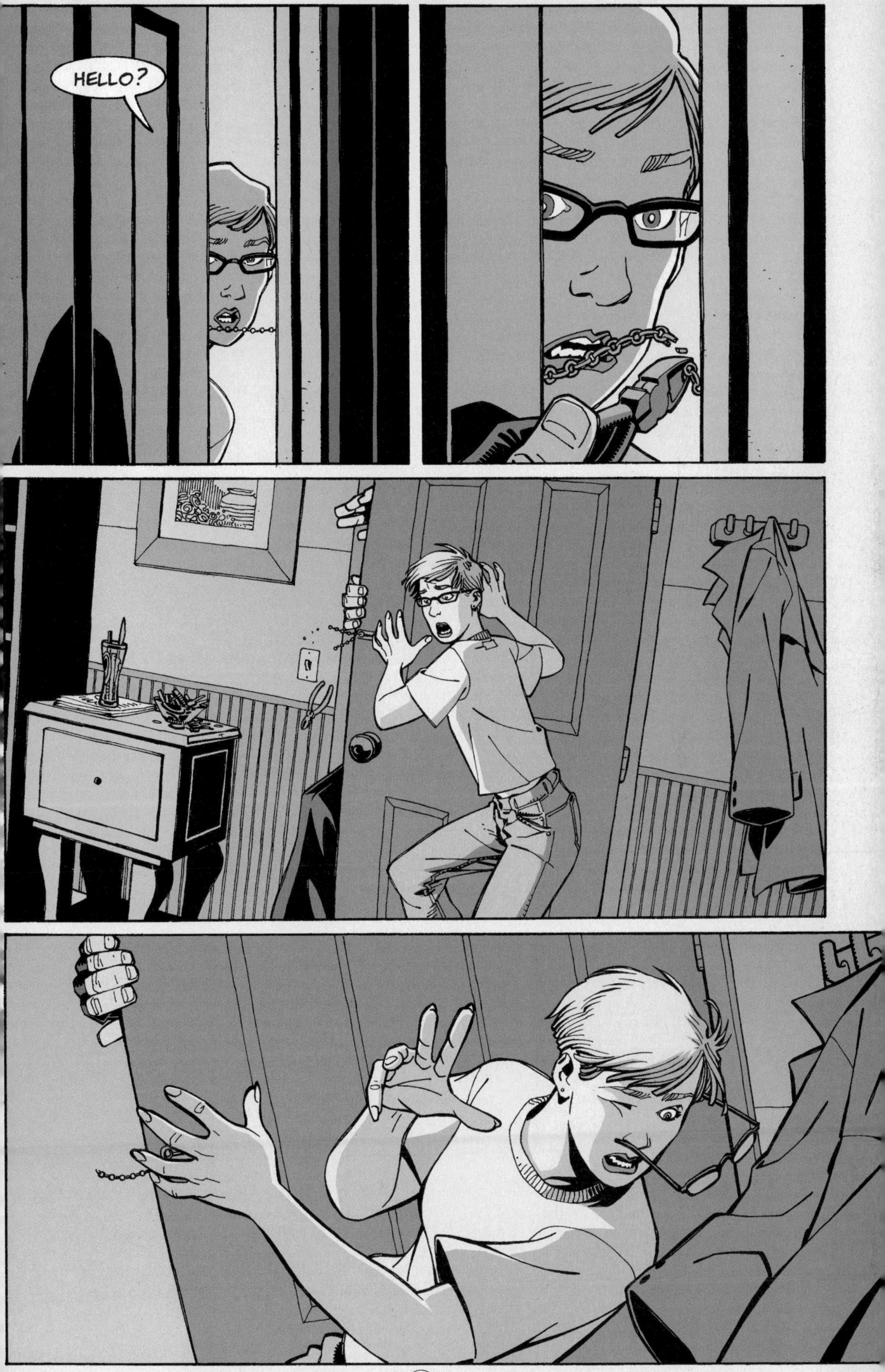

HELLO?

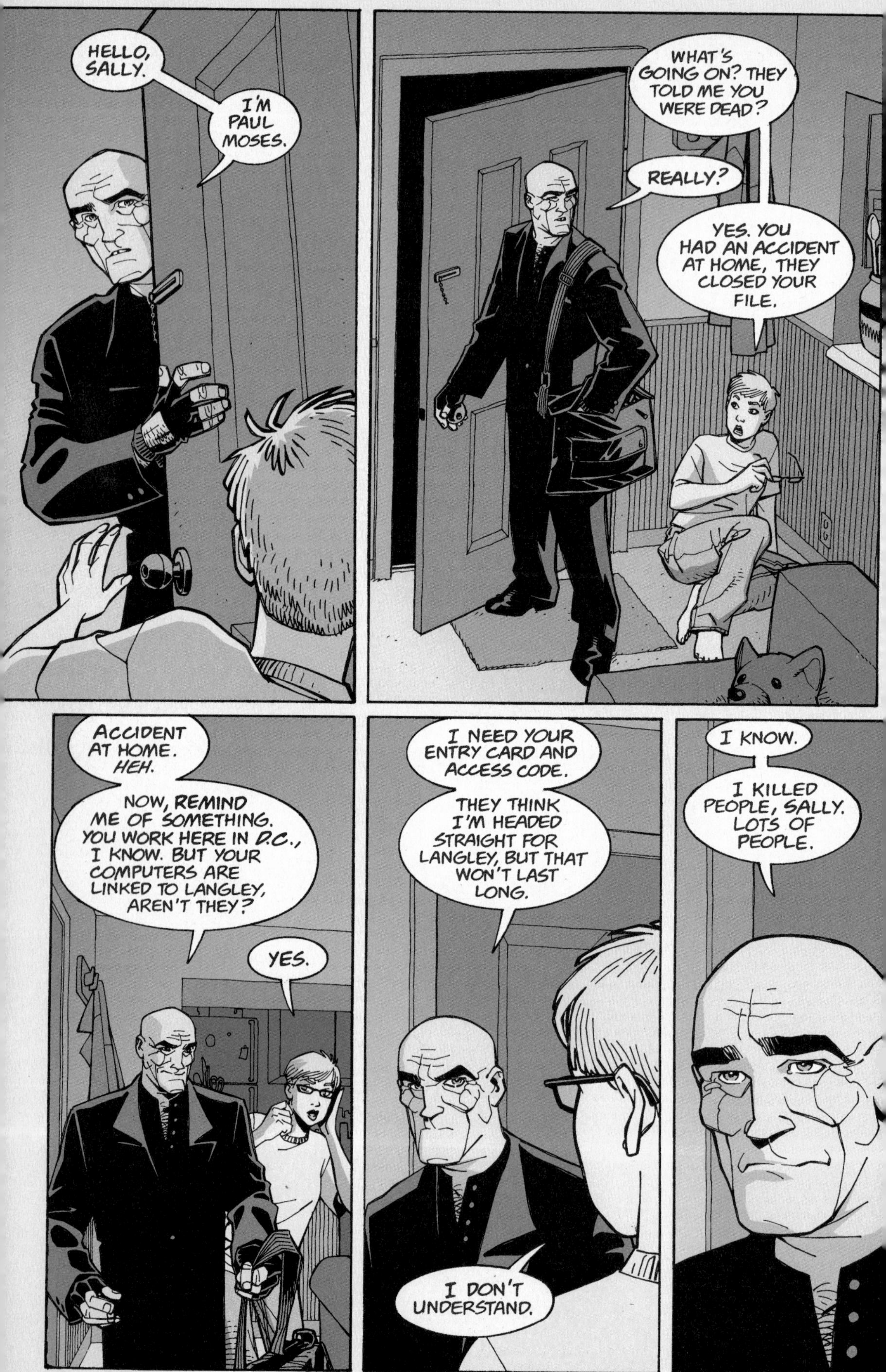
HELLO, SALLY.
I'M PAUL MOSES.
WHAT'S GOING ON? THEY TOLD ME YOU WERE DEAD?
REALLY?
YES. YOU HAD AN ACCIDENT AT HOME, THEY CLOSED YOUR FILE.
ACCIDENT AT HOME. HEH.
NOW, REMIND ME OF SOMETHING. YOU WORK HERE IN D.C., I KNOW. BUT YOUR COMPUTERS ARE LINKED TO LANGLEY, AREN'T THEY?
YES.
I NEED YOUR ENTRY CARD AND ACCESS CODE.
THEY THINK I'M HEADED STRAIGHT FOR LANGLEY, BUT THAT WON'T LAST LONG.
I DON'T UNDERSTAND.
I KNOW.
I KILLED PEOPLE, SALLY. LOTS OF PEOPLE.

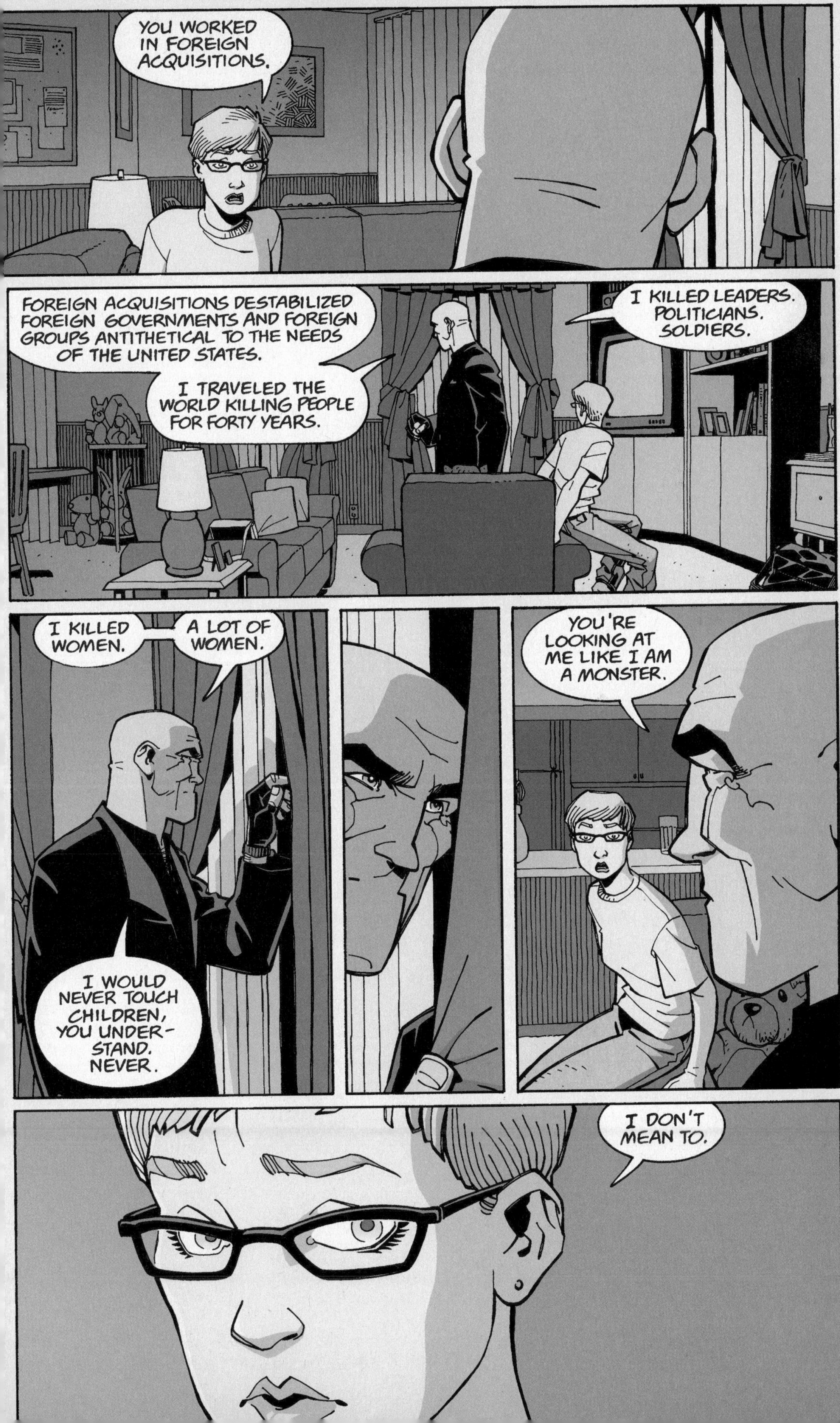
YOU WORKED IN FOREIGN ACQUISITIONS.
FOREIGN ACQUISITIONS DESTABILIZED FOREIGN GOVERNMENTS AND FOREIGN GROUPS ANTITHETICAL TO THE NEEDS OF THE UNITED STATES.
I TRAVELED THE WORLD KILLING PEOPLE FOR FORTY YEARS.
I KILLED LEADERS. POLITICIANS. SOLDIERS.
I KILLED WOMEN.
A LOT OF WOMEN.
I WOULD NEVER TOUCH CHILDREN, YOU UNDER-STAND. NEVER.
YOU'RE LOOKING AT ME LIKE I AM A MONSTER.
I DON'T MEAN TO.

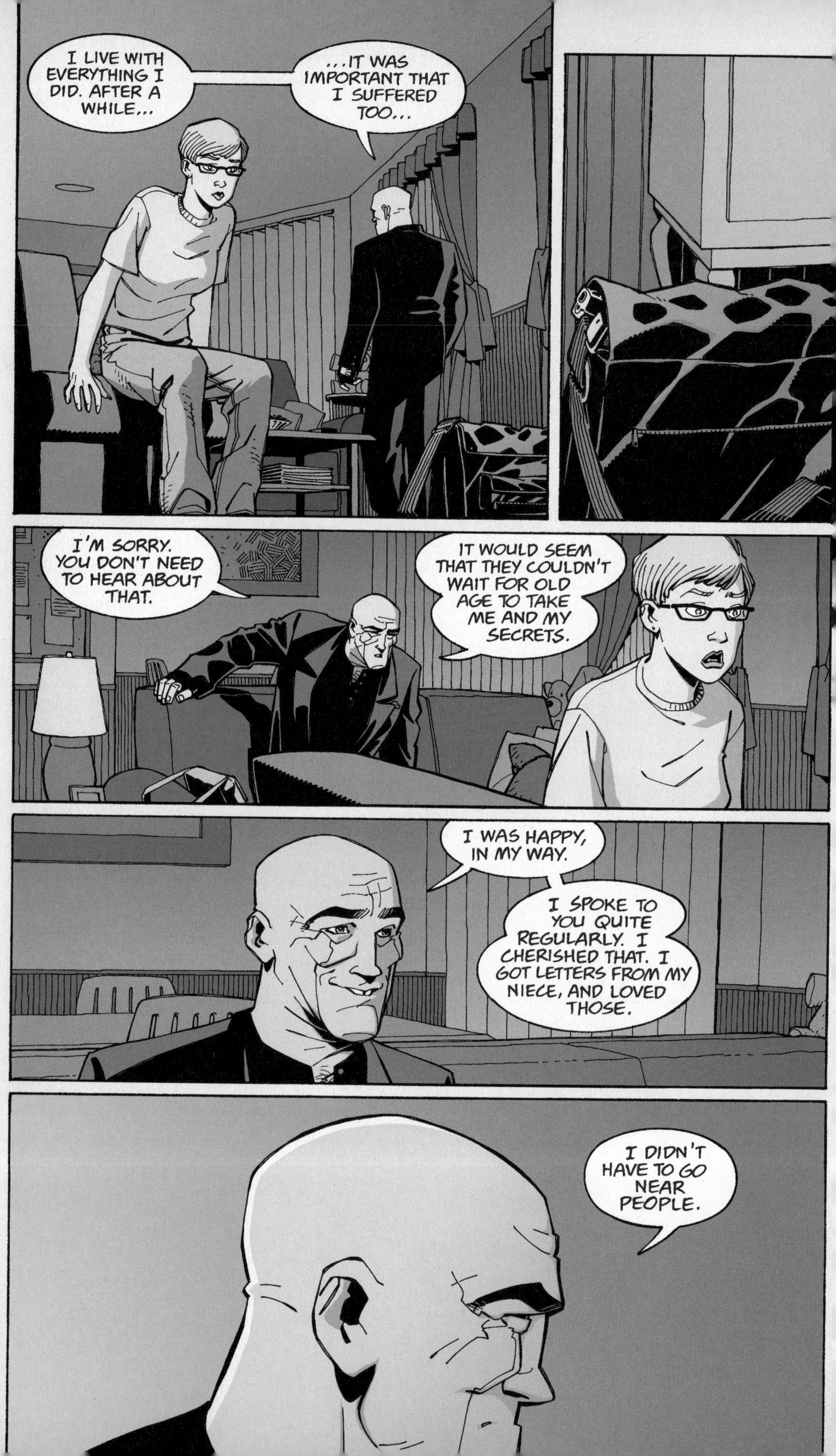
I LIVE WITH EVERYTHING I DID. AFTER A WHILE...
...IT WAS IMPORTANT THAT I SUFFERED TOO...
I'M SORRY. YOU DON'T NEED TO HEAR ABOUT THAT.
IT WOULD SEEM THAT THEY COULDN'T WAIT FOR OLD AGE TO TAKE ME AND MY SECRETS.
I WAS HAPPY, IN MY WAY.
I SPOKE TO YOU QUITE REGULARLY. I CHERISHED THAT. I GOT LETTERS FROM MY NIECE, AND LOVED THOSE.
I DIDN'T HAVE TO GO NEAR PEOPLE.

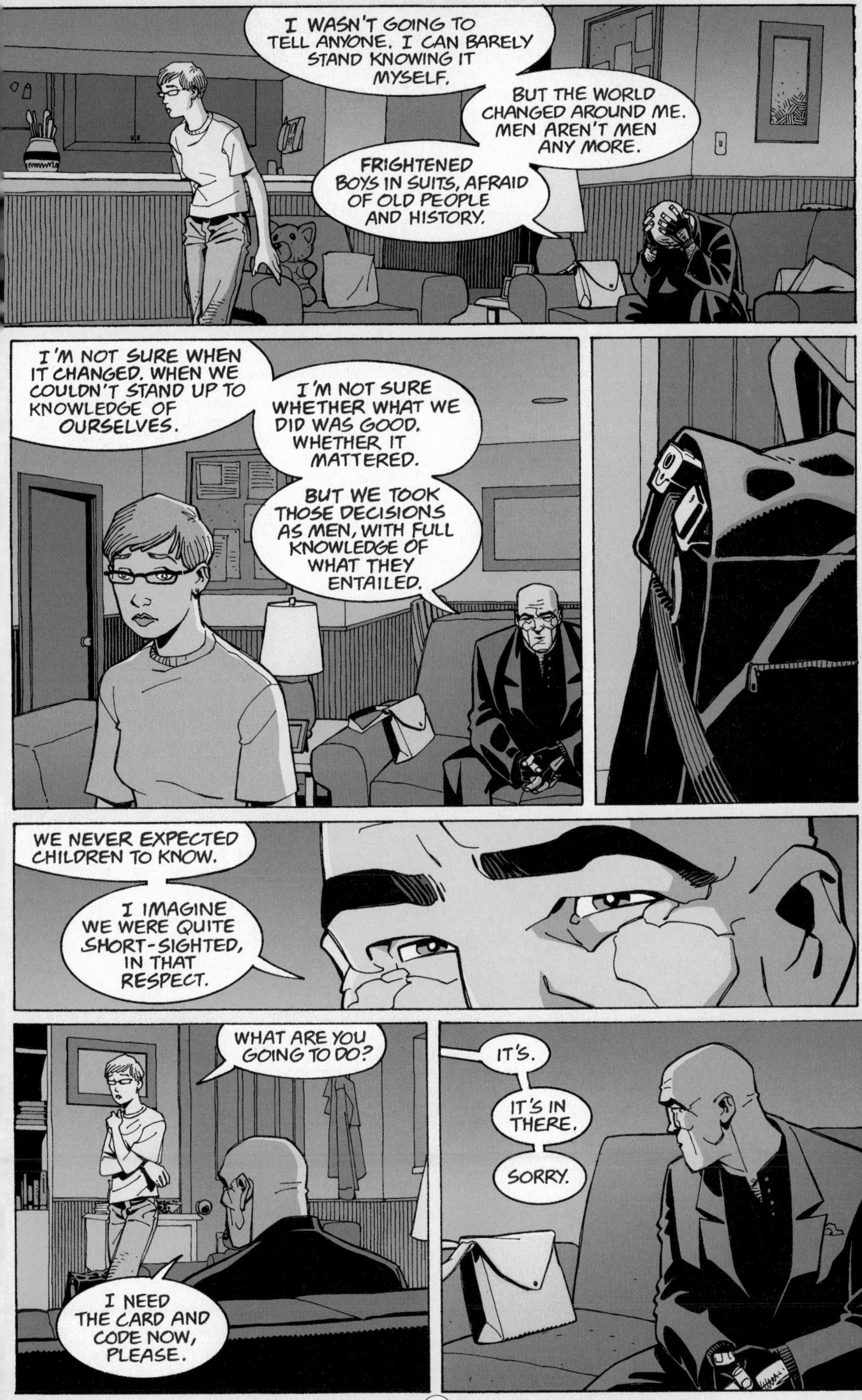
I WASN'T GOING TO TELL ANYONE. I CAN BARELY STAND KNOWING IT MYSELF.
BUT THE WORLD CHANGED AROUND ME. MEN AREN'T MEN ANY MORE.
FRIGHTENED BOYS IN SUITS, AFRAID OF OLD PEOPLE AND HISTORY.
I'M NOT SURE WHEN IT CHANGED. WHEN WE COULDN'T STAND UP TO KNOWLEDGE OF OURSELVES.
I'M NOT SURE WHETHER WHAT WE DID WAS GOOD. WHETHER IT MATTERED.
BUT WE TOOK THOSE DECISIONS AS MEN, WITH FULL KNOWLEDGE OF WHAT THEY ENTAILED.
WE NEVER EXPECTED CHILDREN TO KNOW.
I IMAGINE WE WERE QUITE SHORT-SIGHTED, IN THAT RESPECT.
WHAT ARE YOU GOING TO DO?
I NEED THE CARD AND CODE NOW, PLEASE.
IT'S.
IT'S IN THERE.
SORRY.

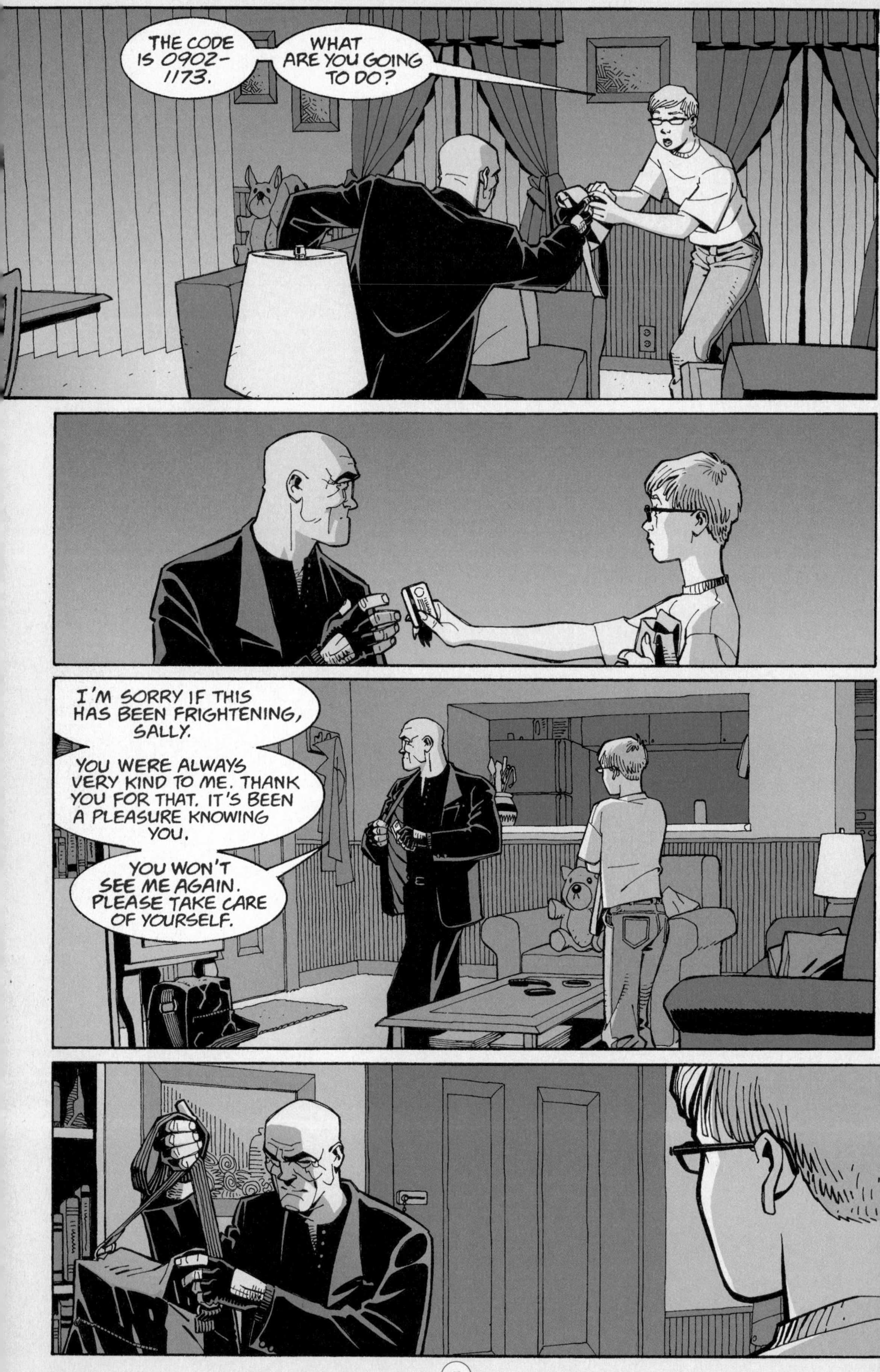
THE CODE IS 0902-1173.
WHAT ARE YOU GOING TO DO?
I'M SORRY IF THIS HAS BEEN FRIGHTENING, SALLY.
YOU WERE ALWAYS VERY KIND TO ME. THANK YOU FOR THAT. IT'S BEEN A PLEASURE KNOWING YOU.
YOU WON'T SEE ME AGAIN. PLEASE TAKE CARE OF YOURSELF.

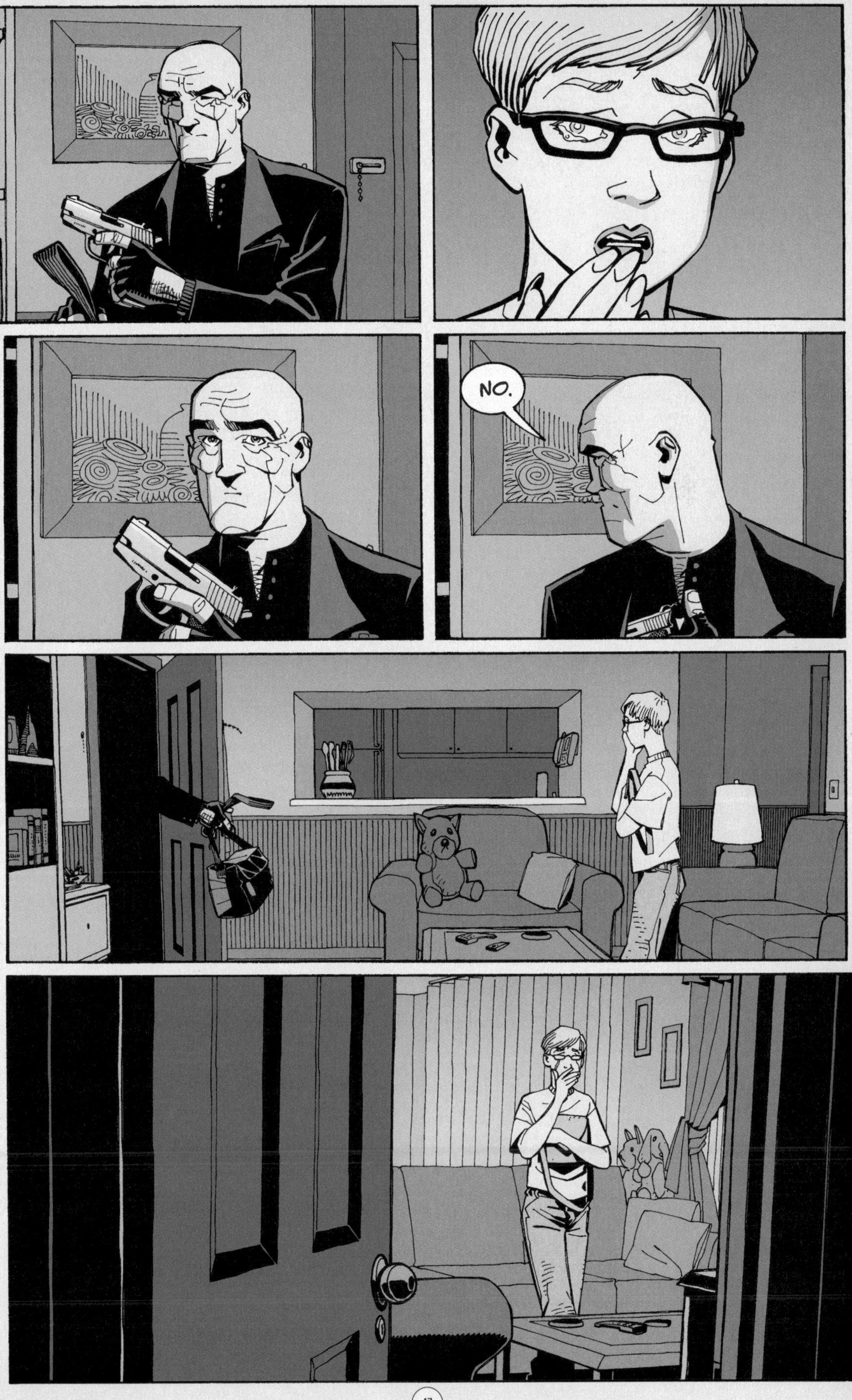
NO.

CAN WE STOP HIM?

I MEAN, THERE'S NO WAY HE CAN BREACH LANGLEY, RIGHT?

WHEN CARTER WAS PRESIDENT, WE WERE ASKED TO RUN A DUMMY OPERATION TO TEST WHITE HOUSE SECURITY.

THE WHITE HOUSE WAS PLACED ON FULL ALERT AT 12 NOON.

AT ONE, CARTER WENT TO THE BATHROOM. HE FOUND THE TOILET FILLED WITH PEANUTS.

PAUL MOSES RESTRAINED HIMSELF. ONLY TWELVE SECURITY AGENTS WERE HOSPITALIZED, AND ALL BUT TWO MADE A FULL RECOVERY.

YOU BEGAN THIS, SIR.

UNDERSTAND THAT YOU HAVE REACTIVATED THE BEST KILLER ON EARTH.

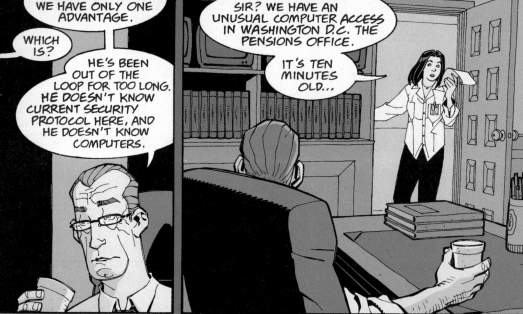

WE HAVE ONLY ONE ADVANTAGE.

WHICH IS?

HE'S BEEN OUT OF THE LOOP FOR TOO LONG. HE DOESN'T KNOW CURRENT SECURITY PROTOCOL HERE, AND HE DOESN'T KNOW COMPUTERS.

SIR? WE HAVE AN UNUSUAL COMPUTER ACCESS IN WASHINGTON D.C. THE PENSIONS OFFICE.

IT'S TEN MINUTES OLD...

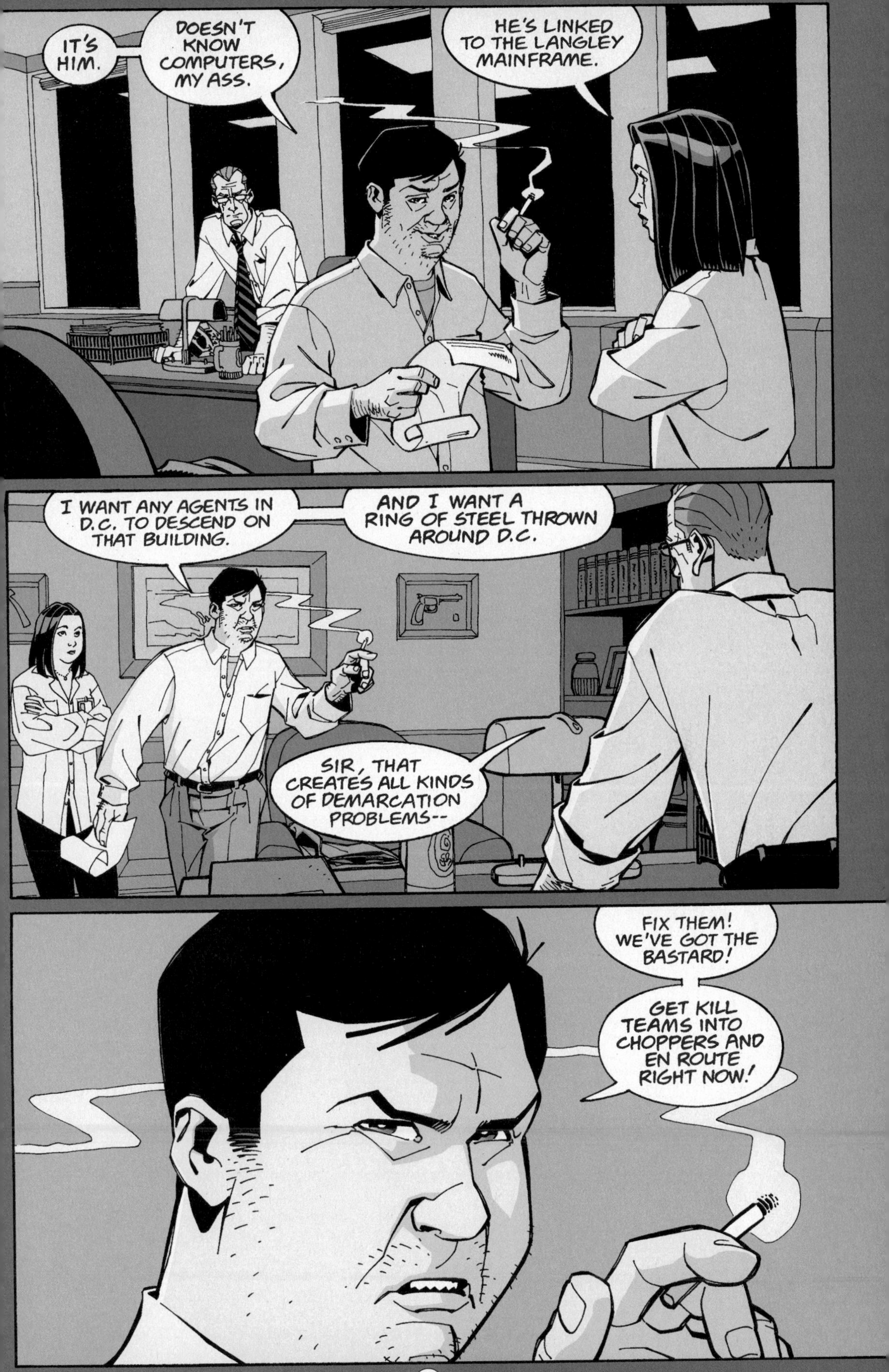
IT'S HIM.
DOESN'T KNOW COMPUTERS, MY ASS.
HE'S LINKED TO THE LANGLEY MAINFRAME.
I WANT ANY AGENTS IN D.C. TO DESCEND ON THAT BUILDING.
AND I WANT A RING OF STEEL THROWN AROUND D.C.
SIR, THAT CREATES ALL KINDS OF DEMARCATION PROBLEMS--
FIX THEM! WE'VE GOT THE BASTARD!
GET KILL TEAMS INTO CHOPPERS AND EN ROUTE RIGHT NOW!

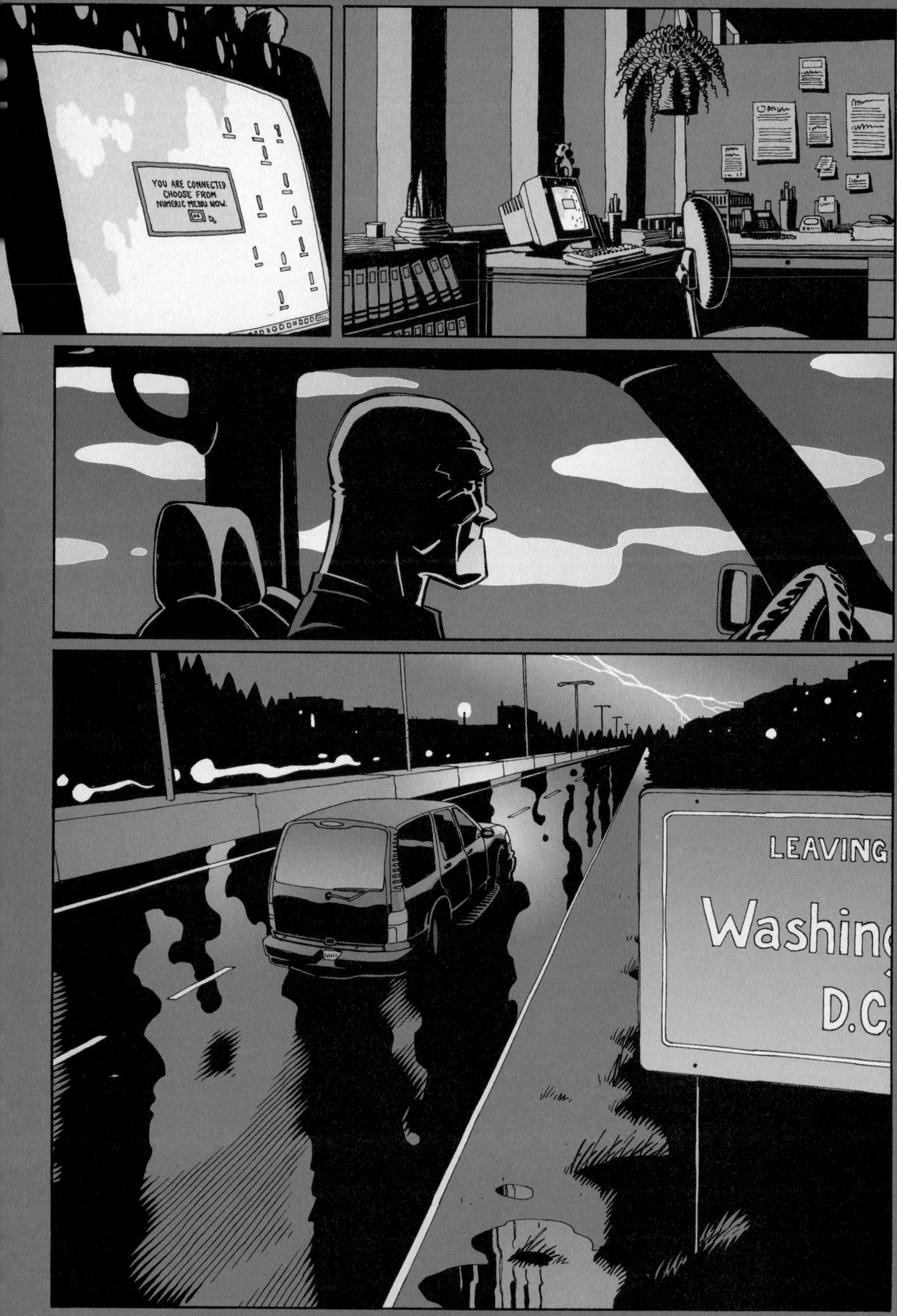
YOU ARE CONNECTED
CHOOSE FROM
NUMERIC MENU NOW.
LEAVING
Washing
D.C.

COVER 3 SKETCHES

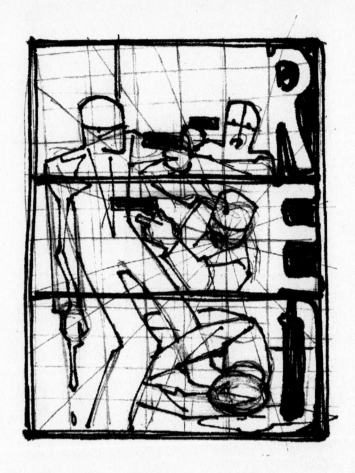

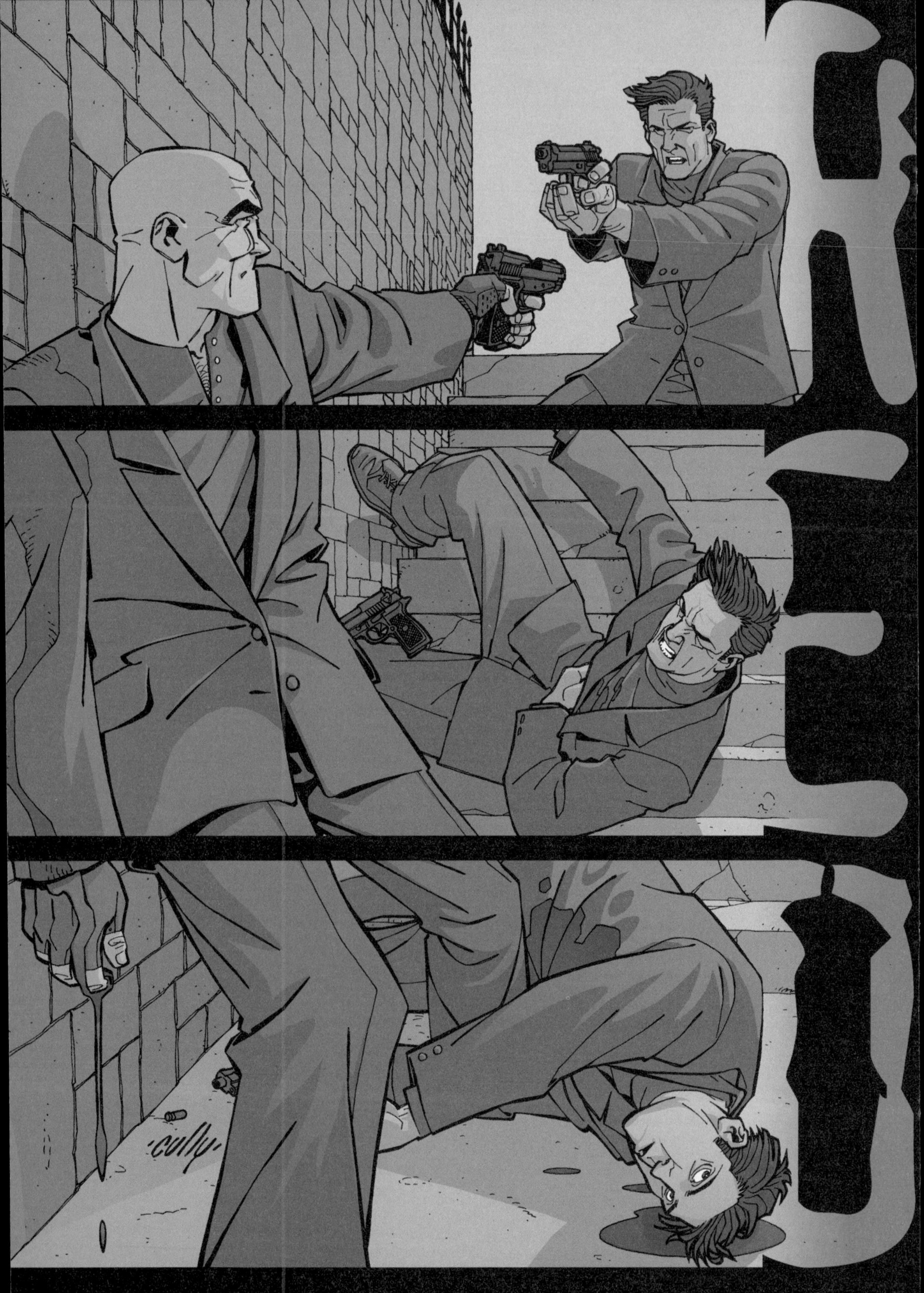

Chapter Three

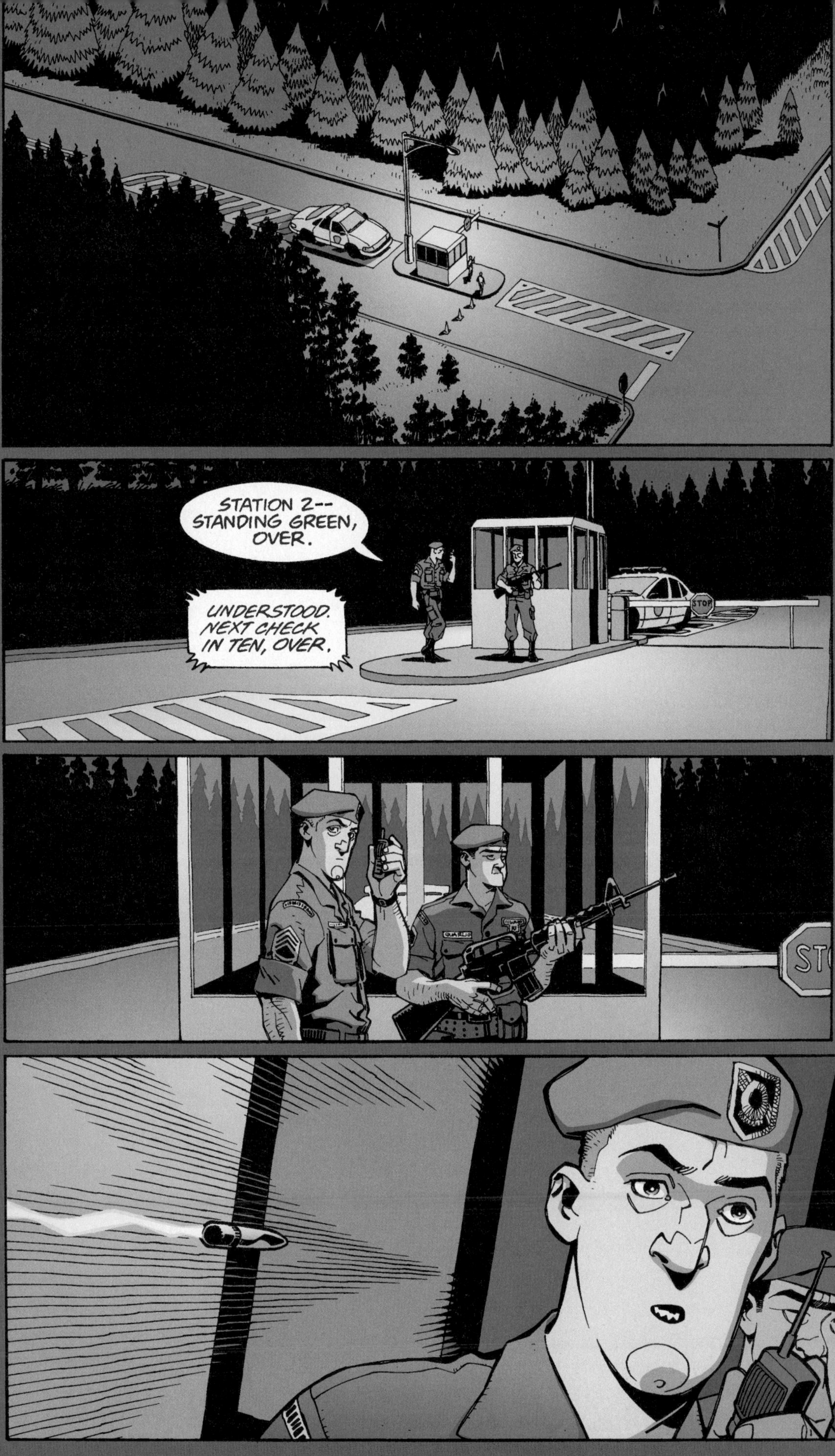

STATION 2-- STANDING GREEN, OVER.
UNDERSTOOD. NEXT CHECK IN TEN, OVER.
STOP

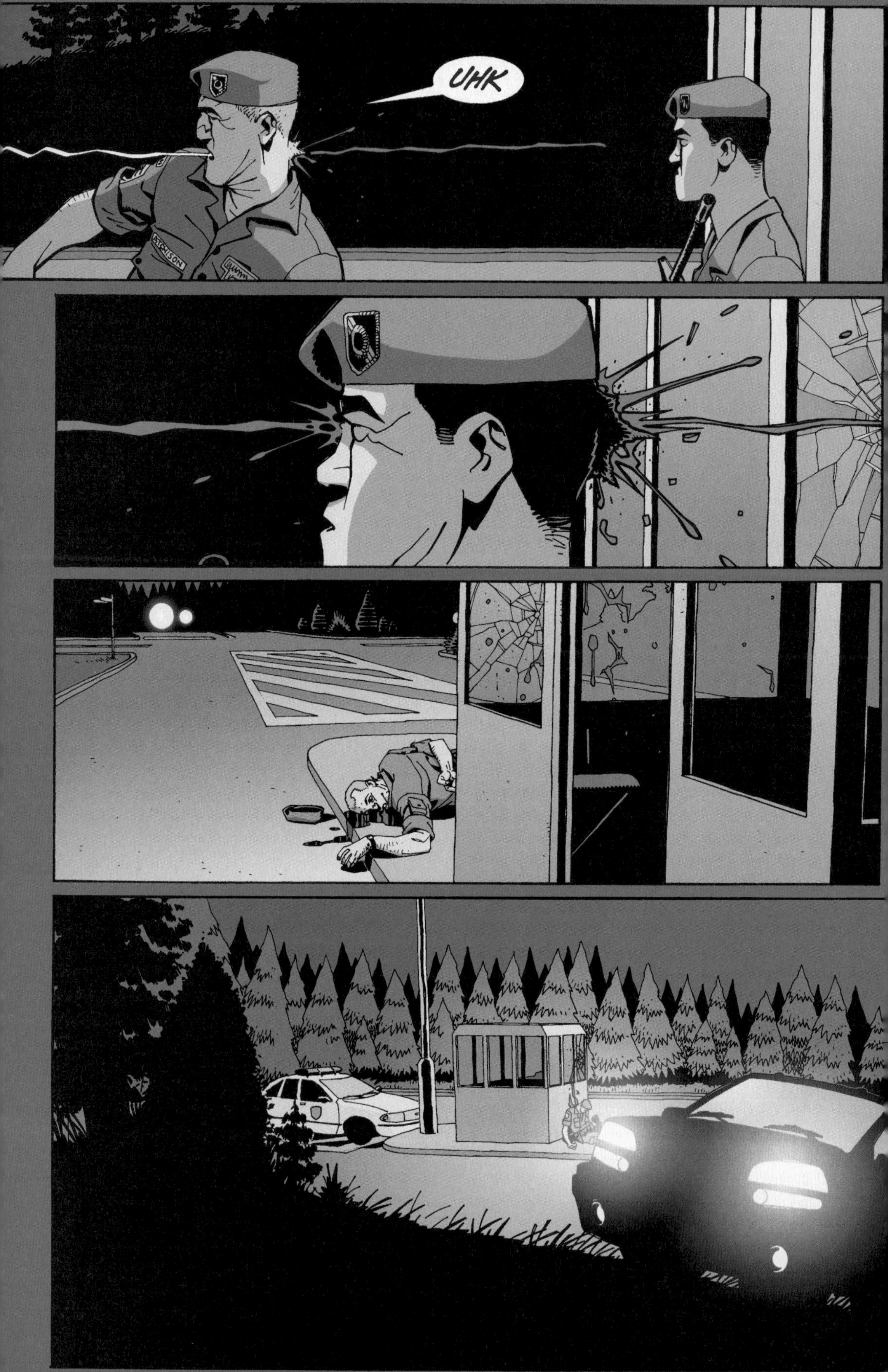
UHK

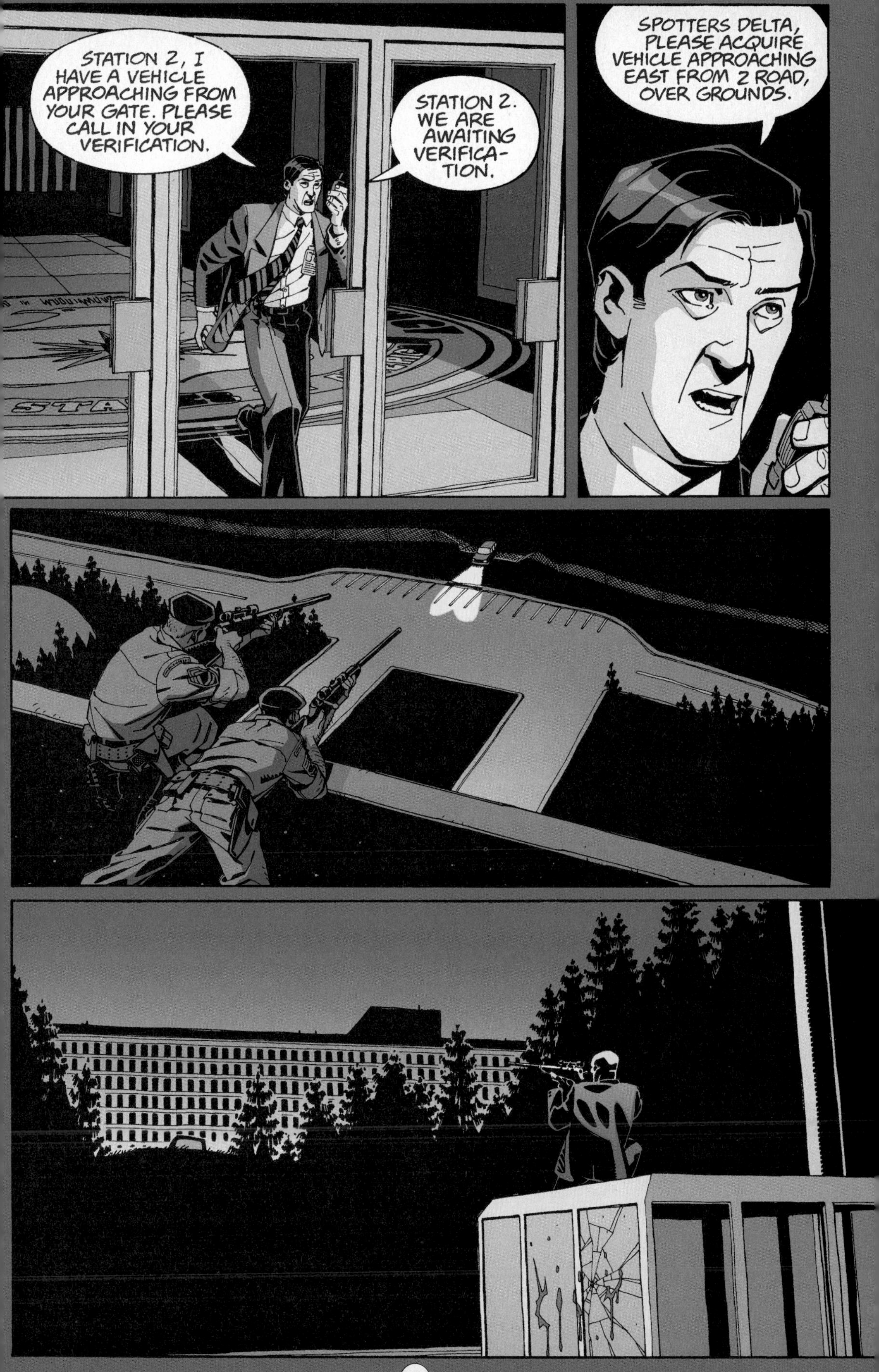
STATION 2, I HAVE A VEHICLE APPROACHING FROM YOUR GATE. PLEASE CALL IN YOUR VERIFICATION.
STATION 2. WE ARE AWAITING VERIFICATION.
SPOTTERS DELTA, PLEASE ACQUIRE VEHICLE APPROACHING EAST FROM 2 ROAD, OVER GROUNDS.

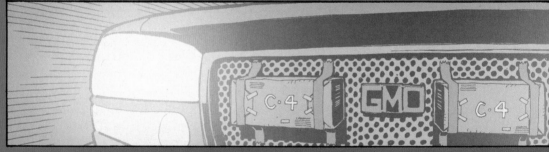

CODE RED.
I REPEAT,
CODE RED--

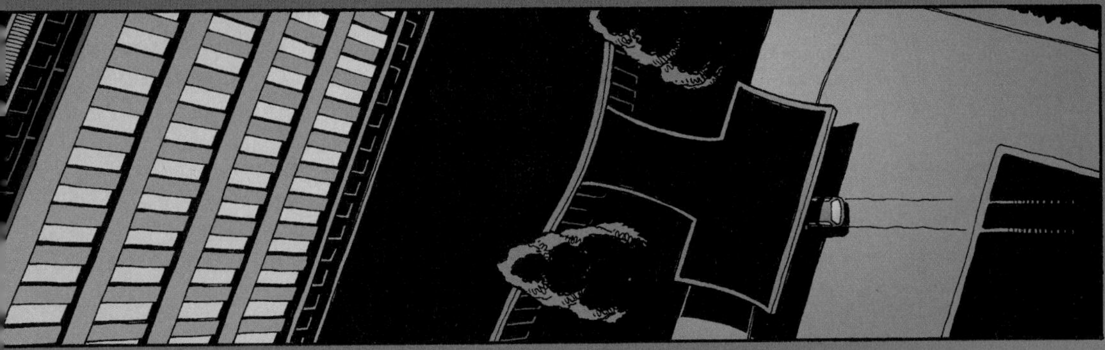

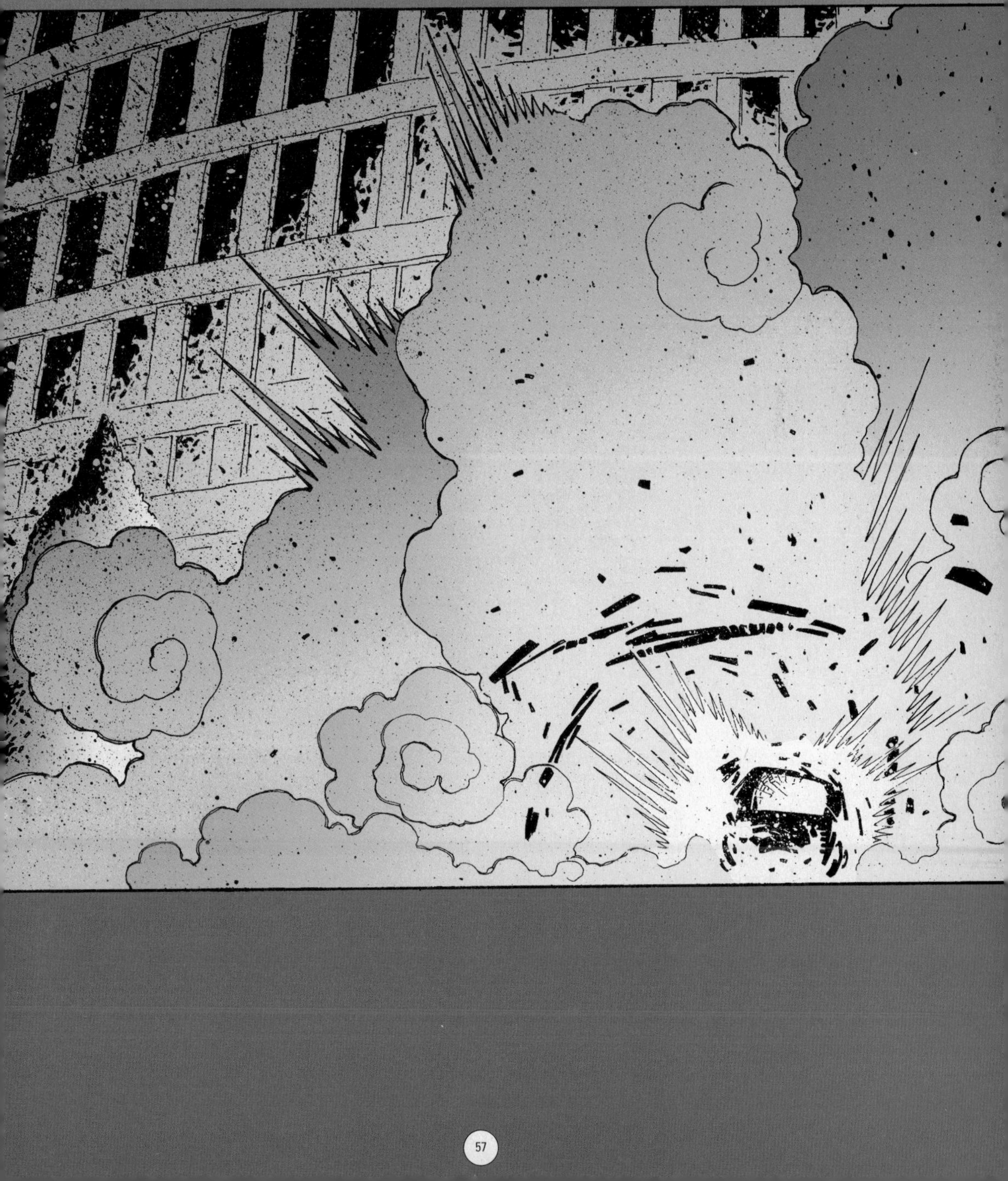

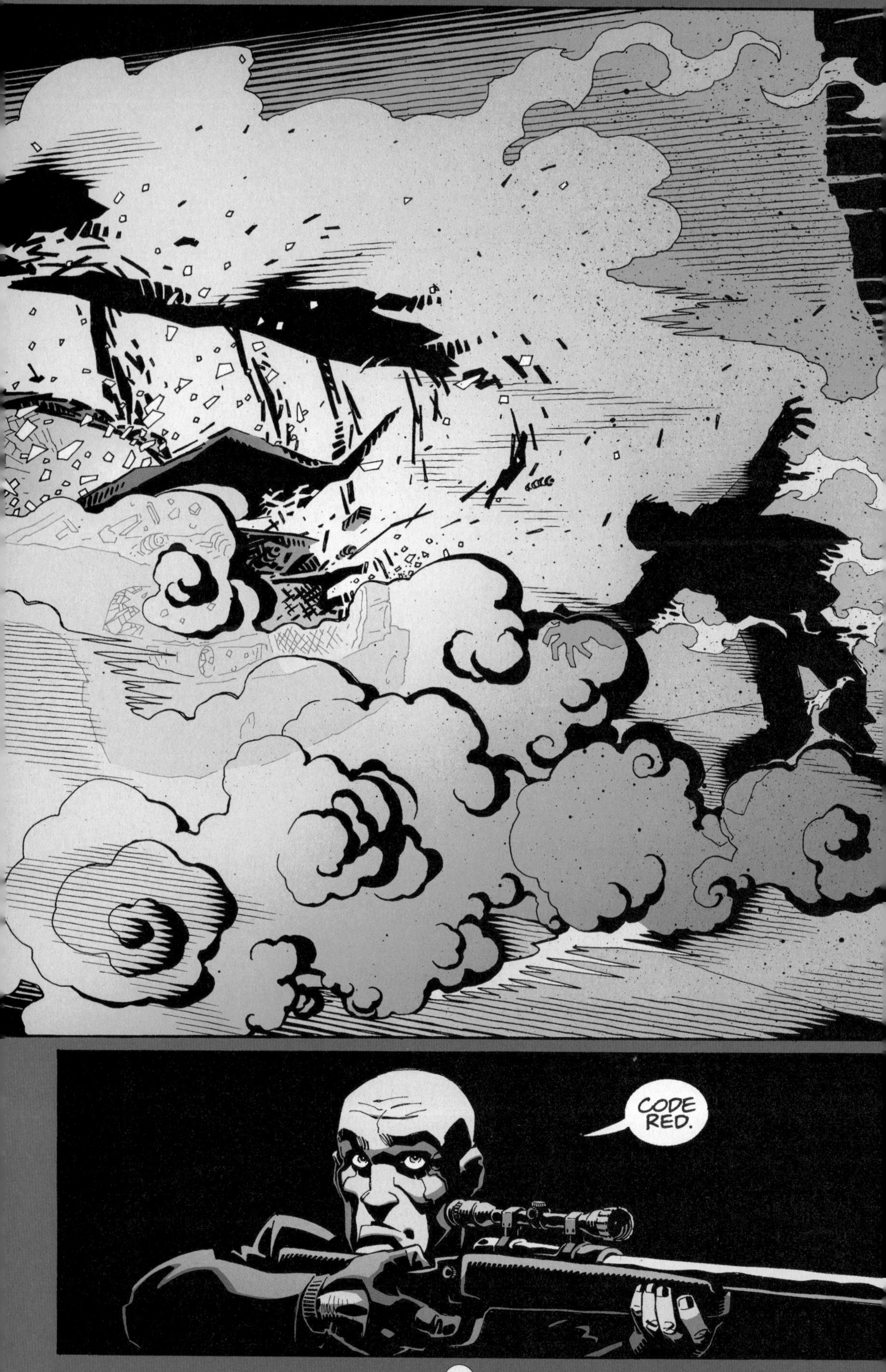
CODE RED.

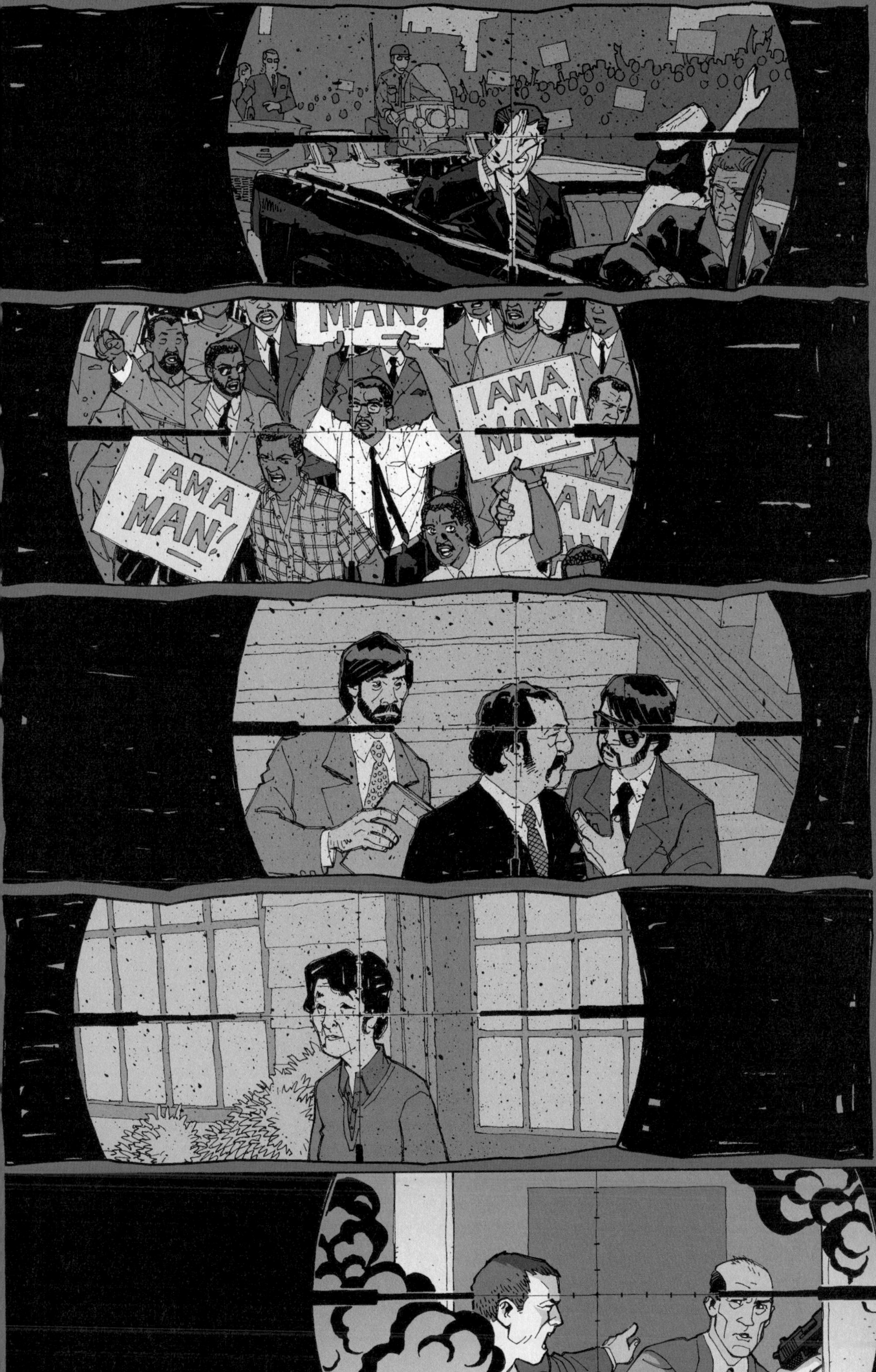
MAN!
I AM A MAN!
I AM A MAN!

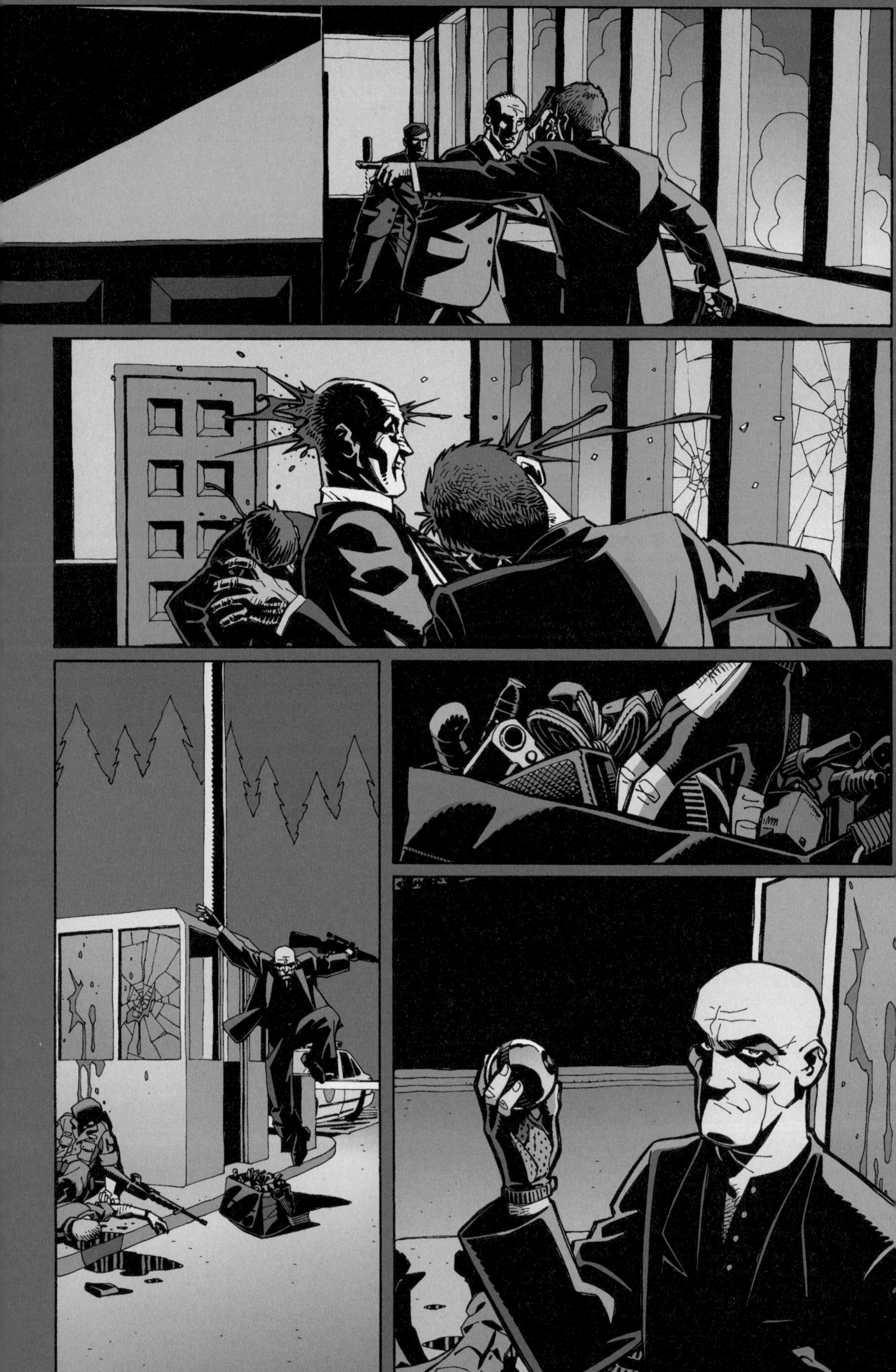

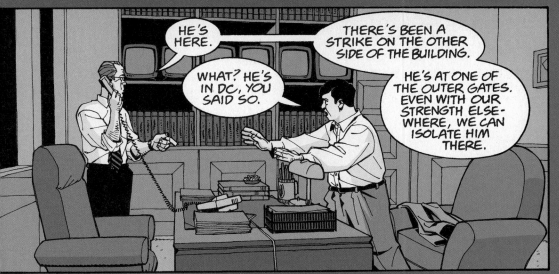

HE'S HERE.

WHAT? HE'S IN DC, YOU SAID SO.

THERE'S BEEN A STRIKE ON THE OTHER SIDE OF THE BUILDING.

HE'S AT ONE OF THE OUTER GATES. EVEN WITH OUR STRENGTH ELSE-WHERE, WE CAN ISOLATE HIM THERE.

DO YOU WANT HIM ALIVE, DIRECTOR?

CHRIST, NO. I DON'T EVEN WANT TO TALK TO HIM, JUST KILL HIM...

EXCUSE ME AGAIN, SIR.

THEY'VE GOT HIM ALREADY?

IT'S PAUL MOSES. HE WANTS TO TALK TO YOU.

I AM LAYING DOWN MY ARMS FOR A MOMENT.

I WANT YOU TO COME OUT AND TALK TO ME.

I WANT YOU TO BE A MAN AND LOOK ME IN THE EYE.

THIS IS KANE. TAKE HIM.

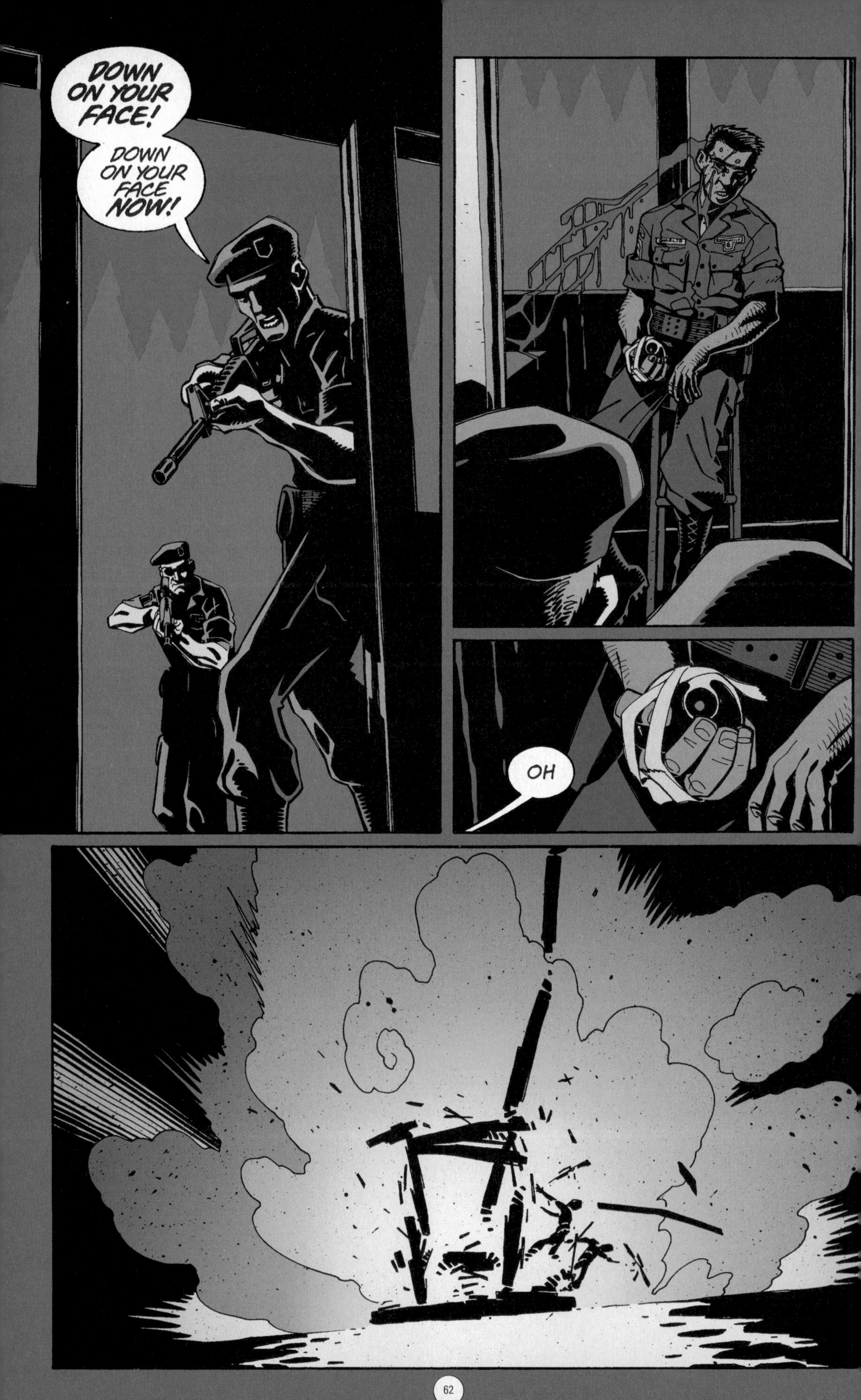
DOWN ON YOUR FACE!
DOWN ON YOUR FACE NOW!
OH

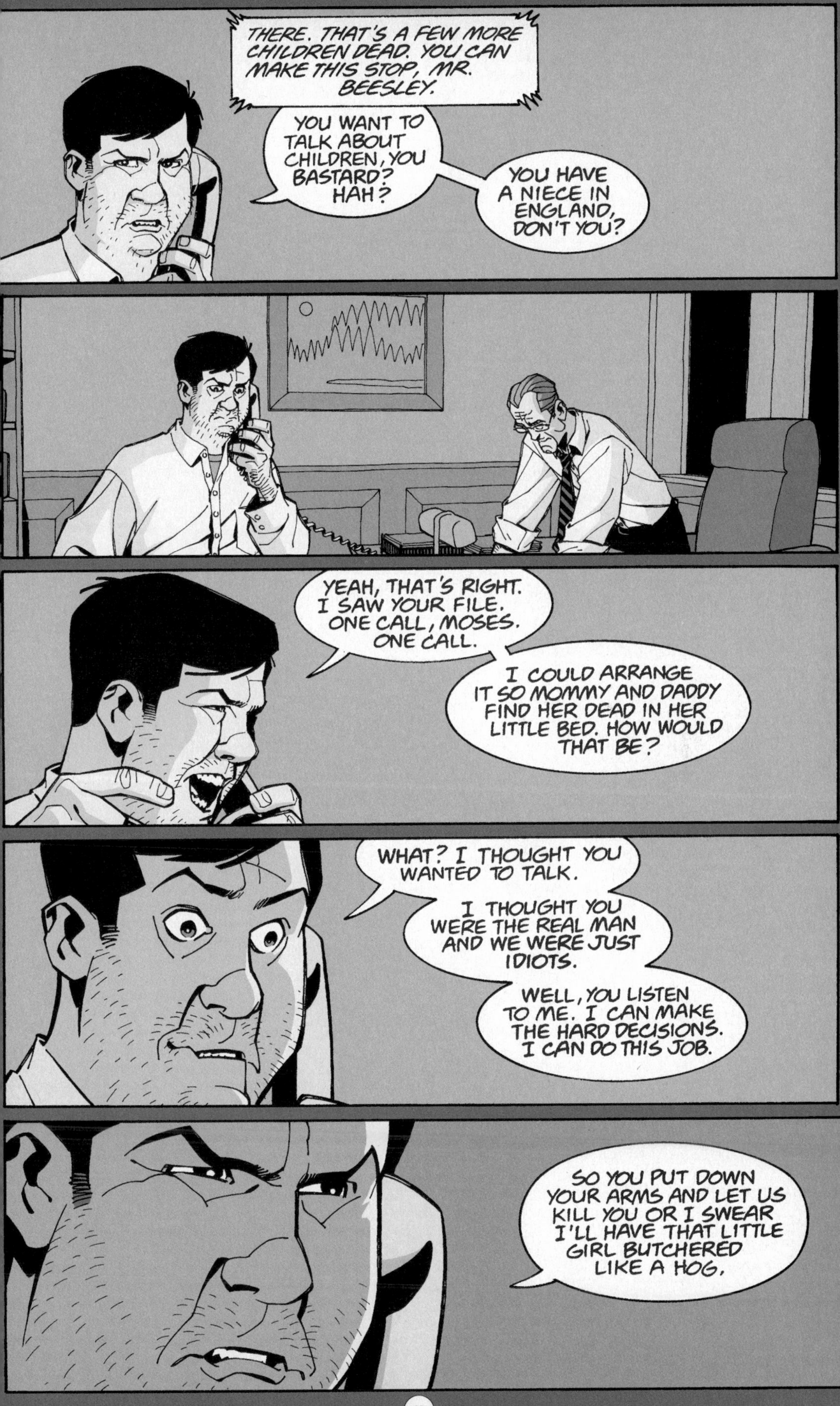
THERE. THAT'S A FEW MORE CHILDREN DEAD. YOU CAN MAKE THIS STOP, MR. BEESLEY.
YOU WANT TO TALK ABOUT CHILDREN, YOU BASTARD? HAH?
YOU HAVE A NIECE IN ENGLAND, DON'T YOU?
YEAH, THAT'S RIGHT. I SAW YOUR FILE. ONE CALL, MOSES. ONE CALL.
I COULD ARRANGE IT SO MOMMY AND DADDY FIND HER DEAD IN HER LITTLE BED. HOW WOULD THAT BE?
WHAT? I THOUGHT YOU WANTED TO TALK.
I THOUGHT YOU WERE THE REAL MAN AND WE WERE JUST IDIOTS.
WELL, YOU LISTEN TO ME. I CAN MAKE THE HARD DECISIONS. I CAN DO THIS JOB.
SO YOU PUT DOWN YOUR ARMS AND LET US KILL YOU OR I SWEAR I'LL HAVE THAT LITTLE GIRL BUTCHERED LIKE A HOG.

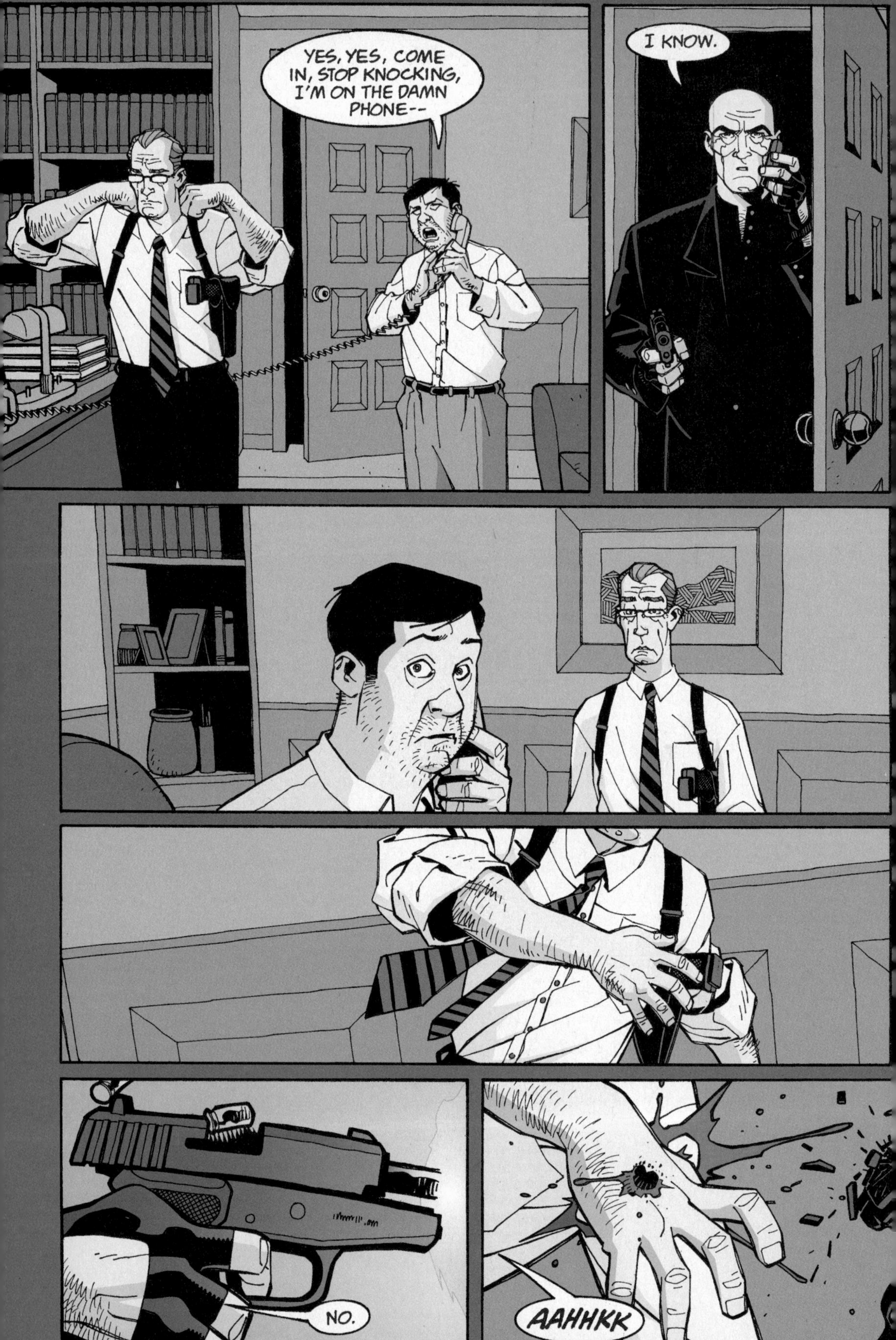
YES, YES, COME IN, STOP KNOCKING, I'M ON THE DAMN PHONE--
I KNOW.
NO.
AAHHKK

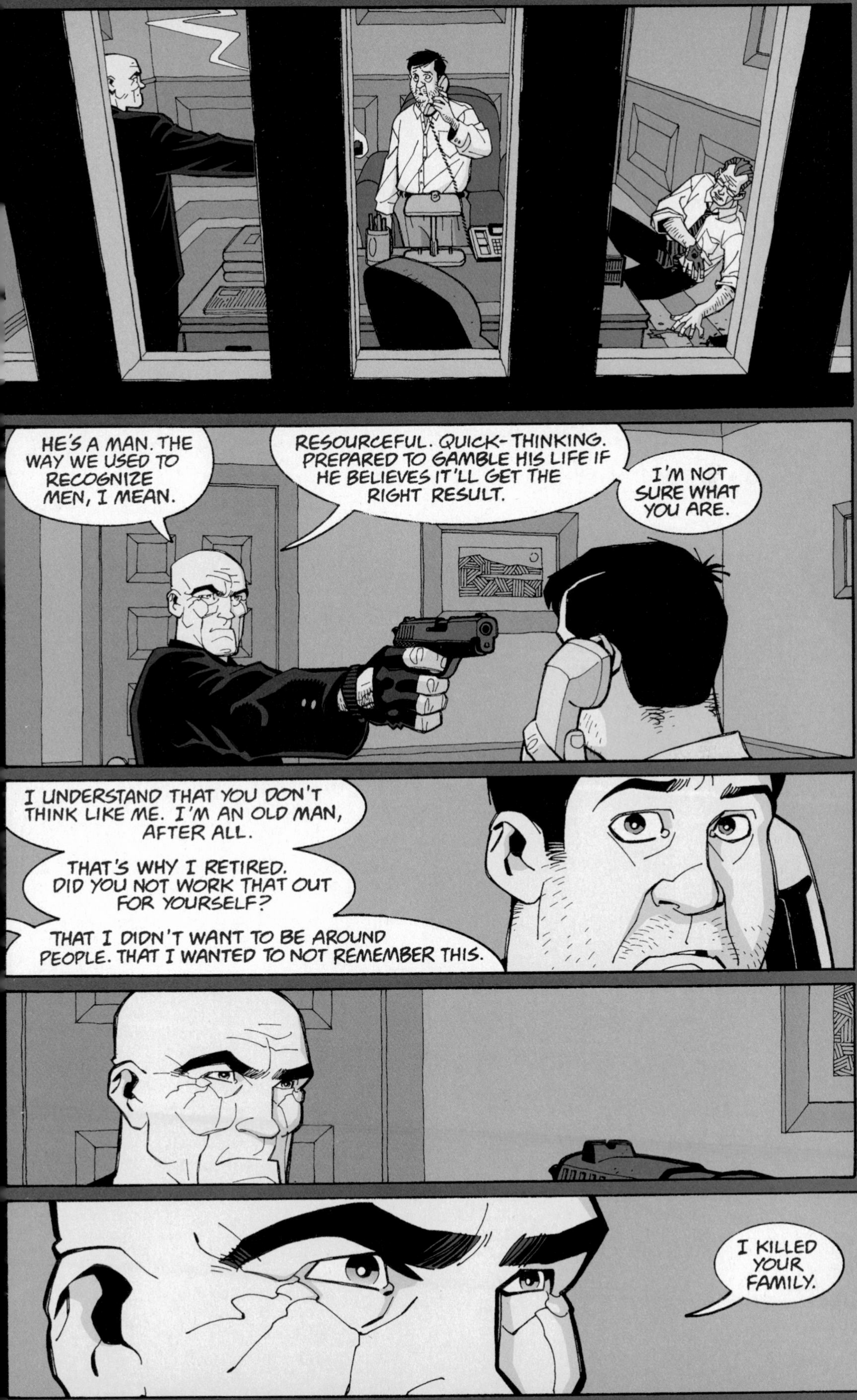
HE'S A MAN. THE WAY WE USED TO RECOGNIZE MEN, I MEAN.
RESOURCEFUL. QUICK-THINKING. PREPARED TO GAMBLE HIS LIFE IF HE BELIEVES IT'LL GET THE RIGHT RESULT.
I'M NOT SURE WHAT YOU ARE.
I UNDERSTAND THAT YOU DON'T THINK LIKE ME. I'M AN OLD MAN, AFTER ALL.
THAT'S WHY I RETIRED. DID YOU NOT WORK THAT OUT FOR YOURSELF?
THAT I DIDN'T WANT TO BE AROUND PEOPLE. THAT I WANTED TO NOT REMEMBER THIS.
I KILLED YOUR FAMILY.

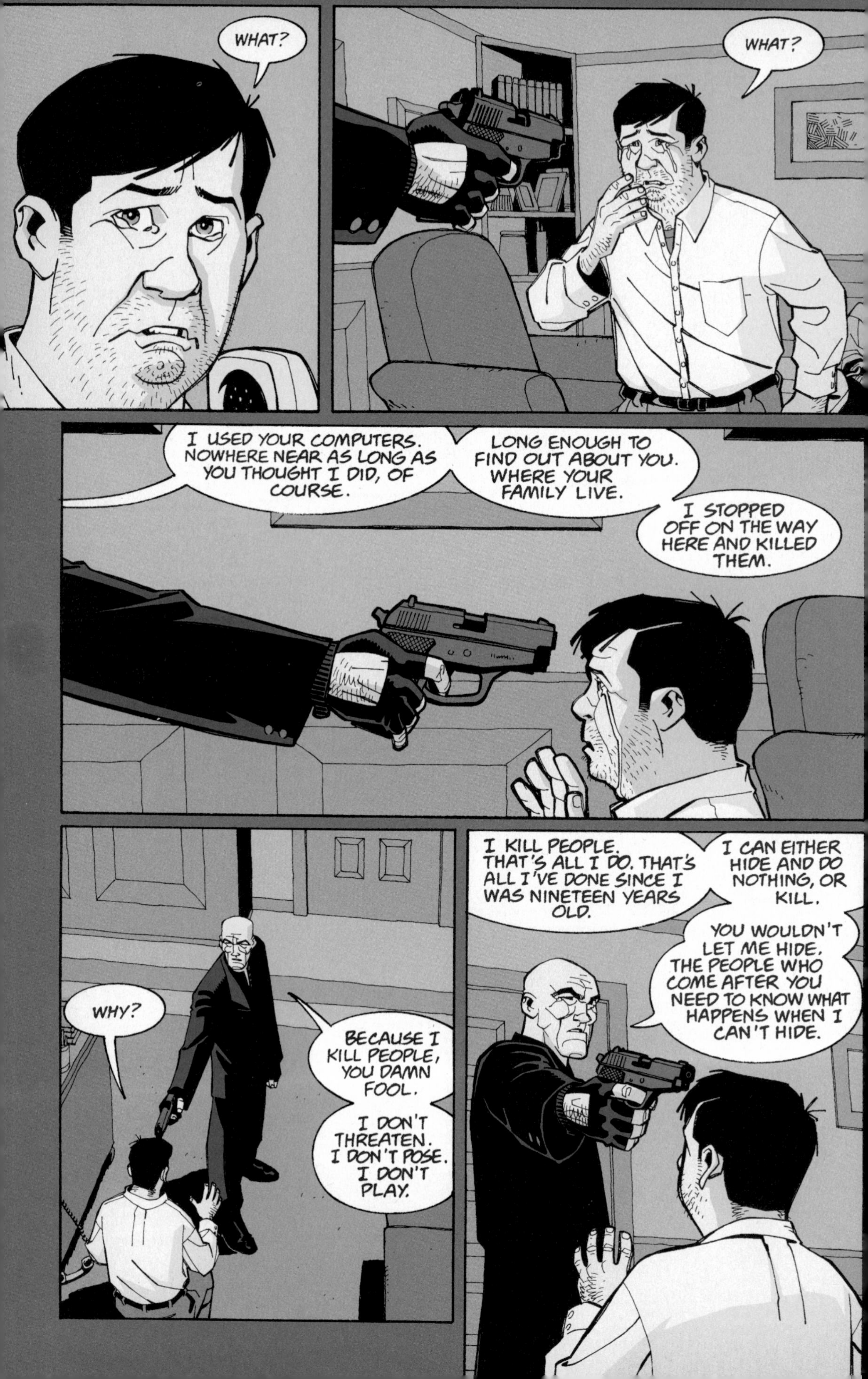
WHAT?
WHAT?
I USED YOUR COMPUTERS. NOWHERE NEAR AS LONG AS YOU THOUGHT I DID, OF COURSE.
LONG ENOUGH TO FIND OUT ABOUT YOU. WHERE YOUR FAMILY LIVE.
I STOPPED OFF ON THE WAY HERE AND KILLED THEM.
WHY?
BECAUSE I KILL PEOPLE, YOU DAMN FOOL.
I DON'T THREATEN. I DON'T POSE. I DON'T PLAY.
I KILL PEOPLE. THAT'S ALL I DO. THAT'S ALL I'VE DONE SINCE I WAS NINETEEN YEARS OLD.
I CAN EITHER HIDE AND DO NOTHING, OR KILL.
YOU WOULDN'T LET ME HIDE. THE PEOPLE WHO COME AFTER YOU NEED TO KNOW WHAT HAPPENS WHEN I CAN'T HIDE.

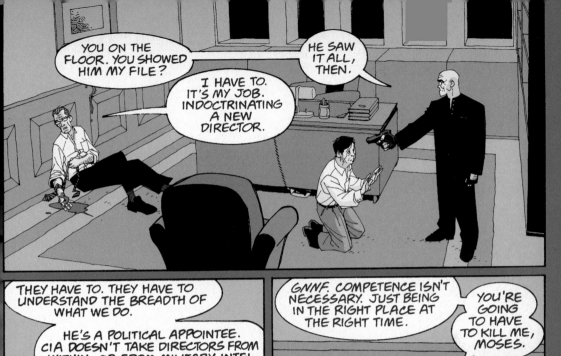

YOU ON THE FLOOR. YOU SHOWED HIM MY FILE?

I HAVE TO. IT'S MY JOB. INDOCTRINATING A NEW DIRECTOR.

HE SAW IT ALL, THEN.

THEY HAVE TO. THEY HAVE TO UNDERSTAND THE BREADTH OF WHAT WE DO.

HE'S A POLITICAL APPOINTEE. CIA DOESN'T TAKE DIRECTORS FROM WITHIN, OR FROM MILITARY INTEL, ANYMORE.

LIKE DISTRICT ATTORNEYS ARE ELECTED, RATHER THAN APPOINTED. LIKE WE ELECT EVERYTHING. WE DON'T JUST --HA--TAKE THE PERSON WHO'S BEST FOR THE TOP JOB AND PUT THEM THERE.

GNNF. COMPETENCE ISN'T NECESSARY. JUST BEING IN THE RIGHT PLACE AT THE RIGHT TIME.

YOU'RE GOING TO HAVE TO KILL ME, MOSES.

BECAUSE YOU WILL CHANGE ALL THAT.

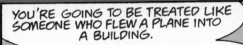

YOU'RE GOING TO BE TREATED LIKE SOMEONE WHO FLEW A PLANE INTO A BUILDING.

WE TRIED TO KILL YOU BECAUSE YOU'RE A MONSTER. WE FAILED TO DO IT RIGHT, AND YOU CAME BACK TO PUNISH US FOR OUR INCOMPETENCE.

YOU WILL HAVE TO KILL ME, AND EVERYONE IN THIS BUILDING, BECAUSE WE WILL RAISE AN ARMY UP AGAINST YOU.

HAVE YOU GOT THE STOMACH FOR THAT?

DO YOU UNDERSTAND THAT YOU CAN NOW ONLY FIND THE PEACE YOU WANT BY DYING?

I'M SORRY YOU WERE CHEATED OUT OF YOUR RETIREMENT. BUT IT'S DONE. AND NOW NOTHING CAN BE THE SAME.

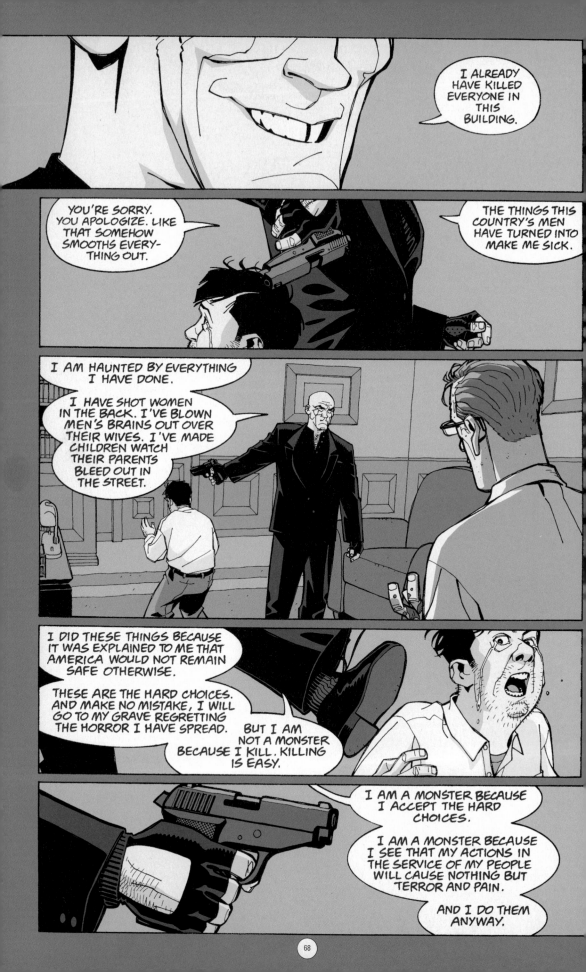

I ALREADY HAVE KILLED EVERYONE IN THIS BUILDING.

YOU'RE SORRY. YOU APOLOGIZE. LIKE THAT SOMEHOW SMOOTHS EVERYTHING OUT.

THE THINGS THIS COUNTRY'S MEN HAVE TURNED INTO MAKE ME SICK.

I AM HAUNTED BY EVERYTHING I HAVE DONE.

I HAVE SHOT WOMEN IN THE BACK. I'VE BLOWN MEN'S BRAINS OUT OVER THEIR WIVES. I'VE MADE CHILDREN WATCH THEIR PARENTS BLEED OUT IN THE STREET.

I DID THESE THINGS BECAUSE IT WAS EXPLAINED TO ME THAT AMERICA WOULD NOT REMAIN SAFE OTHERWISE.

THESE ARE THE HARD CHOICES. AND MAKE NO MISTAKE, I WILL GO TO MY GRAVE REGRETTING THE HORROR I HAVE SPREAD. BUT I AM NOT A MONSTER BECAUSE I KILL. KILLING IS EASY.

I AM A MONSTER BECAUSE I ACCEPT THE HARD CHOICES.

I AM A MONSTER BECAUSE I SEE THAT MY ACTIONS IN THE SERVICE OF MY PEOPLE WILL CAUSE NOTHING BUT TERROR AND PAIN.

AND I DO THEM ANYWAY.

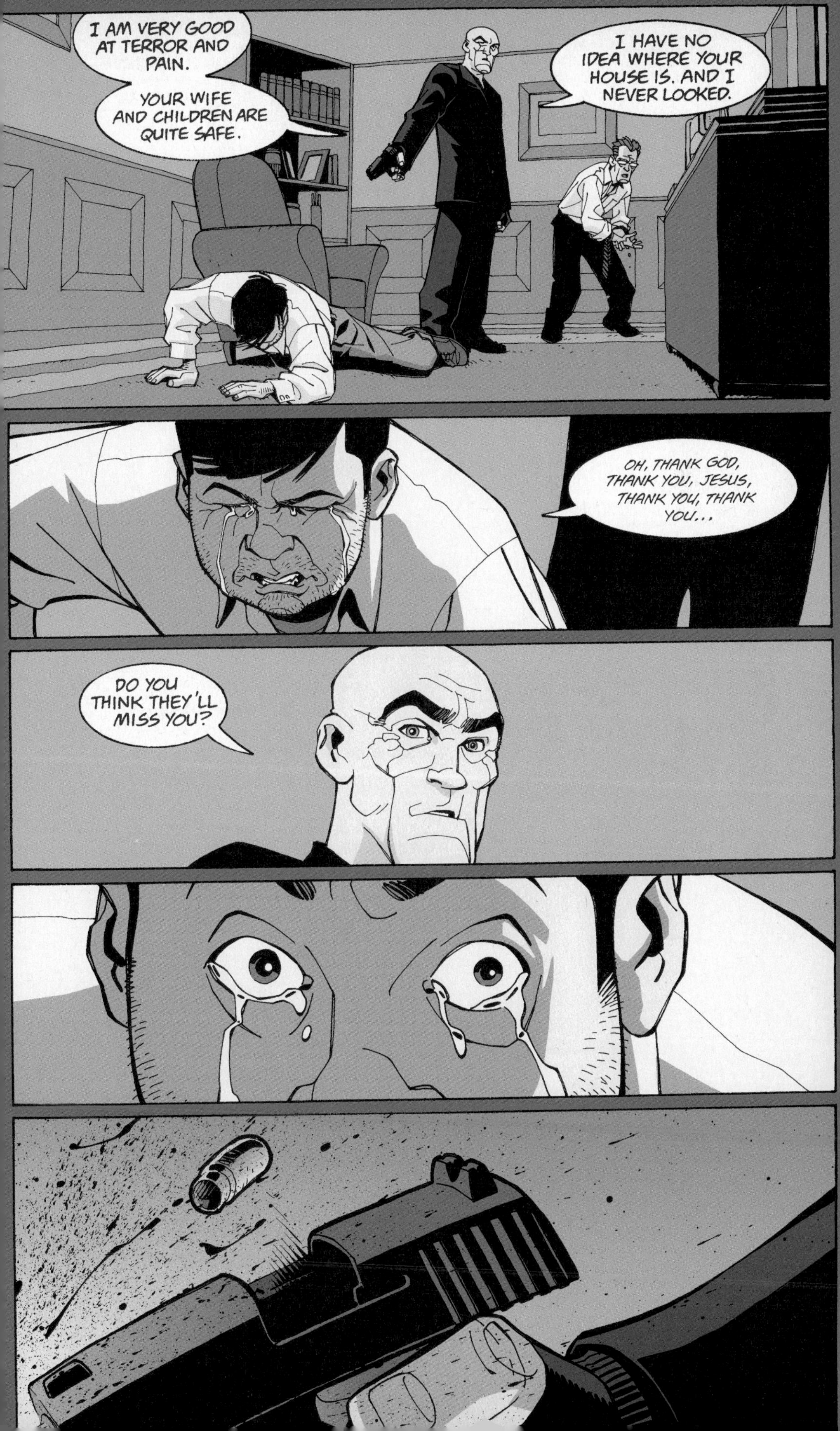
I AM VERY GOOD AT TERROR AND PAIN.
YOUR WIFE AND CHILDREN ARE QUITE SAFE.
I HAVE NO IDEA WHERE YOUR HOUSE IS. AND I NEVER LOOKED.
OH, THANK GOD, THANK YOU, JESUS, THANK YOU, THANK YOU...
DO YOU THINK THEY'LL MISS YOU?

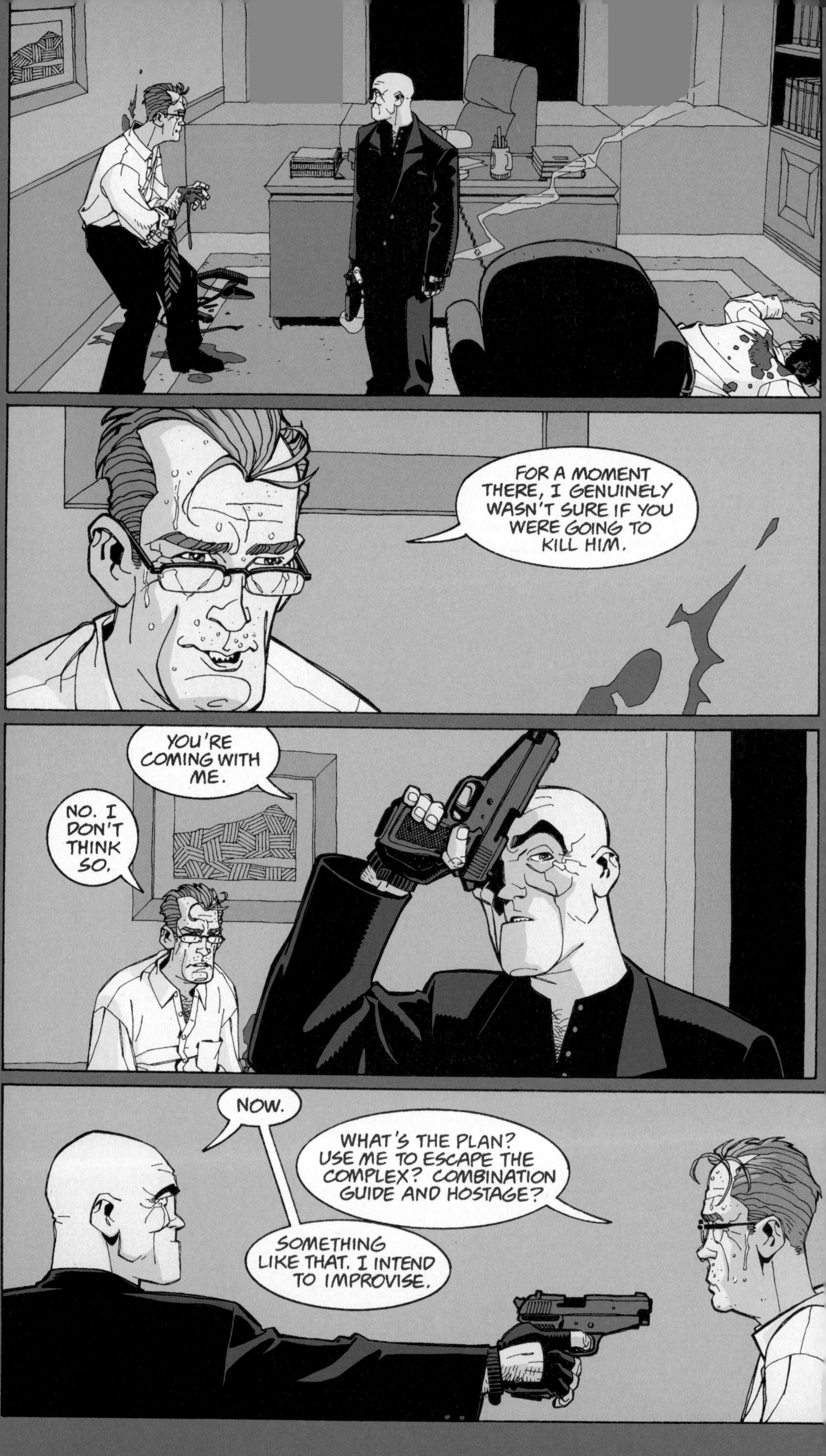
FOR A MOMENT THERE, I GENUINELY WASN'T SURE IF YOU WERE GOING TO KILL HIM.
YOU'RE COMING WITH ME.
NO. I DON'T THINK SO.
NOW.
WHAT'S THE PLAN? USE ME TO ESCAPE THE COMPLEX? COMBINATION GUIDE AND HOSTAGE?
SOMETHING LIKE THAT. I INTEND TO IMPROVISE.

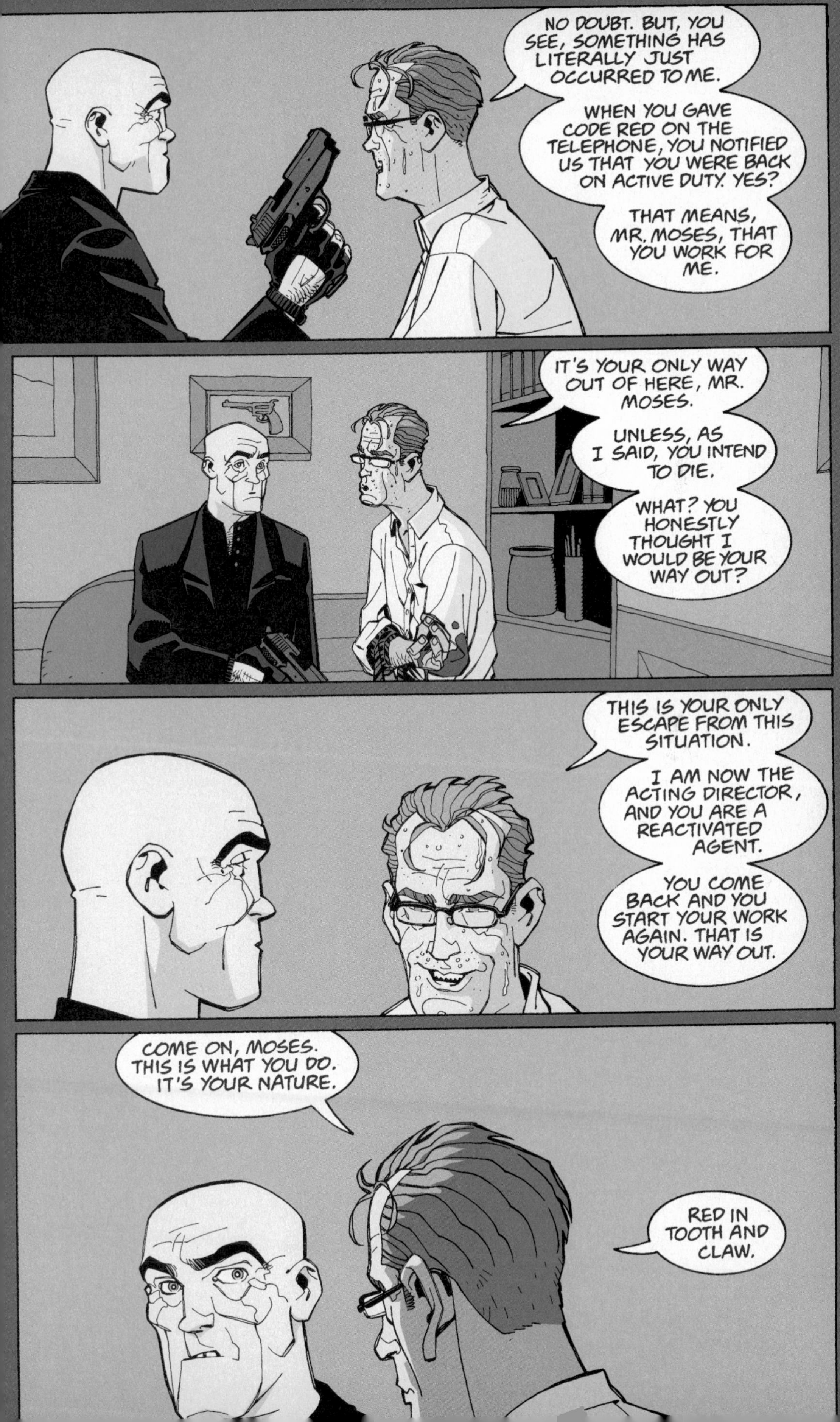
NO DOUBT. BUT, YOU SEE, SOMETHING HAS LITERALLY JUST OCCURRED TO ME.
WHEN YOU GAVE CODE RED ON THE TELEPHONE, YOU NOTIFIED US THAT YOU WERE BACK ON ACTIVE DUTY. YES?
THAT MEANS, MR. MOSES, THAT YOU WORK FOR ME.
IT'S YOUR ONLY WAY OUT OF HERE, MR. MOSES.
UNLESS, AS I SAID, YOU INTEND TO DIE.
WHAT? YOU HONESTLY THOUGHT I WOULD BE YOUR WAY OUT?
THIS IS YOUR ONLY ESCAPE FROM THIS SITUATION.
I AM NOW THE ACTING DIRECTOR, AND YOU ARE A REACTIVATED AGENT.
YOU COME BACK AND YOU START YOUR WORK AGAIN. THAT IS YOUR WAY OUT.
COME ON, MOSES. THIS IS WHAT YOU DO. IT'S YOUR NATURE.
RED IN TOOTH AND CLAW.

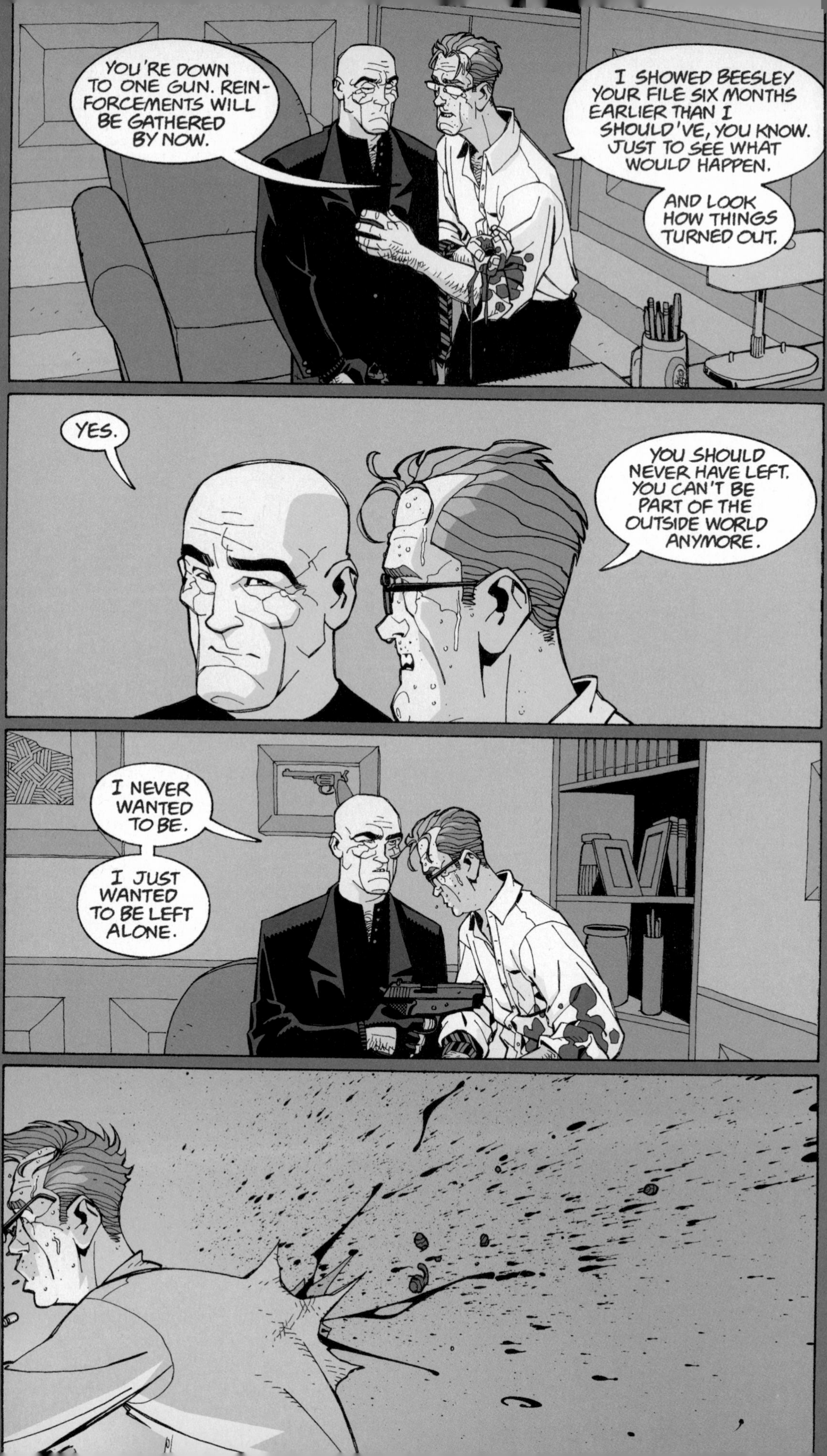
YOU'RE DOWN TO ONE GUN. REIN-FORCEMENTS WILL BE GATHERED BY NOW.
I SHOWED BEESLEY YOUR FILE SIX MONTHS EARLIER THAN I SHOULD'VE, YOU KNOW. JUST TO SEE WHAT WOULD HAPPEN.
AND LOOK HOW THINGS TURNED OUT.
YES.
YOU SHOULD NEVER HAVE LEFT. YOU CAN'T BE PART OF THE OUTSIDE WORLD ANYMORE.
I NEVER WANTED TO BE.
I JUST WANTED TO BE LEFT ALONE.

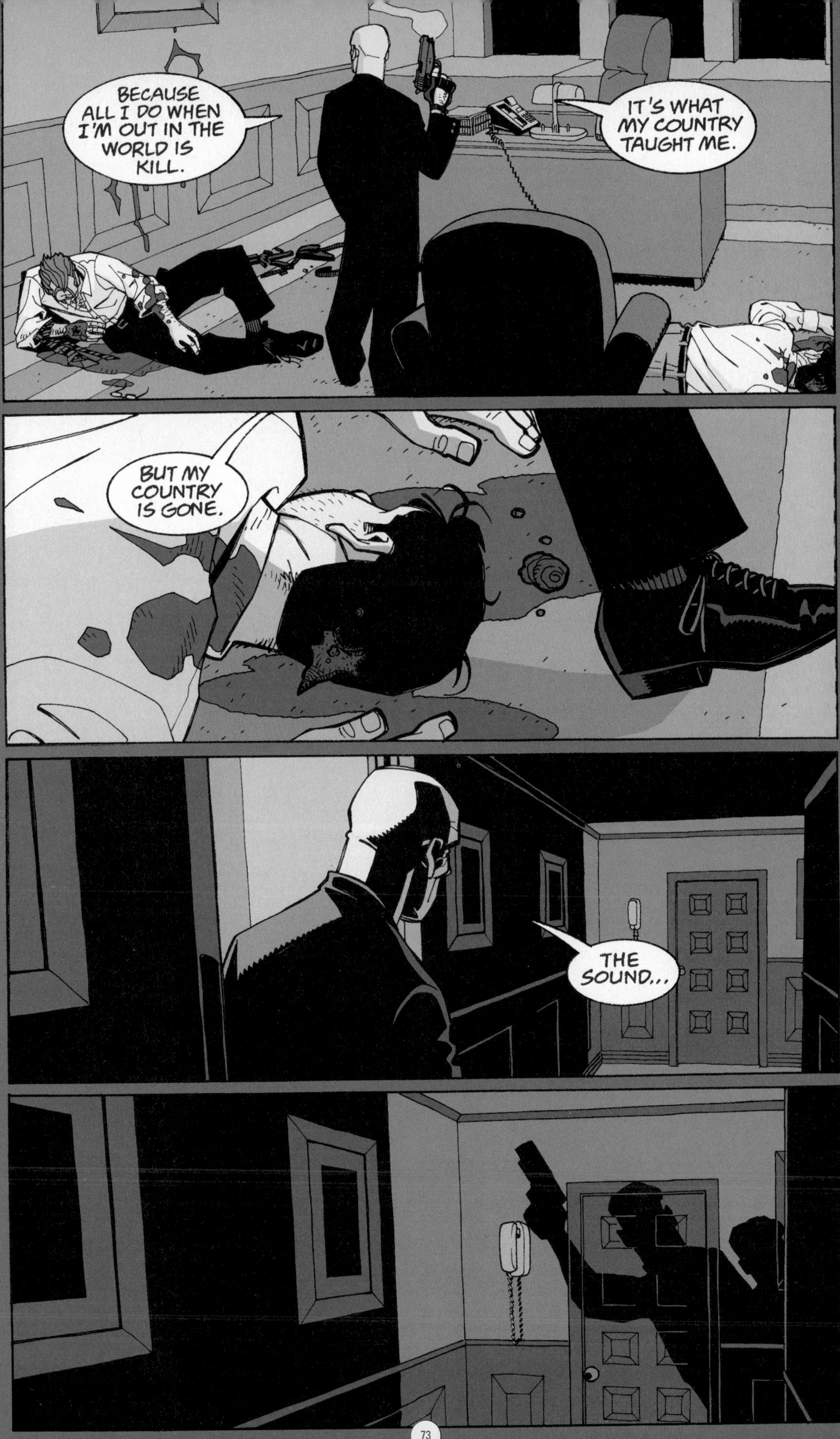
BECAUSE ALL I DO WHEN I'M OUT IN THE WORLD IS KILL.
IT'S WHAT MY COUNTRY TAUGHT ME.
BUT MY COUNTRY IS GONE.
THE SOUND...

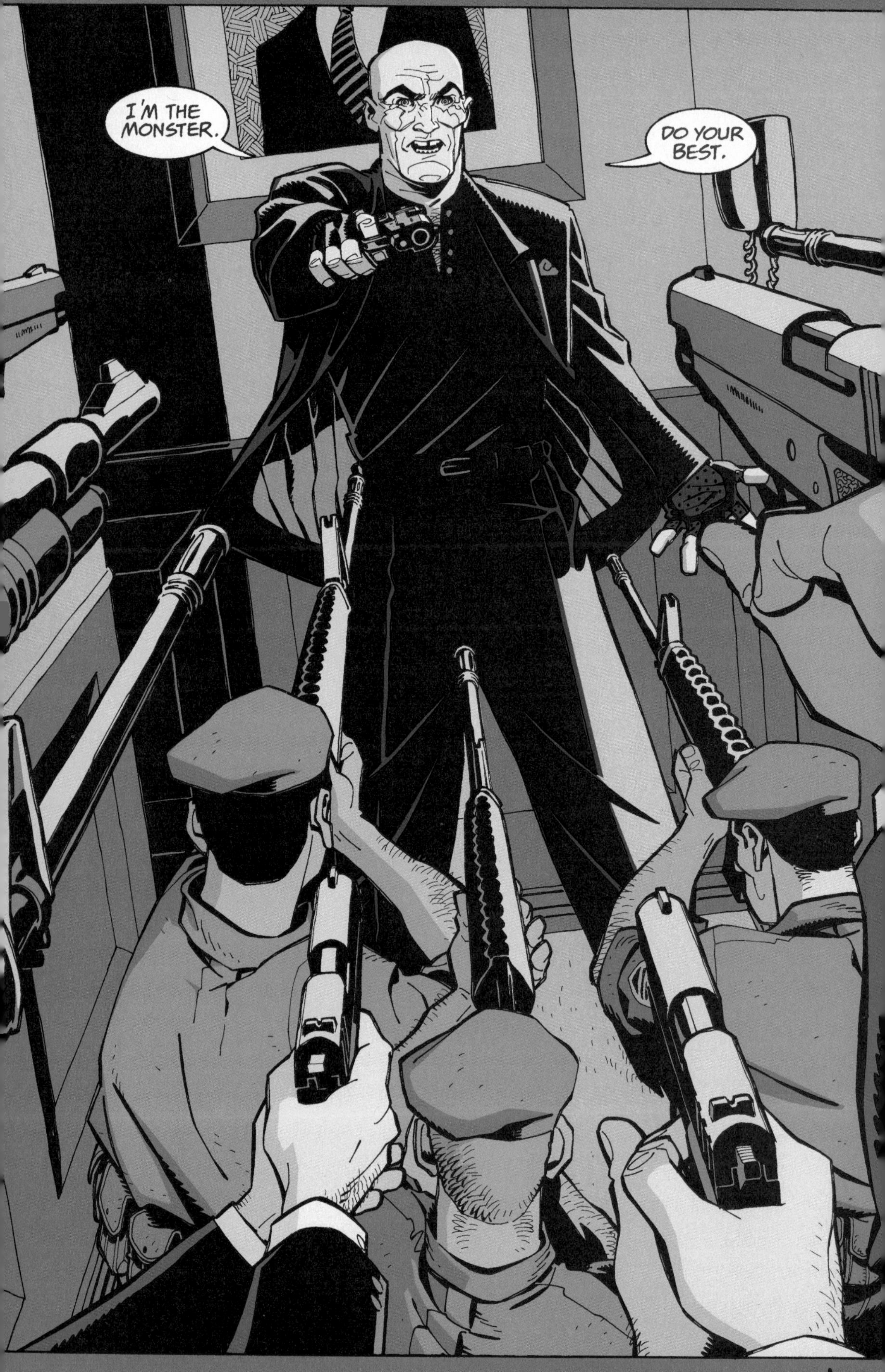
I'M THE MONSTER.
DO YOUR BEST.

end

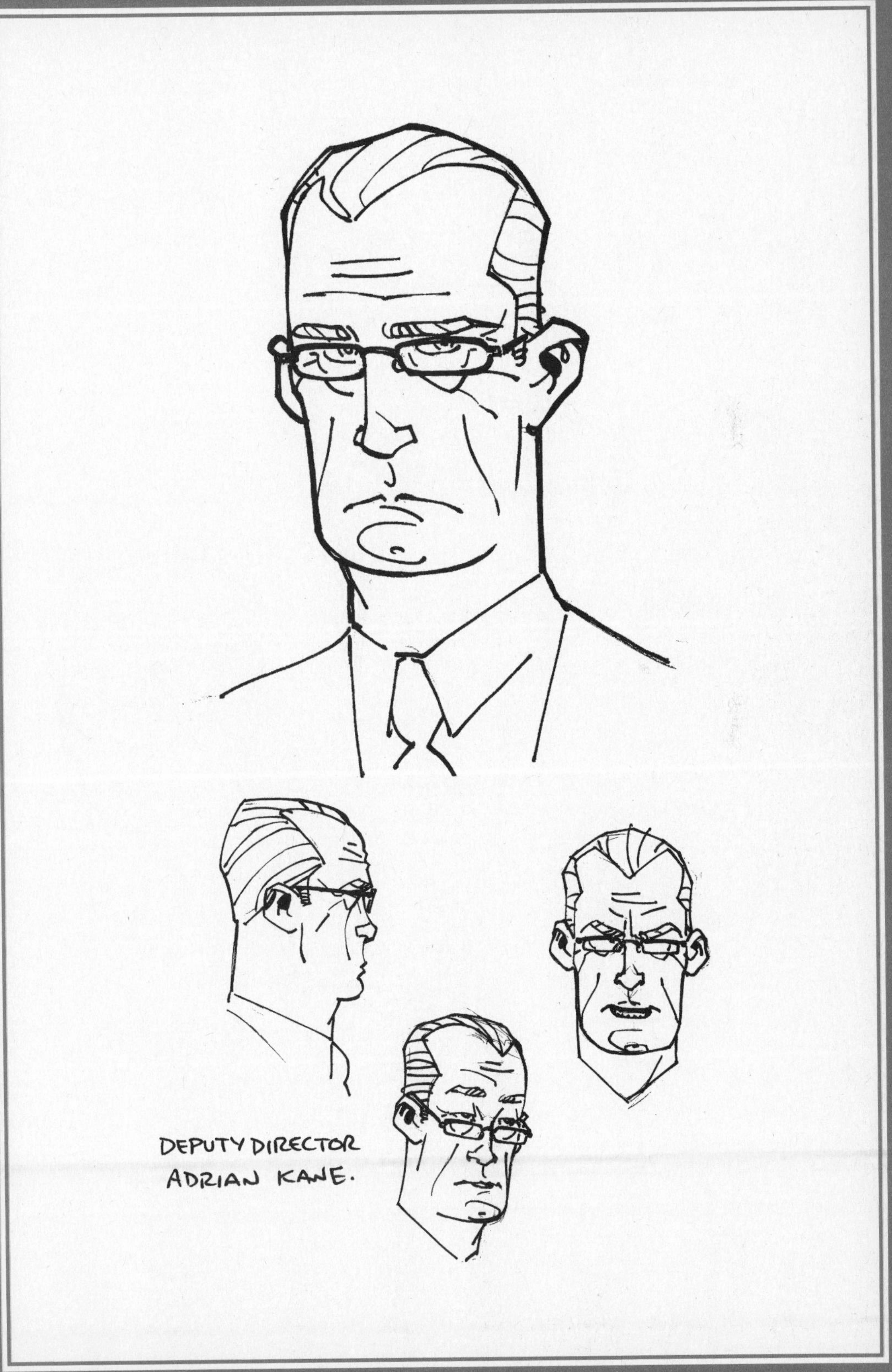
DEPUTY DIRECTOR
ADRIAN KANE.

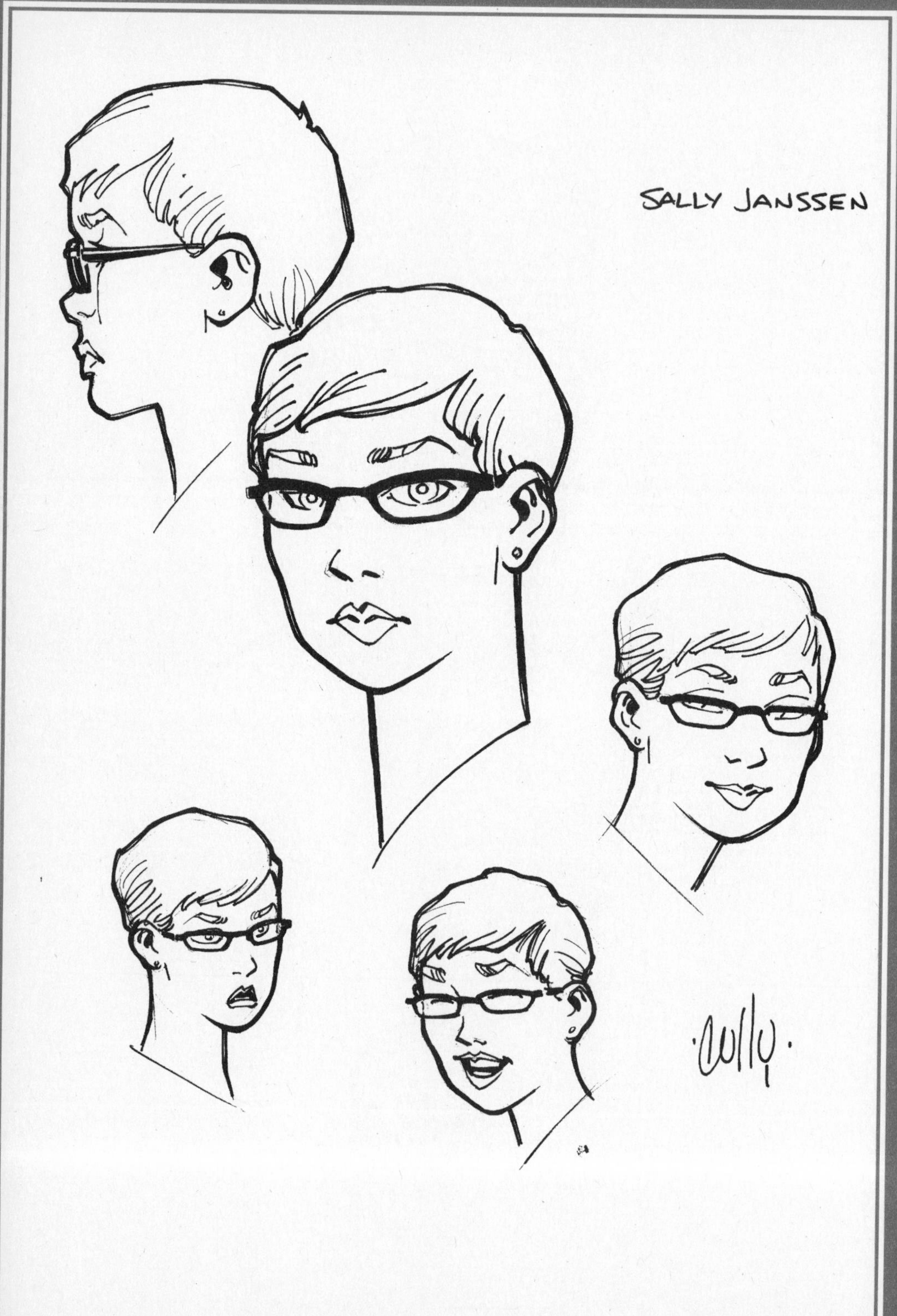
SALLY JANSSEN

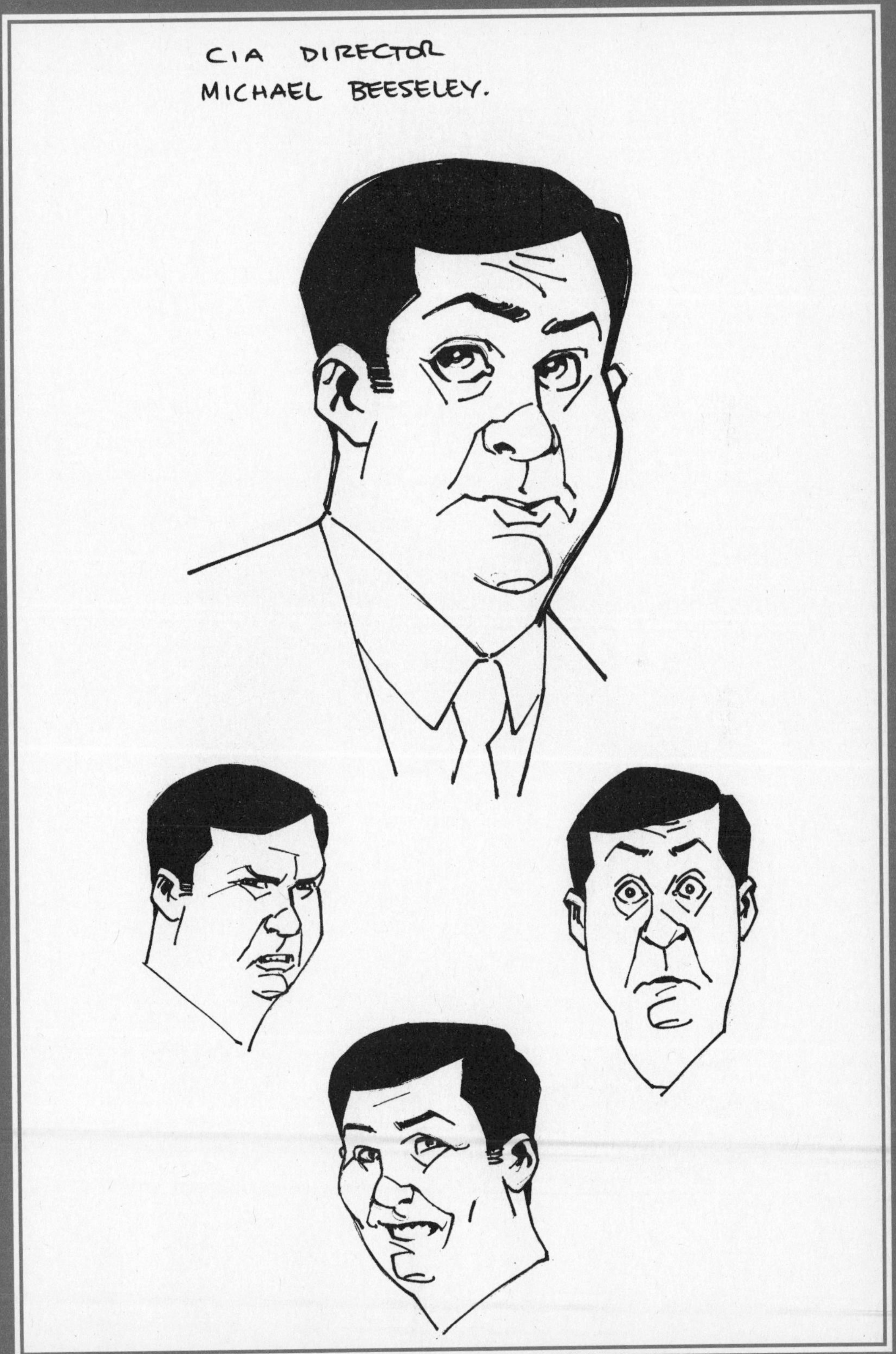
CIA DIRECTOR
MICHAEL BEESELEY.

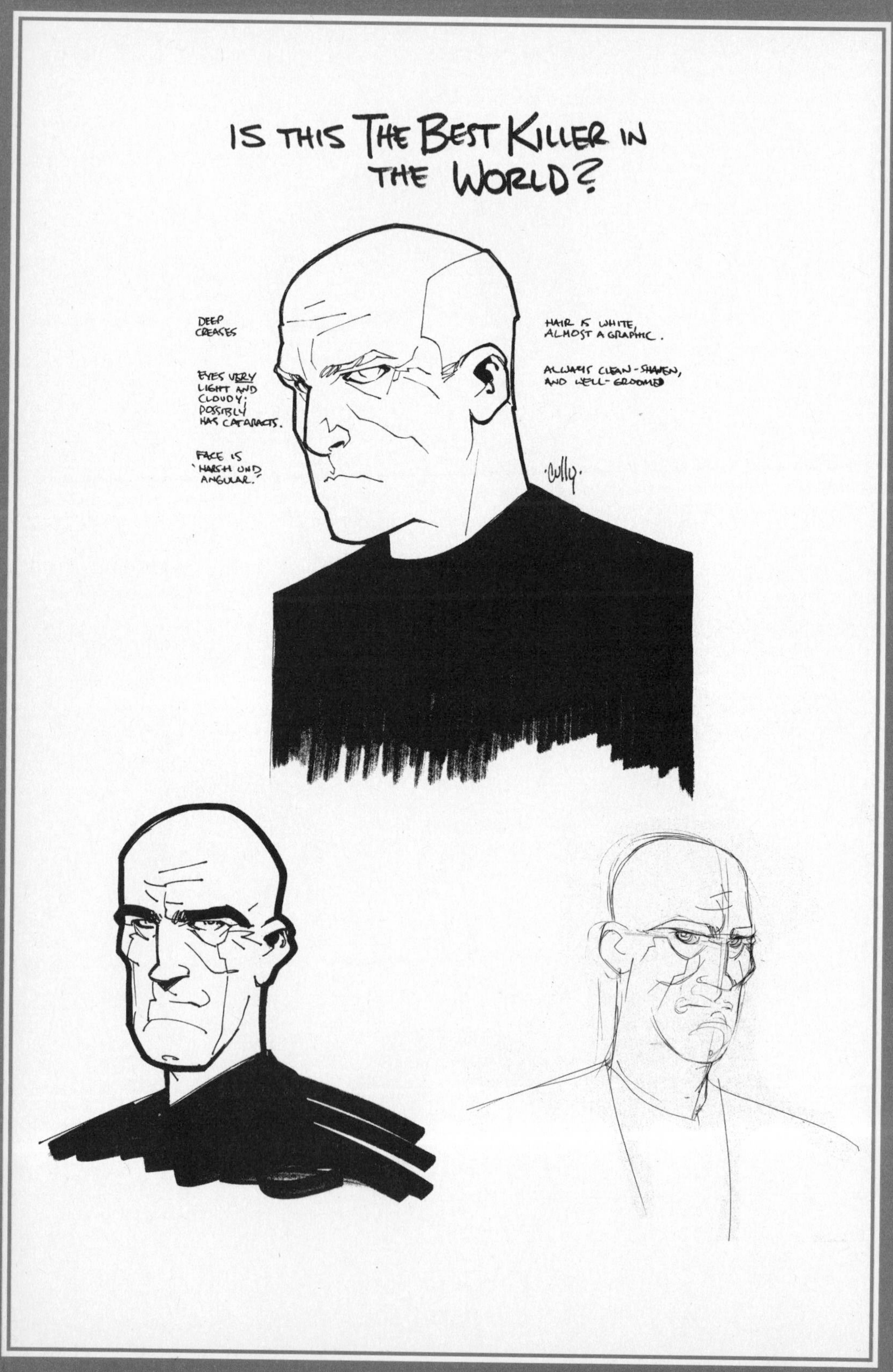
IS THIS THE BEST KILLER IN THE WORLD?
DEEP CREASES
EYES VERY LIGHT AND CLOUDY; POSSIBLY HAS CATARACTS.
FACE IS 'HARSH UND ANGULAR.'
HAIR IS WHITE, ALMOST A GRAPHIC.
ALWAYS CLEAN-SHAVEN, AND WELL-GROOMED
Cully

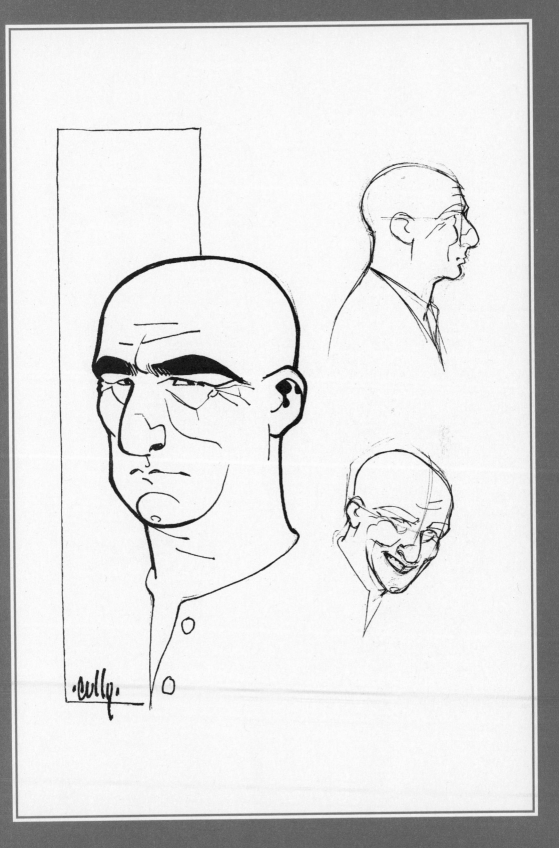

HEADSHOTS

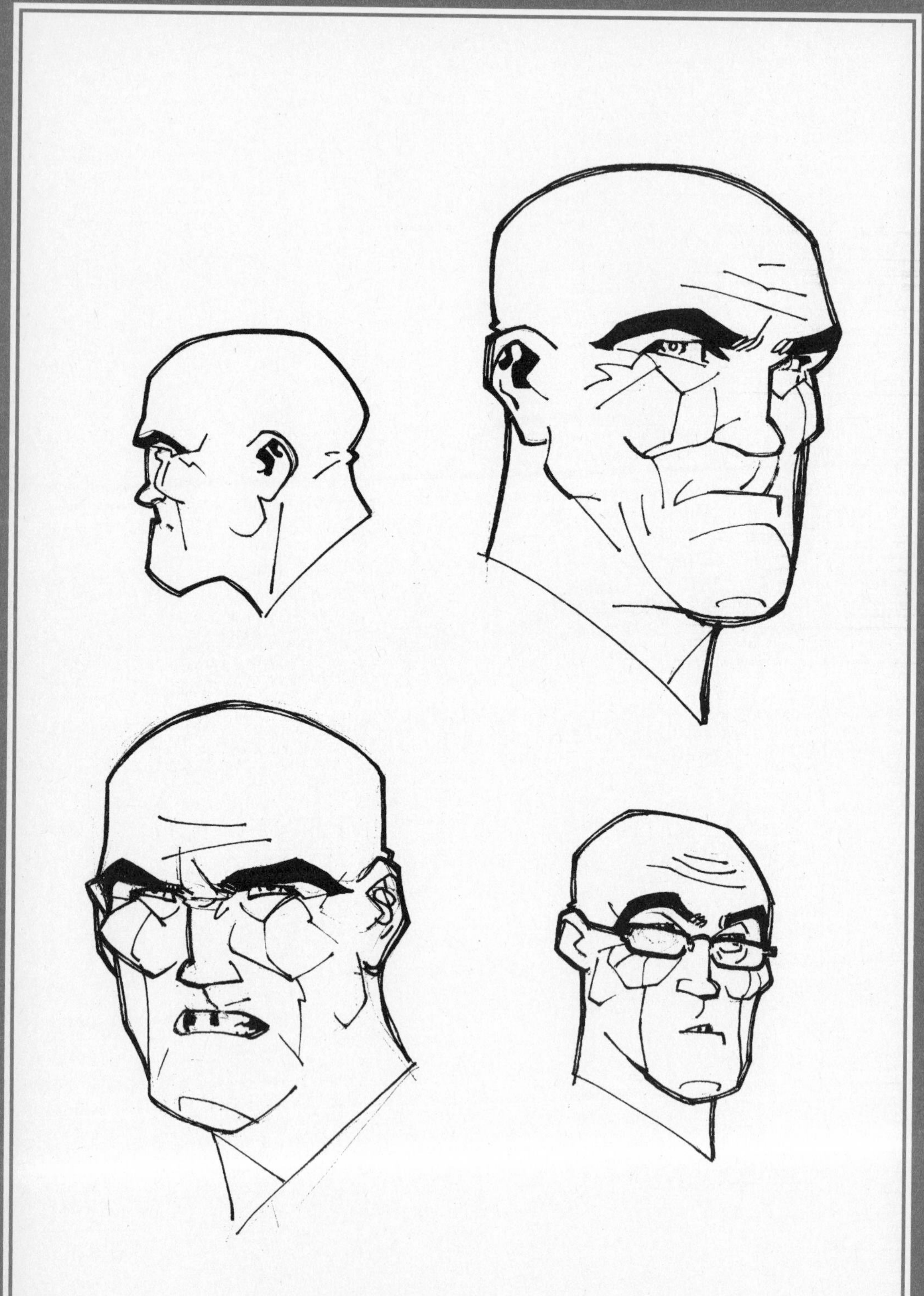

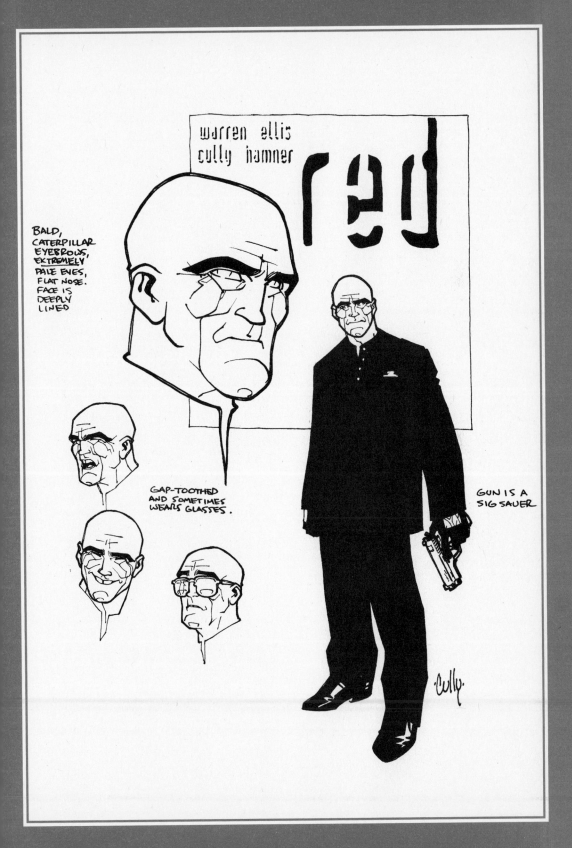

warren ellis
cully hamner
red

BALD,
CATERPILLAR
EYEBROWS,
EXTREMELY
PALE EYES,
FLAT NOSE.
FACE IS
DEEPLY
LINED

GAP-TOOTHED
AND SOMETIMES
WEARS GLASSES.

GUN IS A
SIG SAUER

Cully.

PAGE ONE

Pic 1;
Half the page.

We're looking at the CIA BUILDING in Langley, Virginia, a big glass-and-metal thing – there's plenty of of ref available for it, I'm sure. It's sun-up in Langley, and the sun is coming up big and RED. Langley is surrounded by woodland, and that woodland is BLACK in the rising sun, and black birds are clattering out of the trees across the sun and the burning sky…

LEGEND: # LANGLEY, VIRGINIA

Pic 2;
Inside the building; we look down at two men walking across the famous massive CIA SEAL inset in the marble lobby floor. Sunlight is making its way in here, and it's staining the scene RED too…

The two men are MICHAEL BEESLEY, a man in his late thirties with the eyes of a naïve boy, and ADRIAN KANE, the deputy director of the CIA, older, colder, harder.

BEESLEY: …I MEAN, YES, OKAY, WE CAN'T HIDE THE FACT THAT I'M A POLITICAL APPOINTEE. NEW PRESIDENT, NEW ADMINISTRATION, NEW BROOM.

BEESLEY: AND A NEW BROOM MUST BE SEEN TO BE SWEEPING CLEAN, ADRIAN. YOU DON'T MIND ME CALLING YOU ADRIAN?

KANE: OF COURSE NOT, MR BEESLEY.

Editor's note – Ellis's script is presented here with the original British spelling and punctuation intact.

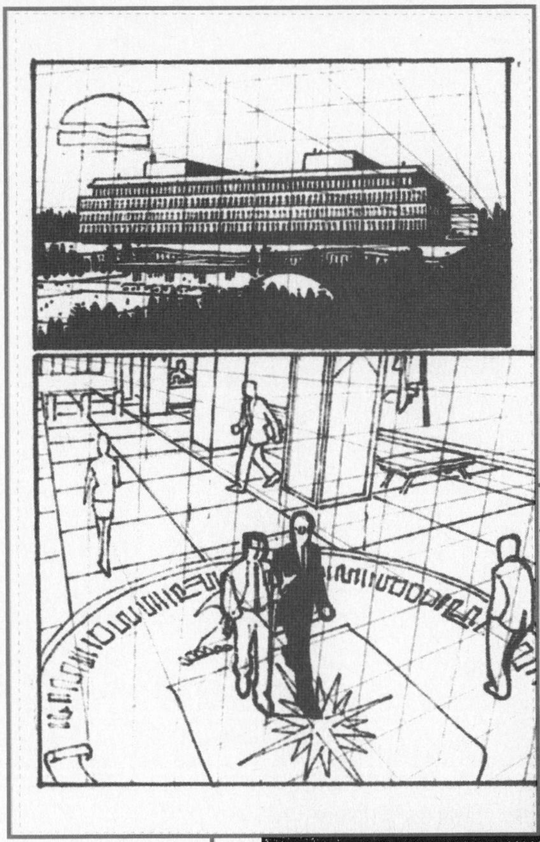

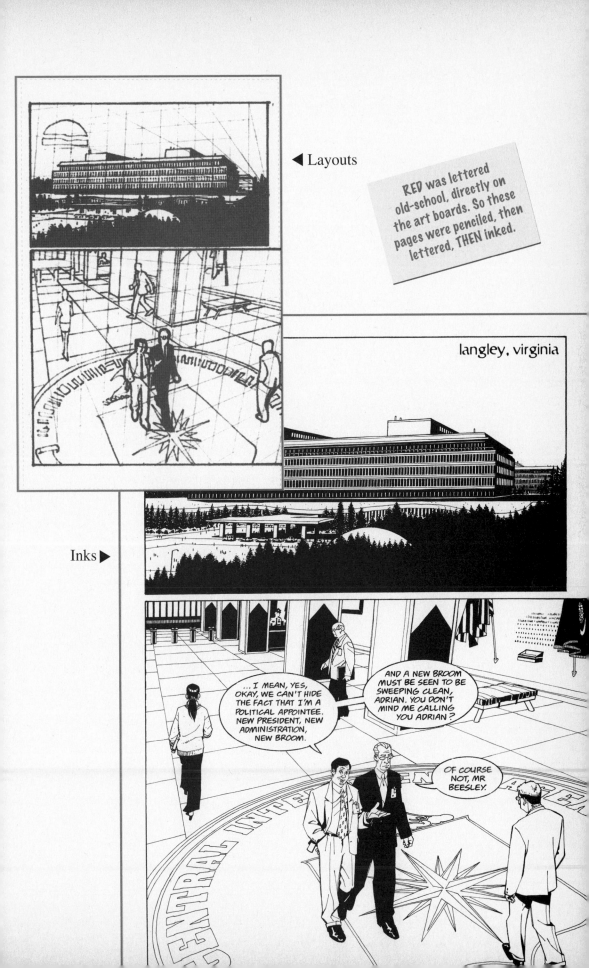

◀ Layouts

RED was lettered old-school, directly on the art boards. So these pages were penciled, then lettered, THEN inked.

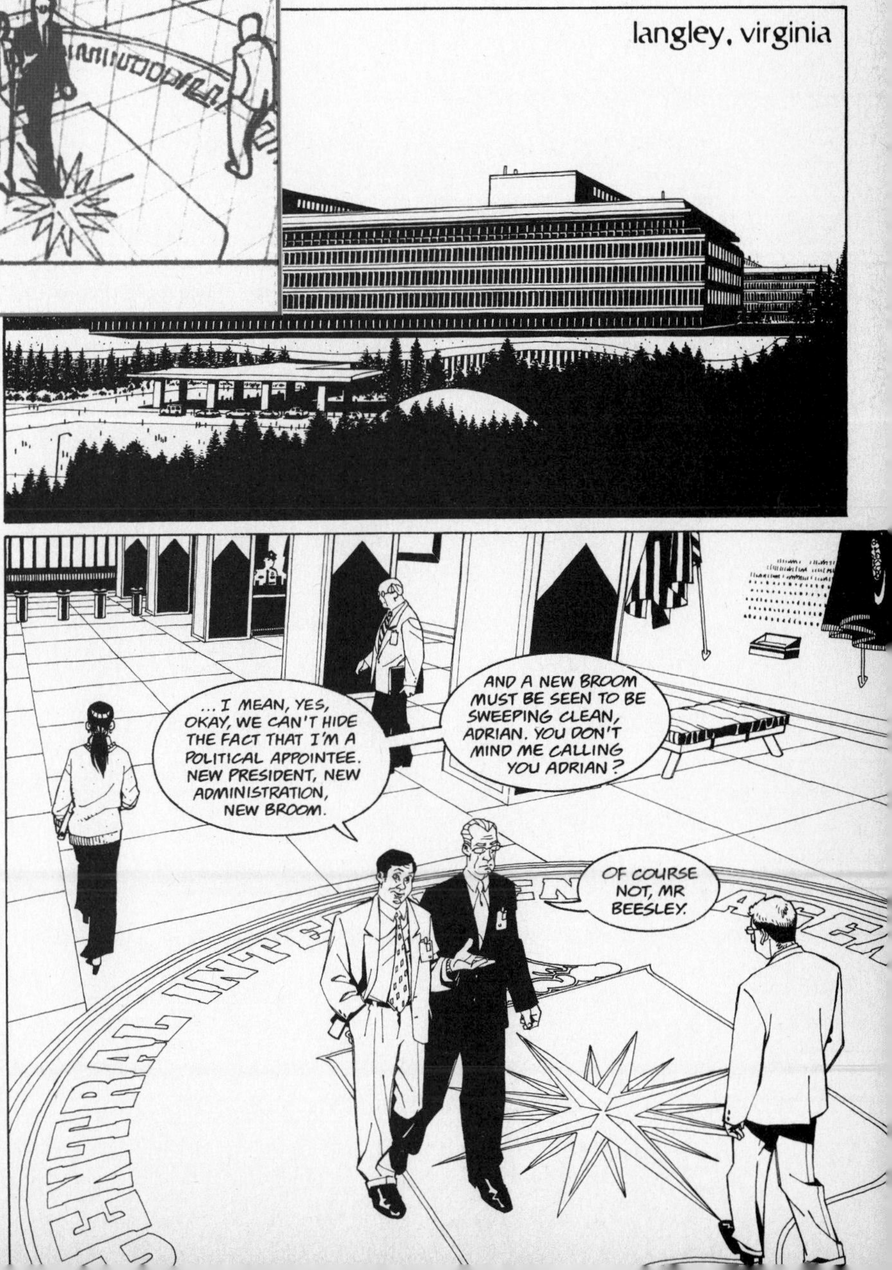

langley, virginia
...I MEAN, YES, OKAY, WE CAN'T HIDE THE FACT THAT I'M A POLITICAL APPOINTEE. NEW PRESIDENT, NEW ADMINISTRATION, NEW BROOM.
AND A NEW BROOM MUST BE SEEN TO BE SWEEPING CLEAN, ADRIAN. YOU DON'T MIND ME CALLING YOU ADRIAN?
OF COURSE NOT, MR BEESLEY.
CENTRAL INTE

Inks ▶

PAGE TWO

Pic 1;
Off the lobby, they turn into a corridor (one side of which is all
windows, letting RED light in), so we can get a good look at them.

BEESLEY: MICHAEL. PLEASE, IT'S MICHAEL. I THINK IT'S
                VERY IMPORTANT WE ALL BE FRIENDS.

BEESLEY: I MEAN, THAT'S WHY I'M HERE. THE PRESIDENT
                WANTS A DIRECTOR OF THE CIA WHO WILL HELP
                HIM AND BE HIS FRIEND.

BEESLEY: THIS IS WHY I SAY, DESPITE THE CIRCUMSTANCE
                OF MY APPOINTMENT, I WANT TO BE A STRONG
                AND EFFECTIVE DIRECTOR.

Pic 2:
Beesley talks too much. He's nervous here - knows he doesn't fit in.
Kane is self-contained, very carefully saying the right things. Both
men in suits, by the way.

KANE: I UNDERSTAND, SIR.

BEESLEY: NO, I MEAN IT. I CAN'T BE MOLLYCODDLED
                THROUGH THIS JOB. I HAVE A BACKGROUND IN
                SECURITY. I CAN MAKE THE HARD DECISIONS.

KANE: OF COURSE, SIR. THAT'S WHY WE'RE GOING TO
                ROOM R THIS MORNING. IT'S A CRUCIAL BRIEFING
                FOR A NEW DIRECTOR.

Pic 3;
Beesley's eyes flick across to Kane. Edgy. Nervous smile.

BEESLEY: YES. ROOM R. CAN YOU TELL ME ANY MORE
                ABOUT THIS?

KANE: NO, SIR.

KANE: ONLY YOU, THE DEPUTY DIRECTOR/INTELLIGENCE
                AND MYSELF AS DEPUTY DIRECTOR/OPERATIONS
                ARE AUTHORISED TO VIEW WHAT'S IN ROOM R.

KANE: YOU'LL UNDERSTAND WHY.

Pic 4;
They stop by a door heavy with electronic locks. Kane takes out a
keycard. The clock above the door reads 7.01.

KANE: ROOM R.

KANE: WE'RE GOING TO WATCH A VIDEOTAPE.

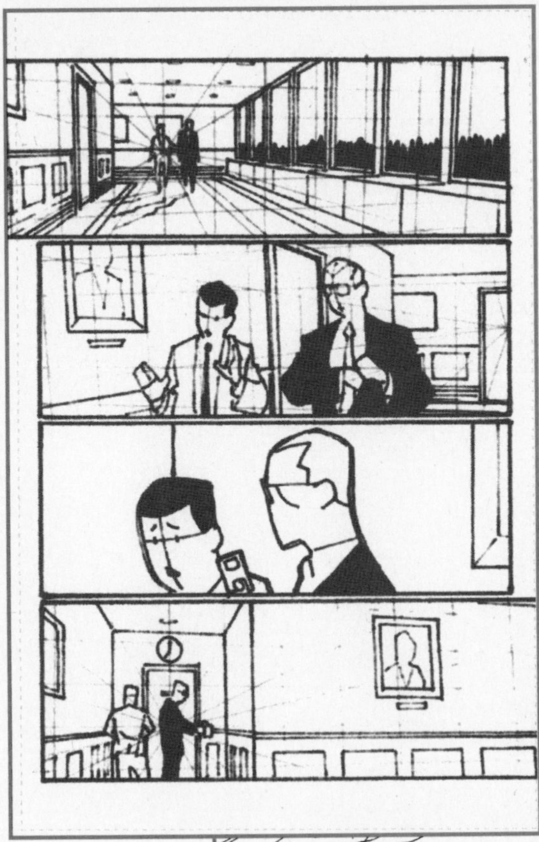

◀ Layouts

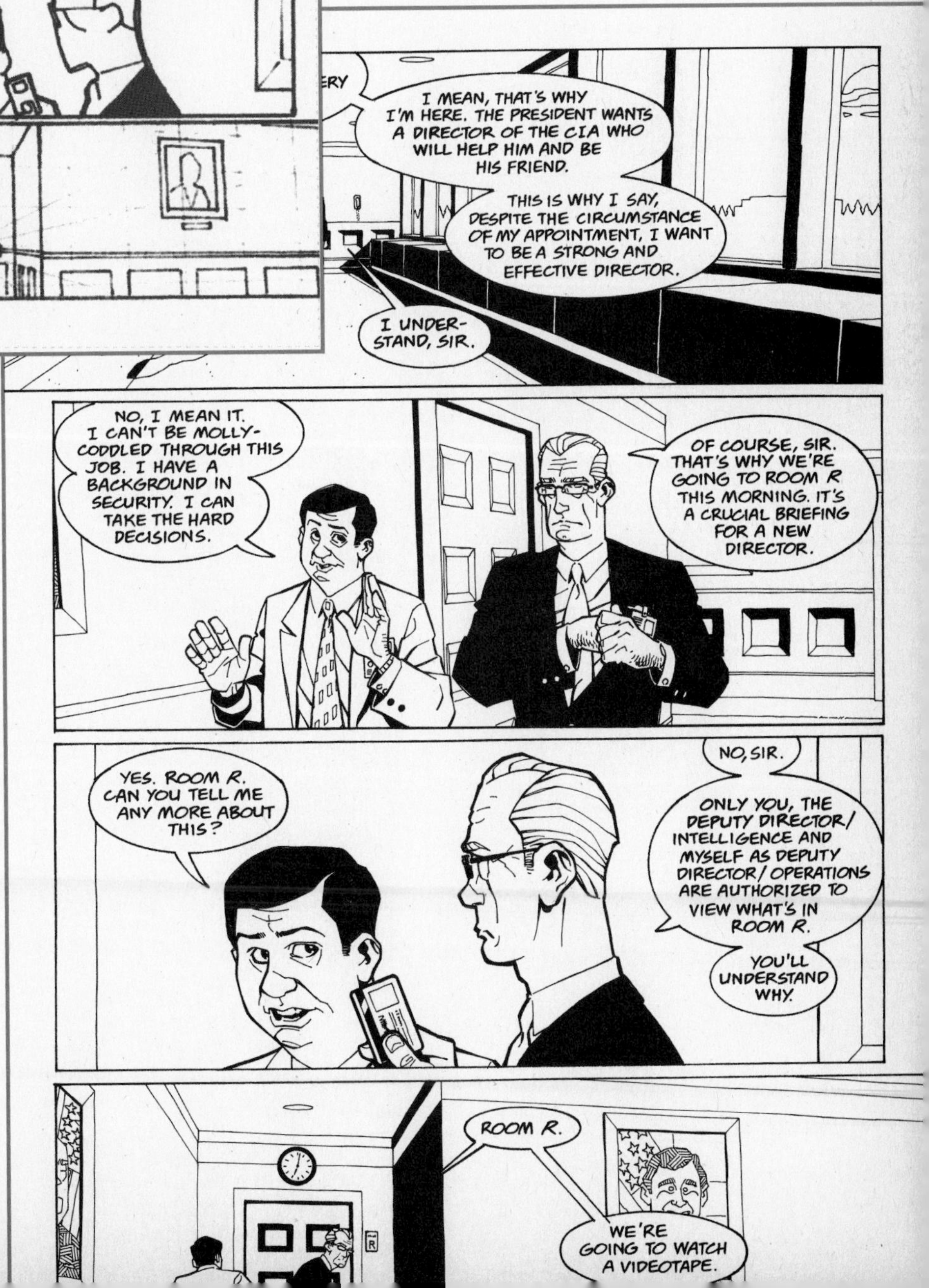

ERY
I MEAN, THAT'S WHY I'M HERE. THE PRESIDENT WANTS A DIRECTOR OF THE CIA WHO WILL HELP HIM AND BE HIS FRIEND.
THIS IS WHY I SAY, DESPITE THE CIRCUMSTANCE OF MY APPOINTMENT, I WANT TO BE A STRONG AND EFFECTIVE DIRECTOR.
I UNDER-STAND, SIR.
NO, I MEAN IT. I CAN'T BE MOLLY-CODDLED THROUGH THIS JOB. I HAVE A BACKGROUND IN SECURITY. I CAN TAKE THE HARD DECISIONS.
OF COURSE, SIR. THAT'S WHY WE'RE GOING TO ROOM R THIS MORNING. IT'S A CRUCIAL BRIEFING FOR A NEW DIRECTOR.
YES. ROOM R. CAN YOU TELL ME ANY MORE ABOUT THIS?
NO, SIR.
ONLY YOU, THE DEPUTY DIRECTOR/ INTELLIGENCE AND MYSELF AS DEPUTY DIRECTOR/ OPERATIONS ARE AUTHORIZED TO VIEW WHAT'S IN ROOM R.
YOU'LL UNDERSTAND WHY.
ROOM R.
WE'RE GOING TO WATCH A VIDEOTAPE.

Inks ▶

PAGE THREE

Pic 1;
Repeat previous pic, but with no-one in front of it, and the clock reading 8.11.

(no dialogue)

Pic 2;
Repeat pic: but with the clock at 8.47, and Kane and Beesley exiting the door. The room is lit RED within.

(no dialogue)

Pic 3;
Beesley is white, soaked in sweat. Hands clenched. Kane has seen it before, and is still entirely composed.

(no dialogue)

Pic 4;
Beesley's eyes are wild. He sinks against the wall next to the door as Kane locks it off.

BEESLEY: DO YOU HAVE A CIGARETTE?

KANE: NO, SIR.

BEESLEY: I WANT A CIGARETTE.

Pic 5;
Beesley stares at the ceiling.

BEESLEY: MY GOD.

BEESLEY: ONE MAN.

BEESLEY: MY GOD.

Pic 6;
And tips his head back down, squeezing his eyes shut.

BEESLEY: WE'VE GOT TO KILL HIM.

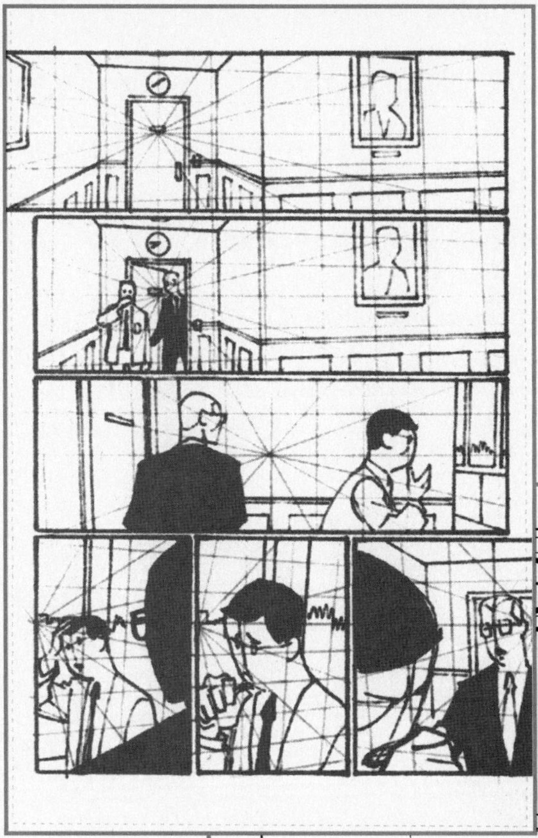

◀ Layouts

Inks ▶

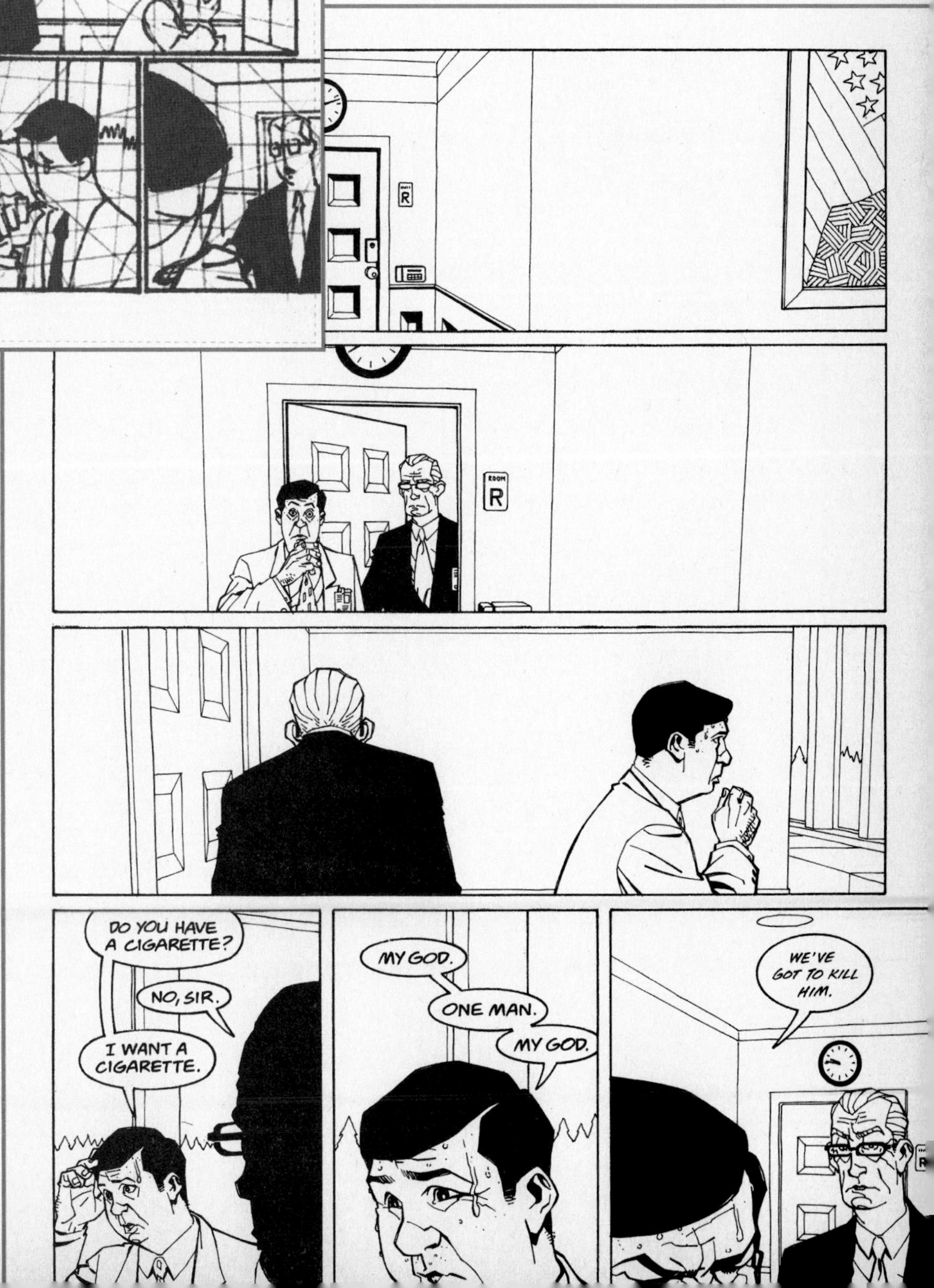
DO YOU HAVE A CIGARETTE?
NO, SIR.
I WANT A CIGARETTE.
MY GOD.
ONE MAN.
MY GOD.
WE'VE GOT TO KILL HIM.

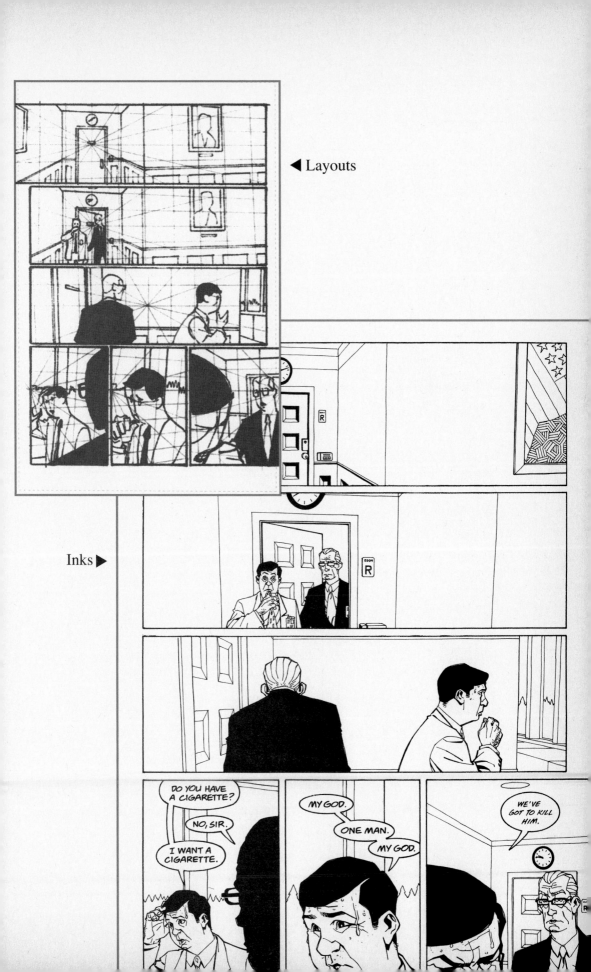

PAGE FOUR

Pic 1;
Kane looks at Beesley, concern in his face for the first time.

KANE: SIR, HE'S RETIRED. HE'S BEEN RETIRED A LONG TIME. HE IS ENTIRELY SAFE. IT'S A STABLE SITUATION.

KANE: AND, FRANKLY, HE'S NO LONGER YOUNG.

KANE: HIS DISPOSITION IS NOT AN ISSUE HERE. THE ROOM R BRIEFING IS TO GROUND A NEW DIRECTOR IN--

Pic 2;
Beesley turns, hissing at Kane. He is not stable. He does not have the personality to do this job. And he's showing it, and he doesn't care. Like Nixon, or Dubya, he's an aggressive incompetent.

BEESLEY: I DON'T CARE.

BEESLEY: IF ANYONE FOUND OUT--

KANE: NO-ONE'S GOING TO FIND OUT.

Pic 3;
Beesley stabs a finger in front of Kane's face. Kane glares.

BEESLEY: YOU'RE DAMNED RIGHT.

BEESLEY: WE CAN'T EVEN HAVE SOMEONE OUTSIDE THIS BUILDING WITH THAT KNOWLEDGE IN THEIR HEAD.

BEESLEY: IF, IF PEOPLE **KNEW**…

Pic 4;
Beesley turns away, passes a hand across his eyes - his body language is all over the place, he's losing it…

BEESLEY: I MEAN, WE'RE TRYING TO BUILD A NEW WORLD ORDER HERE. THE FOREIGN POLICY, LEADING THE WORLD…

BEESLEY: NO. WE HAVE TO ELIMINATE ALL TRACES OF THIS, THIS...

BEESLEY: NO-ONE CAN KNOW THIS EVEN HAPPENED. THAT THE WORLD WAS EVEN LIKE THIS.

Pic 5;
Beesley walks quickly down the corridor, away from us…

BEESLEY: HE DIES.

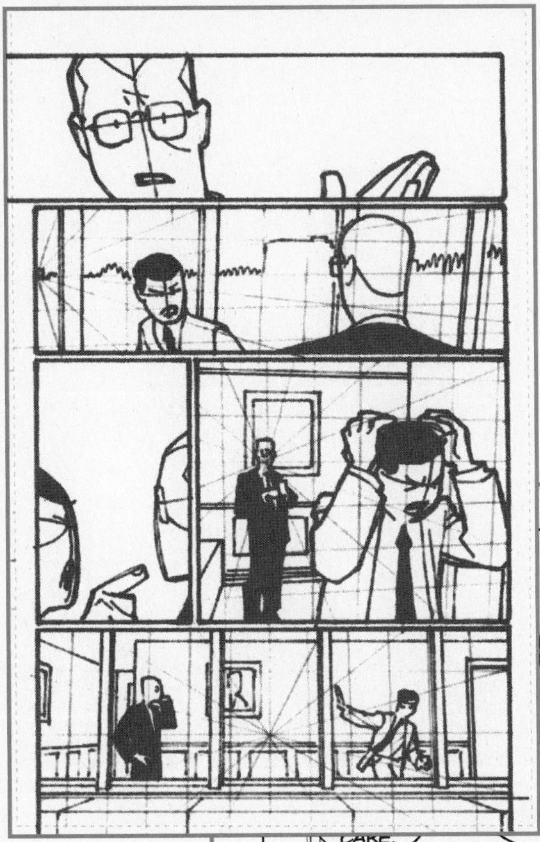

◀ Layouts

Inks ▶

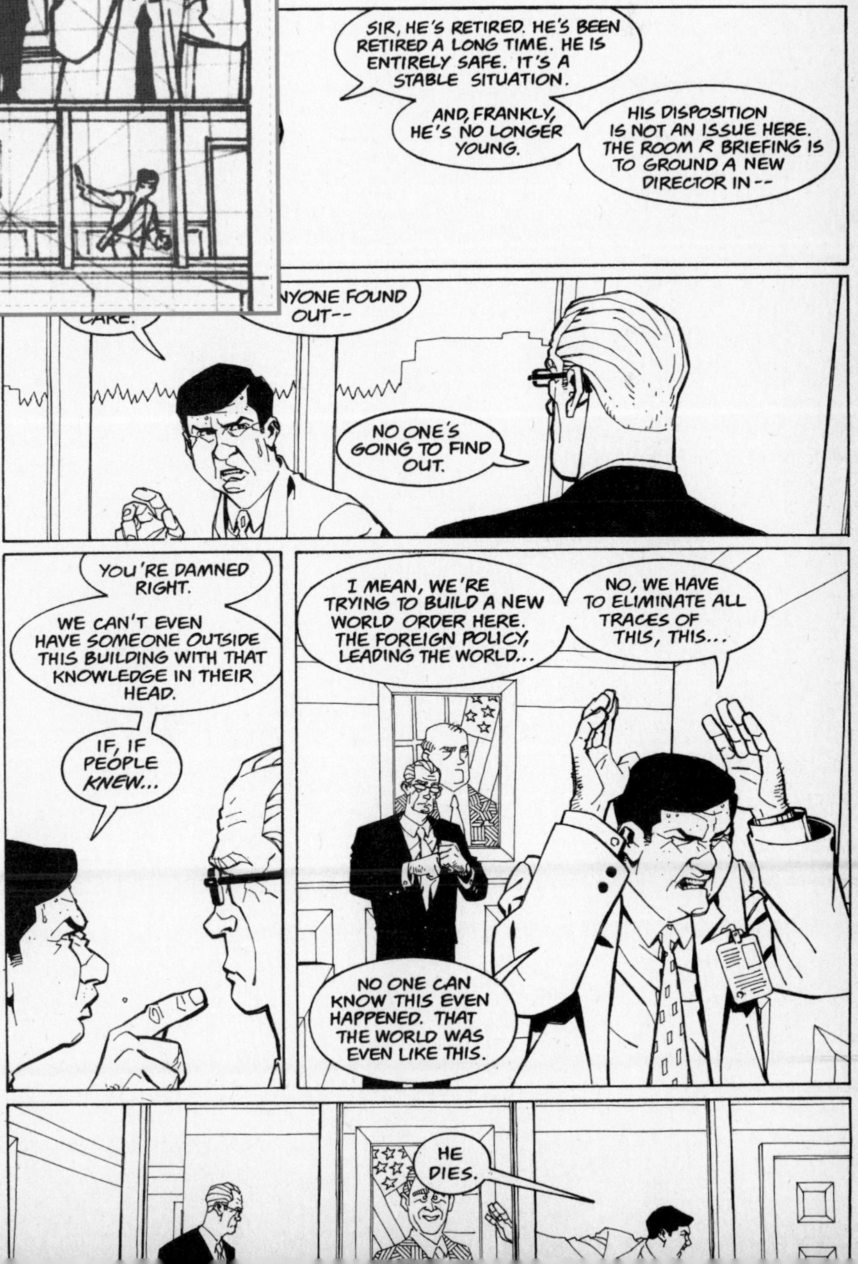

SIR, HE'S RETIRED. HE'S BEEN RETIRED A LONG TIME. HE IS ENTIRELY SAFE. IT'S A STABLE SITUATION.
AND, FRANKLY, HE'S NO LONGER YOUNG.
HIS DISPOSITION IS NOT AN ISSUE HERE. THE ROOM R BRIEFING IS TO GROUND A NEW DIRECTOR IN--
NO ONE'S GOING TO FIND OUT.
YOU'RE DAMNED RIGHT.
WE CAN'T EVEN HAVE SOMEONE OUTSIDE THIS BUILDING WITH THAT KNOWLEDGE IN THEIR HEAD.
IF, IF PEOPLE KNEW...
I MEAN, WE'RE TRYING TO BUILD A NEW WORLD ORDER HERE. THE FOREIGN POLICY, LEADING THE WORLD...
NO, WE HAVE TO ELIMINATE ALL TRACES OF THIS, THIS...
NO ONE CAN KNOW THIS EVEN HAPPENED. THAT THE WORLD WAS EVEN LIKE THIS.
HE DIES.

Pic 1;
OPEN ON: A large home set in its own grounds, under a STORM. The
storm thunders, lightning stabbing down...

TITLES: RED

Pic 2;
Inside the house: lightning flashes outside, blasting harsh blue
light through the broad windows of a living room area. Only one
armchair, but lots of objets d'art, antiques, primitive and native
arts. Eccentric and expensive – an ornate, grotesque African mask
here, a handpainted boomerang there – this is the home of someone
who's travelled the world many, many times.

CREDITS: written by WARREN ELLIS and
                                 illustrated by CULLY HAMNER

Pic 3;
The house goes dark again, and we move through a corridor, low and
quick like an assassin, headed towards another blue-lit room…

CREDITS: with color art by David Self
                                 and lettering by John Costanza
                                 edited by Ben Abernathy and John Layman

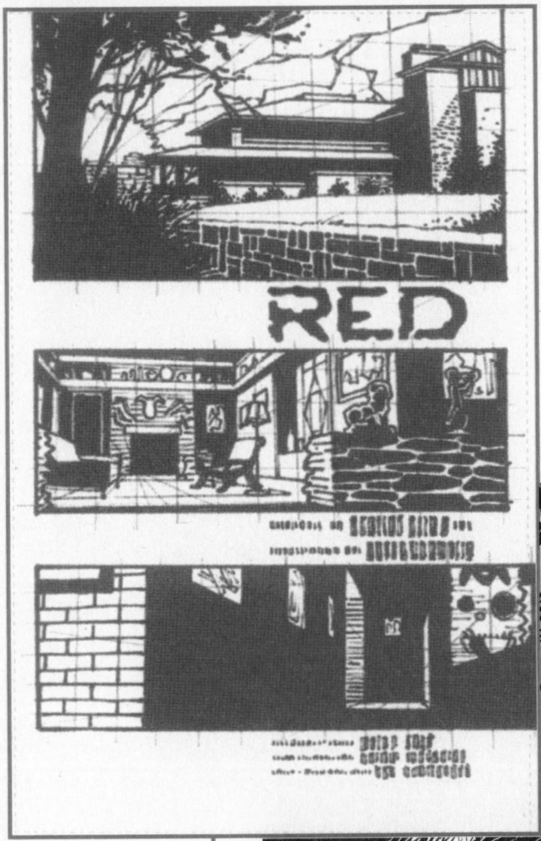

RED

◀ Layouts

Inks ▶

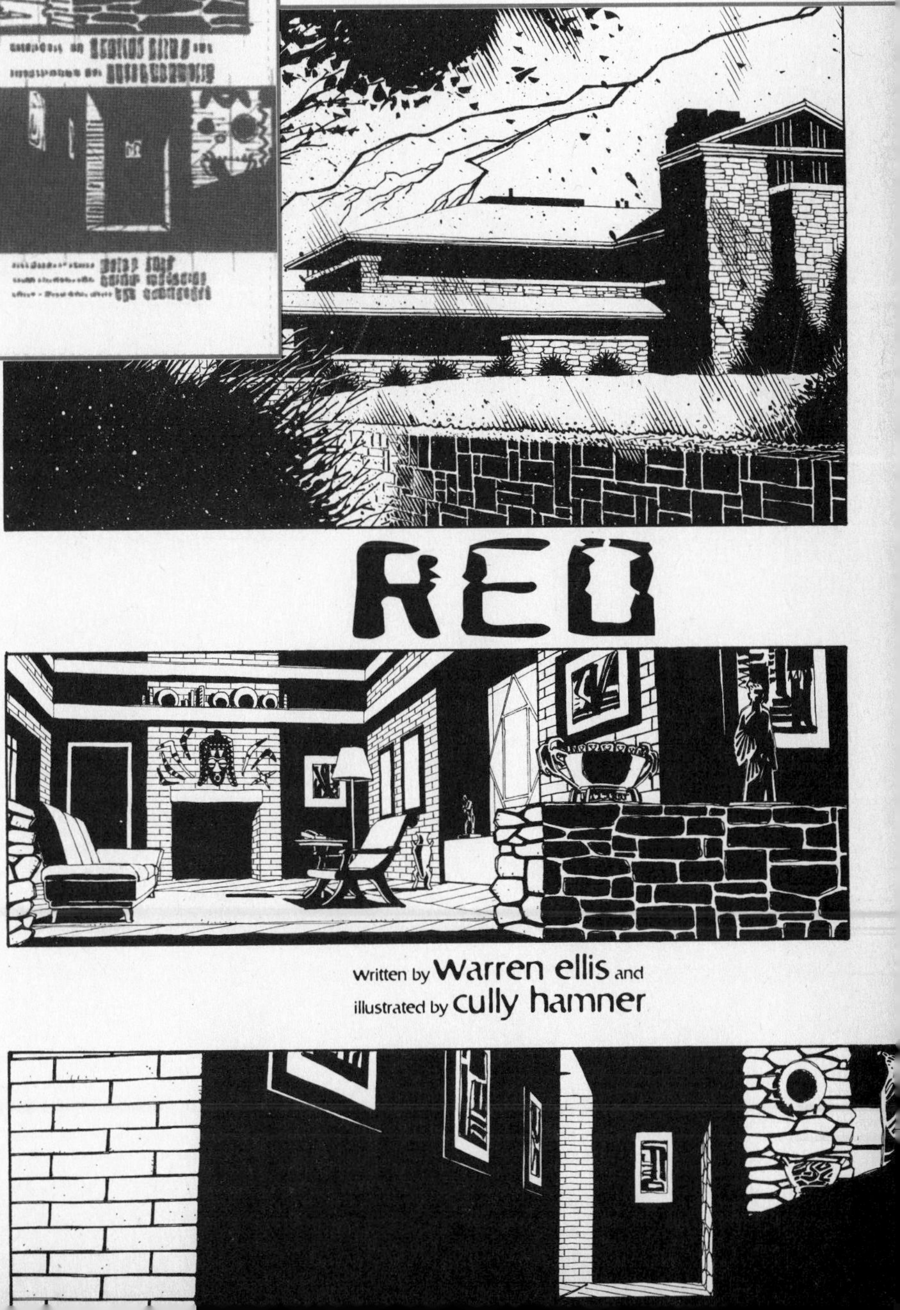

RED
written by warren ellis and
illustrated by cully hamner

PAGE SIX

Pic 1;
…The KITCHEN. There is PAUL MOSES, nude, standing at the sink and
looking out of the broad windows at the storm. His back is to us, in
our low sniper POV.

(no dialogue)

Pic 2;
Move in on MOSES: hard, but no longer young. When he looks up, we see
his eyes; eyes that have seen terrible things, things that have
marked him. He stares out at the storm, obviously awoken by it.

(no dialogue)

Pic 3;
Lightning.

(no dialogue)

Pic 4;
He shudders as the bang of deep thunder follows...

MOSES: THE SOUND...

Pic 5;
Over his shoulder; his kitchen window looks out on a leafy garden,
fronds and branches lit up by the lightning…

(no dialogue)

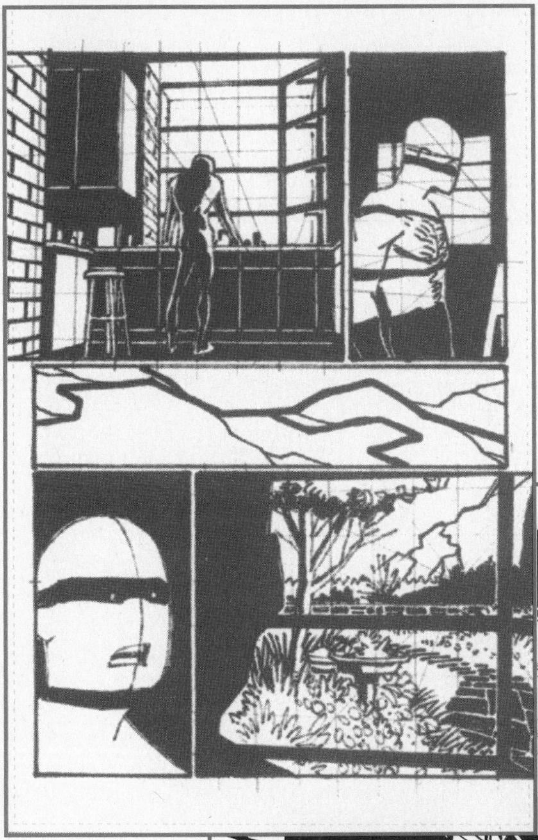

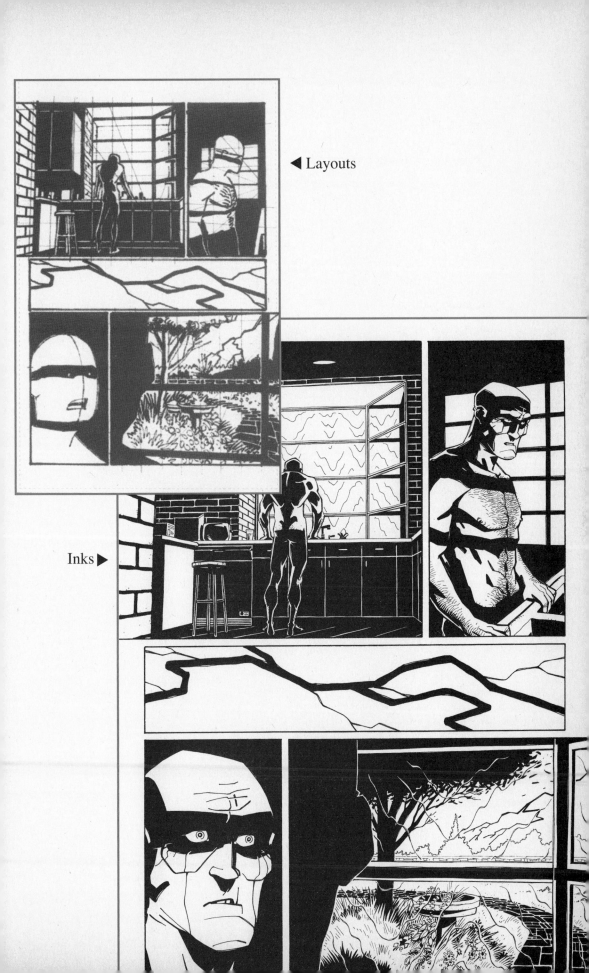

◀ Layouts

Inks ▶

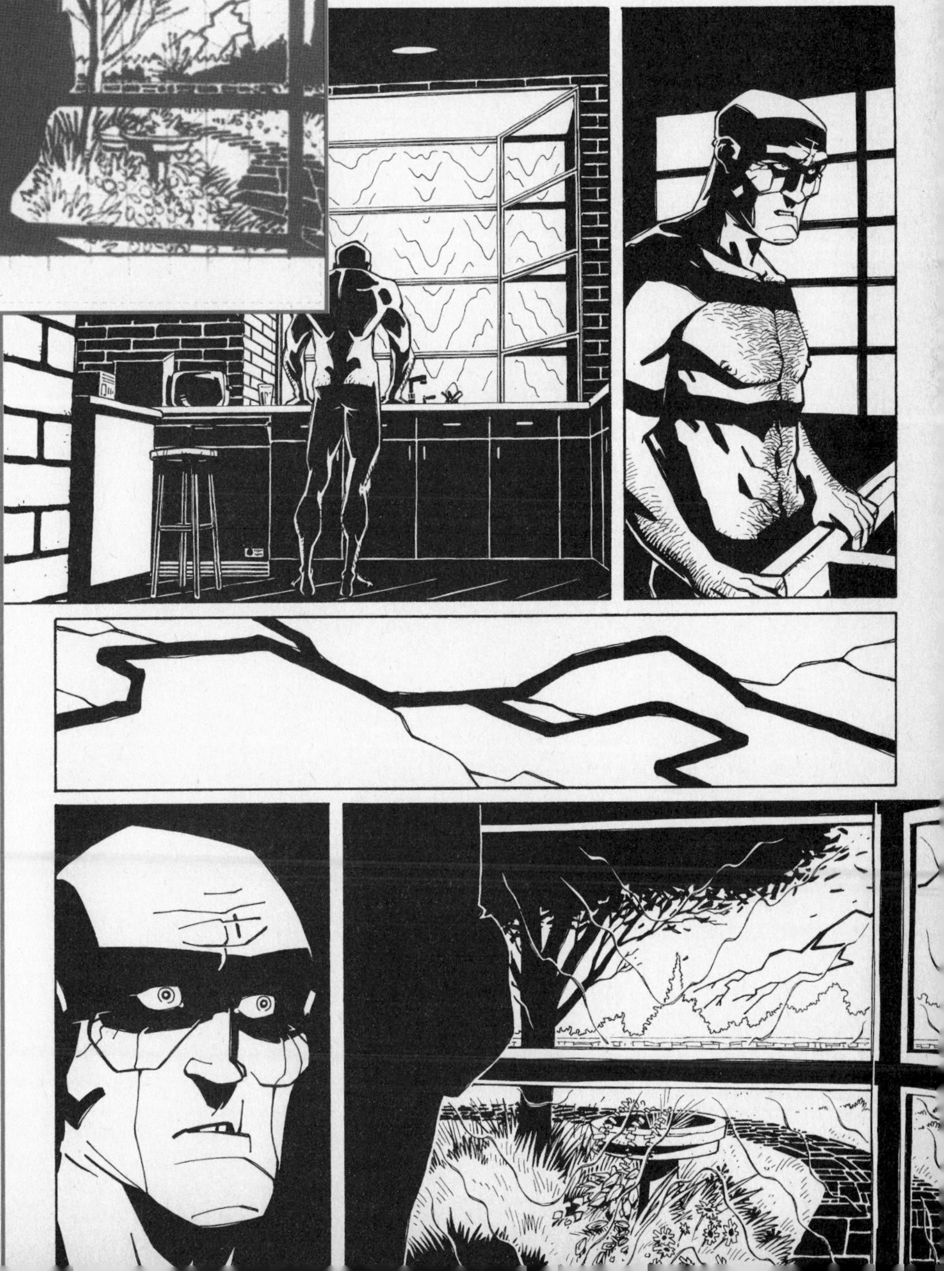

PAGE SEVEN

Pic 1;
FLASHBACK: EXT. JUNGLE - NIGHT

A YOUNG ASIAN MAN standing in mud in torrential rain at night,
pleading with us, lightning splitting the sky and lighting up the
fronds and branches --

(no dialogue)

Pic 2;
-- and if there's thunder, it's the roar of the GUN in our hand,
blowing the top of his head off.

(no dialogue)

Pic 3;
FLASHBACK: EXT. ALLEY - NIGHT

Under a storm again, as our PISTOL cuts down a WOMAN from behind as
lightning cracks again --

(no dialogue)

Pic 4;
-- black blood spurting out of her into our eyes --

(no dialogue)

Pic 5;
-- an ALL-BLACK PANEL --

(no dialogue)

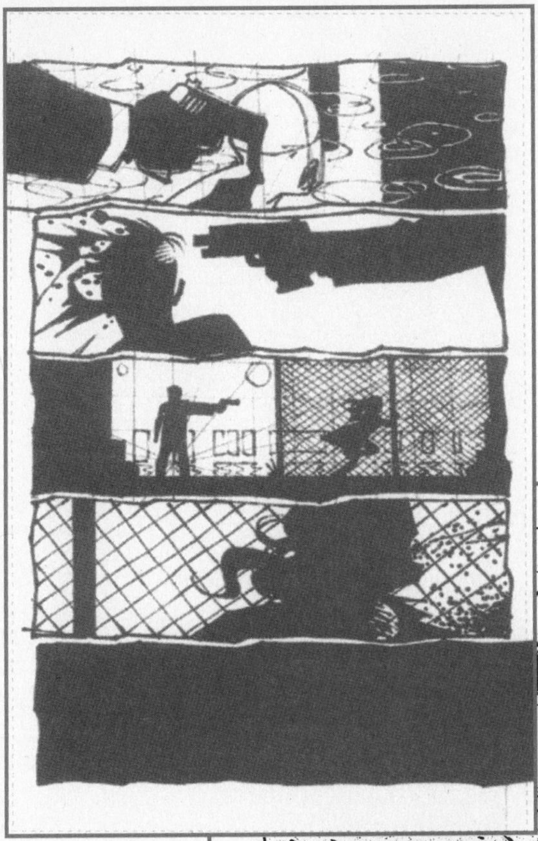

◀ Layouts

Inks ▶

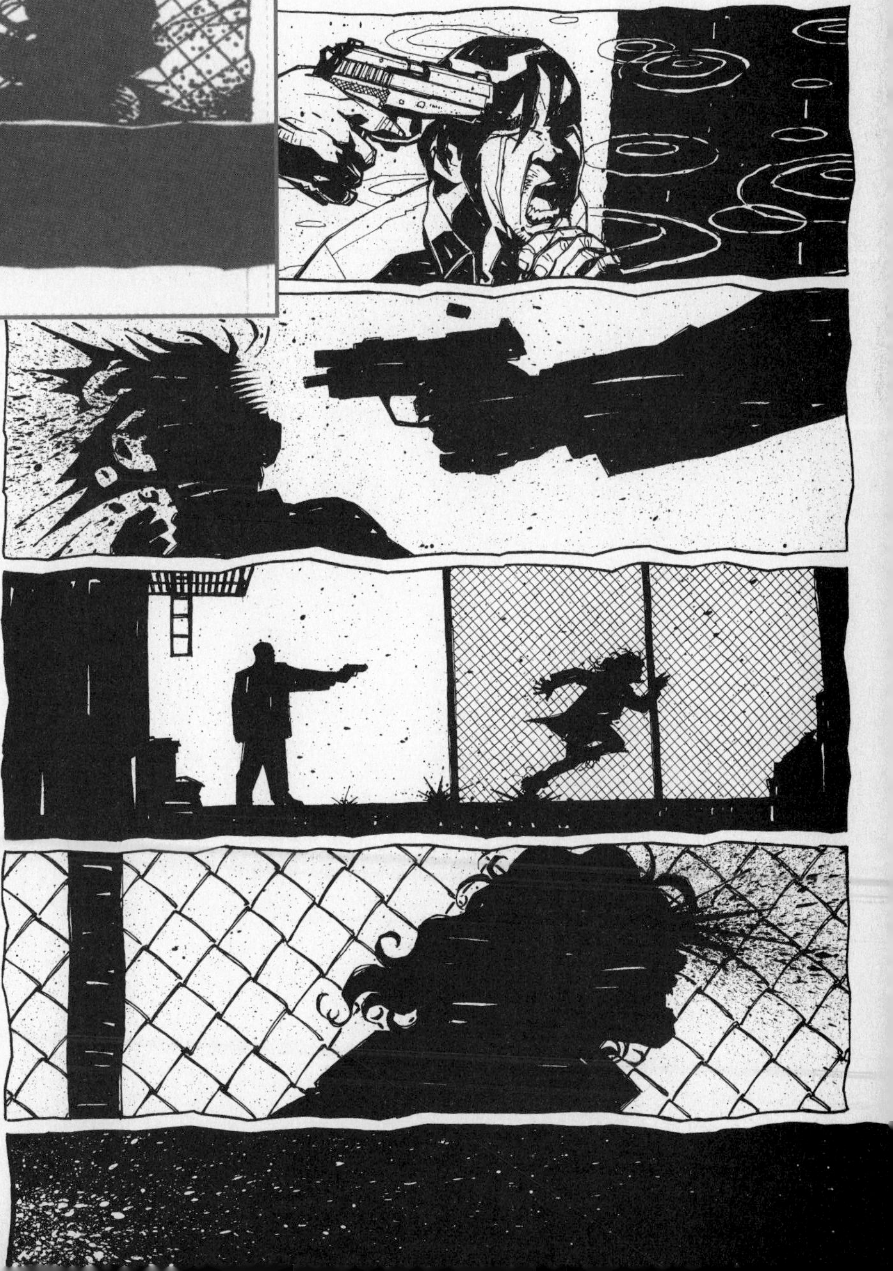

PAGE EIGHT

Pic 1;
-- LIGHTNING flashing --

(no dialogue)

Pic 2;
END FLASHBACK:
as Moses judders again with the bang of the storm, lightning's glare
flashing over him. It's the memories that the gunfire-crack of
thunder brings that are keeping him awake tonight.

(no dialogue)

Pic 3;
His hands are on the edge of the metal sink. His fingers twist and
writhe - and press into the metal. The metal depresses under his
fingers.

(no dialogue)

Pic 4;
Close up on his face, on profile. He bites his lips, and there's the
start of tears at the edges of his tightly closed eyes.

(no dialogue)

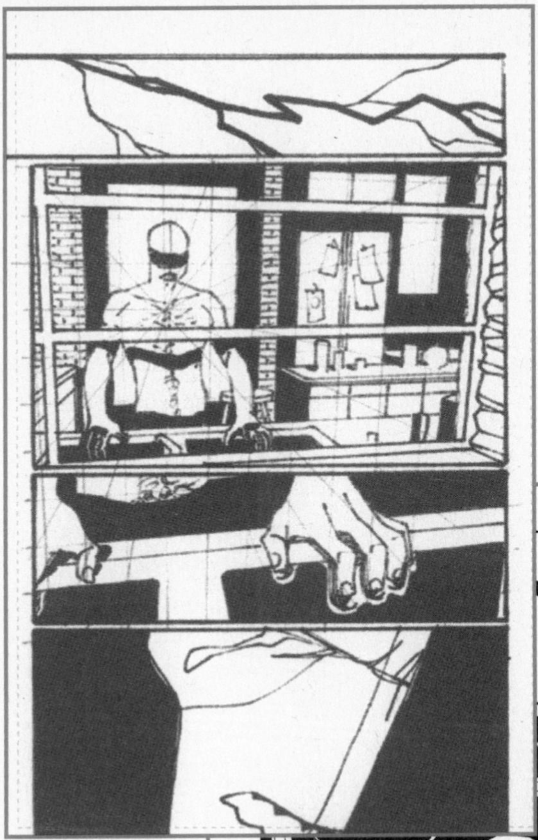

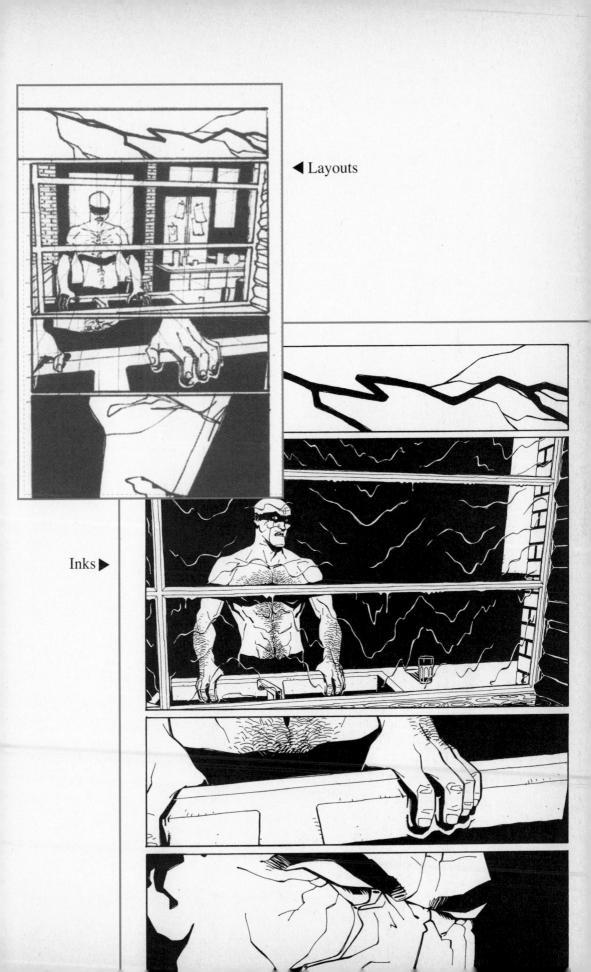

◀ Layouts

Inks ▶

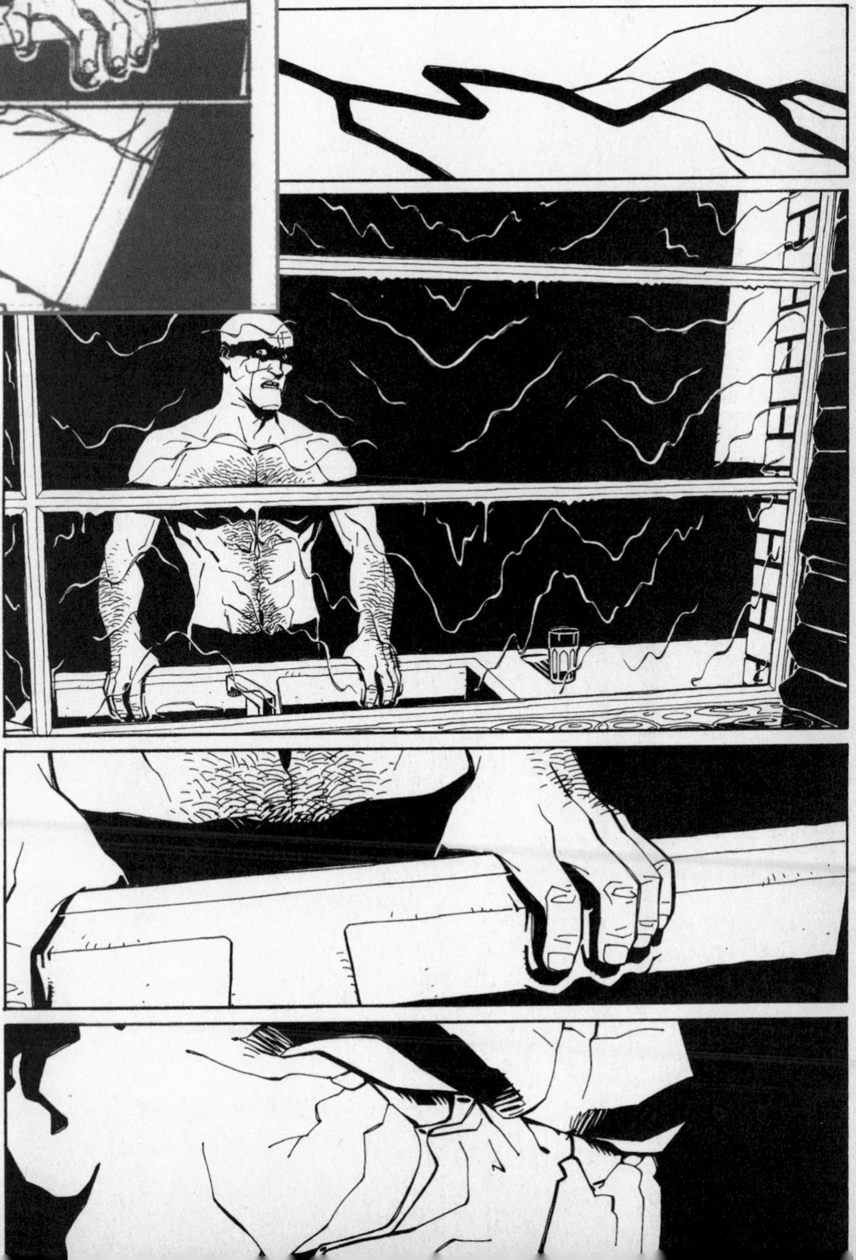

PAGE NINE

Pic 1;
CUT TO; THE HOUSE, under brilliant morning daylight. Use the same POV you used to intro the house on Page One. But now, y'know, it's a pretty place. Give it half the page easy.

(no dialogue)

Pic 2;
CUT TO; The kitchen sink, under daylight. Water running into it from the faucet. Finger depressions clearly visible in the metal.

(no dialogue)

Pic 3;
Pull back: Paul stands by the sink, drinking down a large glass of water. White shirt, white trousers. Room filled with light.

(no dialogue)

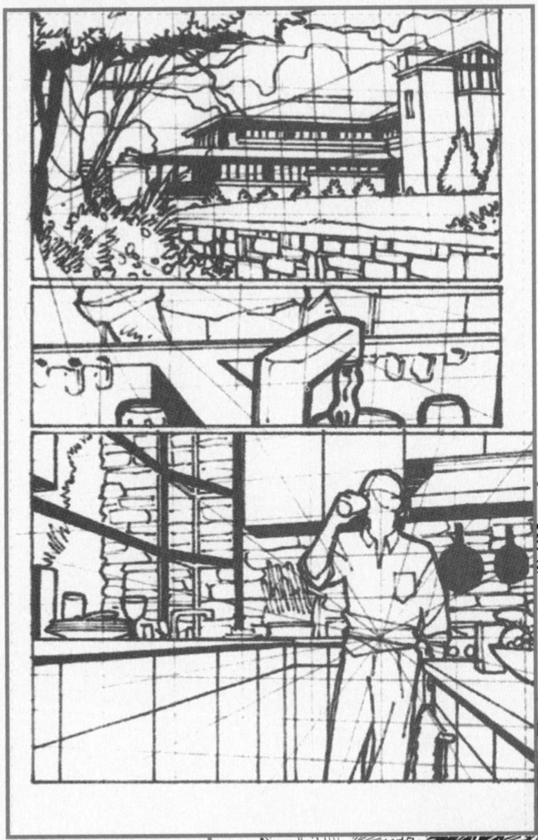

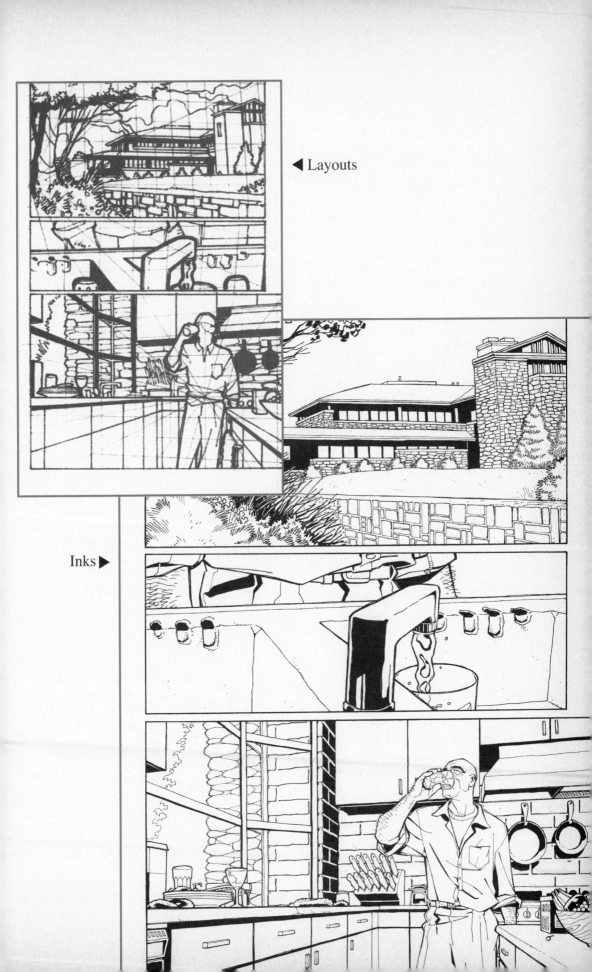

◀ Layouts

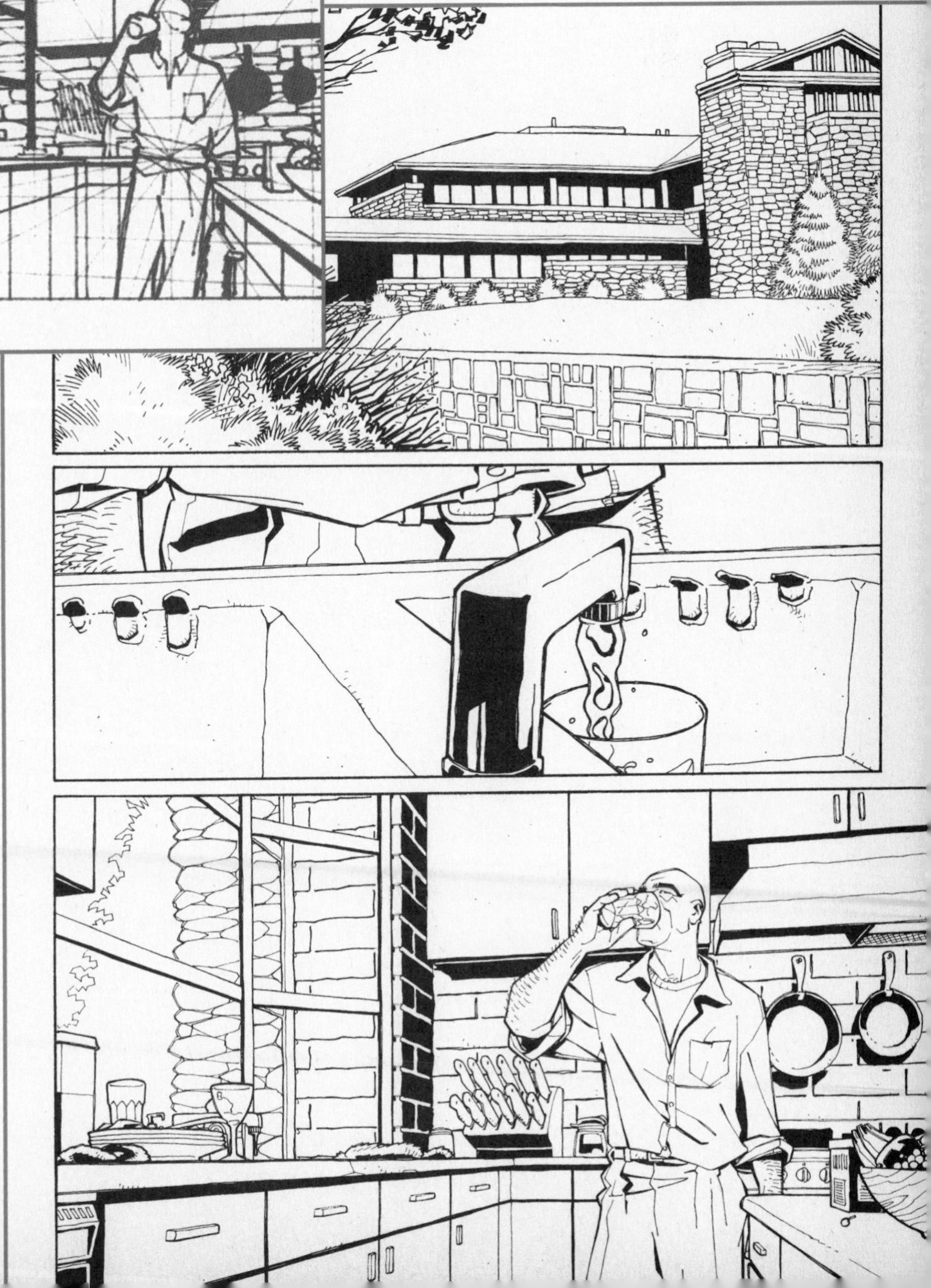

Inks ▶

Pic 1;
Later, with coffee, he sits in a comfortable old chair by a table with a phone and a lamp on. He's dialling. There's an opened letter by the phone, and an index card.

Pic 2;
The call goes through, and he sips at his coffee. In the foreground, though, we look at the INDEX CARD. It has two numbers on it. CASE OFFICER (SALLY) – 555-919-8845 HOME – 555-999-0000.

FROM PHONE:	OPERATOR. STATUS, PLEASE.
PAUL:	GREEN.
FROM PHONE:	INACTIVE OFFICER STATUS CONFIRMED. CONNECTING YOUR CALL NOW, MR MOSES.

Pic 3;
Paul grins as a familiar voice comes on the line.

FROM PHONE:	GOOD MORNING, PAUL.
PAUL:	HELLO, SALLY. HOW'S LIFE AT LANGLEY?

Pic 4;
CUT TO: SALLY JANSSEN, in her office. Shabby government office, a few lonely pot plants, rain batting at her window. Sally is a Nordic blonde, beautiful, strong and pale. A sadly cheerful woman – genuinely nice, but in a life that does nothing for her.

SALLY:	I KEEP TELLING YOU, RETIREMENT HANDLING ISN'T AT LANGLEY, PAUL…
FROM PHONE:	I KNOW, I KNOW. OLD HABIT. YOU KNOW WHAT I MEAN. HOW'S IT GOING?
SALLY:	IT'S GOING DULL. I SHOULD'VE HAD A JOB AT THE AGENCY LIKE YOURS. YOU SAW THE WORLD, I SEE A POT PLANT I CAN'T KEEP ALIVE.

Pic 5;
Paul smiles over his coffee.

PAUL:	THE DATING'S GOING WELL, THEN?

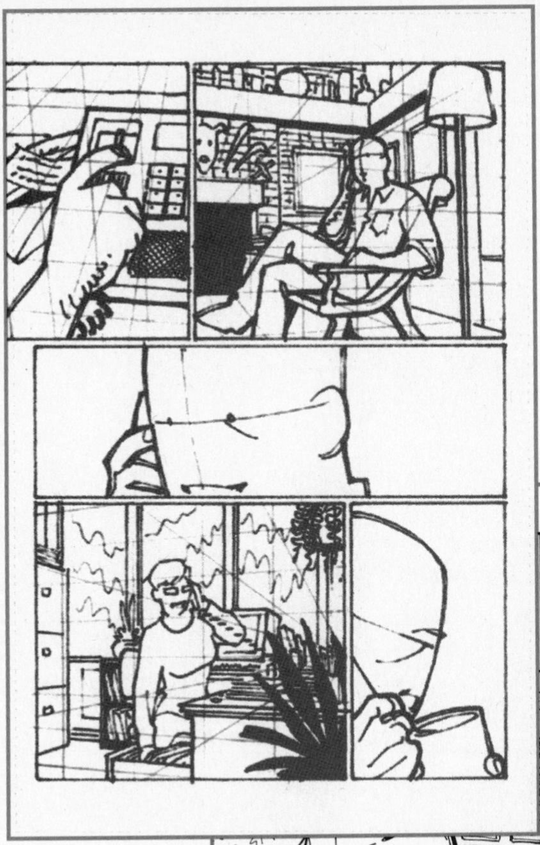

◀ Layouts

Inks ▶

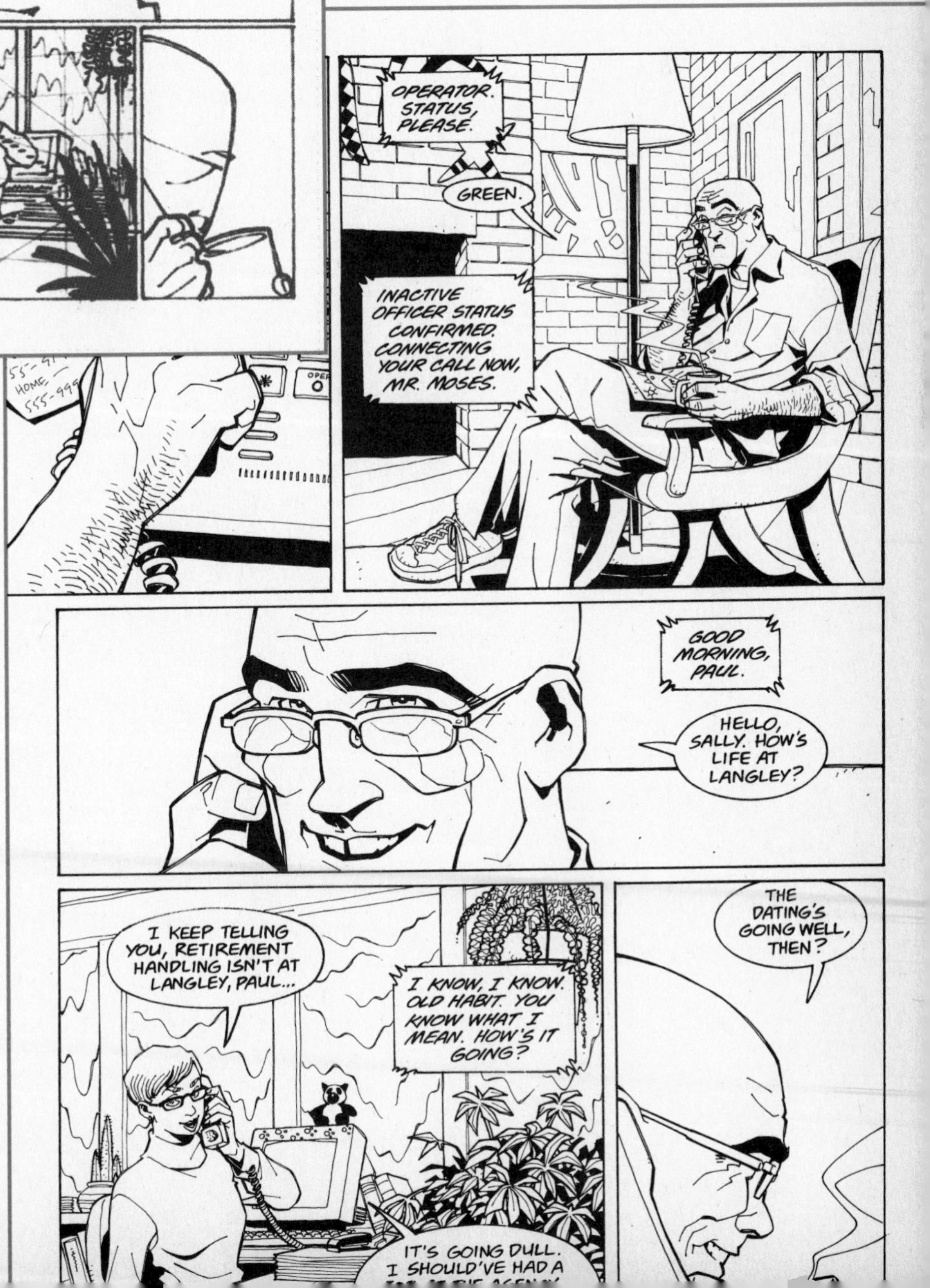
OPERATOR. STATUS, PLEASE.
GREEN.
INACTIVE OFFICER STATUS CONFIRMED. CONNECTING YOUR CALL NOW, MR. MOSES.
GOOD MORNING, PAUL.
HELLO, SALLY. HOW'S LIFE AT LANGLEY?
I KEEP TELLING YOU, RETIREMENT HANDLING ISN'T AT LANGLEY, PAUL...
I KNOW, I KNOW. OLD HABIT. YOU KNOW WHAT I MEAN. HOW'S IT GOING?
THE DATING'S GOING WELL, THEN?
IT'S GOING DULL. I SHOULD'VE HAD A

PAGE ELEVEN

Pic 1;
Sally smiles ruefully, pulling a worksheet and a pen…

SALLY: OH, HA HA. LET'S MOVE ON TO THE OFFICIAL STUFF BEFORE I START CRYING.

FROM PHONE: EVERYTHING'S FINE…

SALLY: PENSION PAYMENT CLEARED? NO UTILITIES OUTSTANDING? FINANCES STRAIGHT? HEARD FROM YOUR CUTE LITTLE NIECE?

Pic 2;
Paul picks up the letter, smiles at it as he talks.

PAUL: GOT THIS WEEK'S LETTER THIS MORNING. SHE JUST HAD HER FIRST GYMKHANA. SHE DID A DRAWING OF HER HORSE.

FROM PHONE: WHAT PART OF ENGLAND ARE THEY IN AGAIN?

PAUL: NORFOLK, THE EAST COAST. IT'S PRETTY THERE.

Pic 3;
Sally settles her head on her chin, faintly wistful.

SALLY: HOW COME YOU NEVER HAD KIDS?

PAUL: NEVER HAD THE TIME. THE AGENCY HAD ME SHOOTING ALL OVER THE WORLD FOR DECADES.

SALLY: FOREIGN ACQUISITIONS, RIGHT? SEEING THE WORLD, BUYING STUFF. TOUGH LIFE.

Pic 4;
She looks up, waves - someone off-panel is demanding her attention.

SALLY: THAT'S THE KIND OF AGENCY JOB I WANTED. NOT KEEPING AN OFFICE WARM, AND NOT GETTING SHOT AT OR SOMETHING--JUST SEEING THE WORLD…

PAUL: THE WORLD ISN'T ALL IT'S MADE OUT TO BE, SALLY--

SALLY: EXCUSE ME, PAUL, I GOTTA GO, SOMEONE'S MOUTHING THE WORD "URGENT MEETING" AT ME AND WAVING THEIR HANDS A LOT…

Pic 5;
Paul smiles sadly. He likes her, likes the connection.

PAUL: OKAY…YES, NEXT WEEK, WE CAN TALK MORE THEN.

PAUL: BYE.

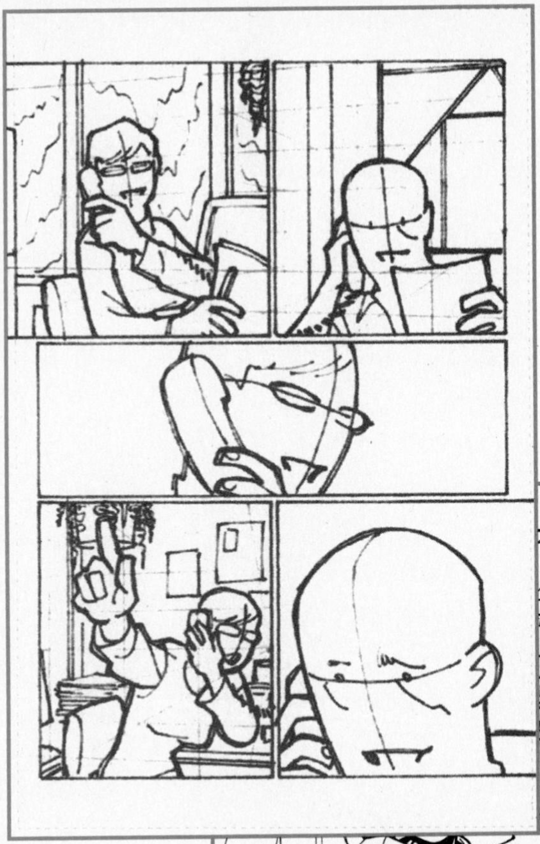

◀ Layouts

Inks ▶

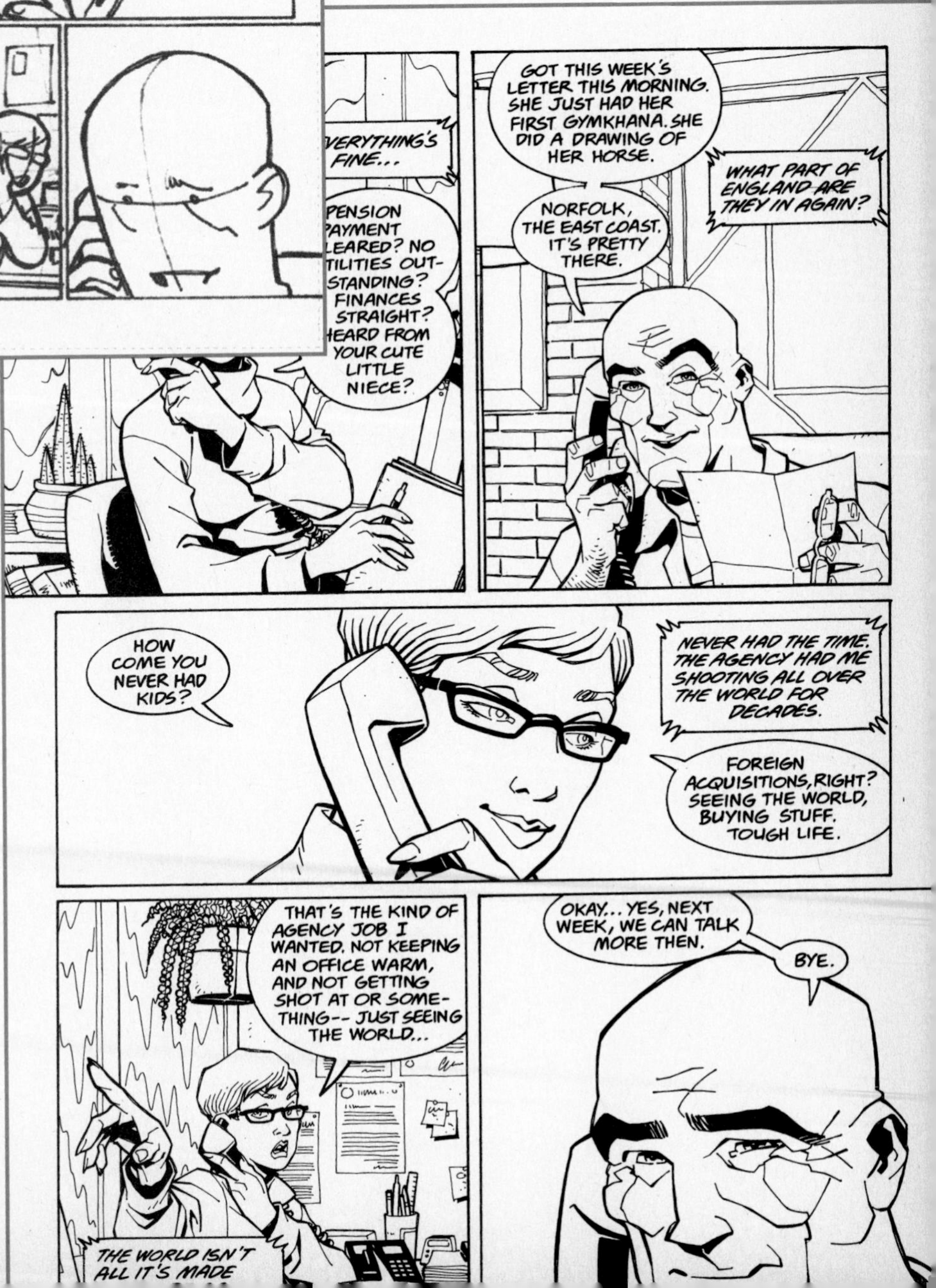
VERYTHING'S FINE...
PENSION PAYMENT LEARED? NO TILITIES OUT-STANDING? FINANCES STRAIGHT? HEARD FROM YOUR CUTE LITTLE NIECE?
GOT THIS WEEK'S LETTER THIS MORNING. SHE JUST HAD HER FIRST GYMKHANA. SHE DID A DRAWING OF HER HORSE.
WHAT PART OF ENGLAND ARE THEY IN AGAIN?
NORFOLK, THE EAST COAST. IT'S PRETTY THERE.
HOW COME YOU NEVER HAD KIDS?
NEVER HAD THE TIME. THE AGENCY HAD ME SHOOTING ALL OVER THE WORLD FOR DECADES.
FOREIGN ACQUISITIONS, RIGHT? SEEING THE WORLD, BUYING STUFF. TOUGH LIFE.
THAT'S THE KIND OF AGENCY JOB I WANTED. NOT KEEPING AN OFFICE WARM, AND NOT GETTING SHOT AT OR SOME-THING-- JUST SEEING THE WORLD...
THE WORLD ISN'T ALL IT'S MADE
OKAY... YES, NEXT WEEK, WE CAN TALK MORE THEN.
BYE.

PAGE TWELVE

Pic 1;
CUT TO: Paul in a chair in his garden, a drink by his side, reading a book in the peaceful warmth.

(no dialogue)

Pic 2:
CUT TO: Paul walking away from his house, wearing a hat to keep the sun off… just a contented stroll in the late afternoon…

(no dialogue)

Pic 3;
CUT TO; Paul returning to the front door of his house, key in hand. The sun's almost down, the sky is angry colours, shadows are thick and dark…

(no dialogue)

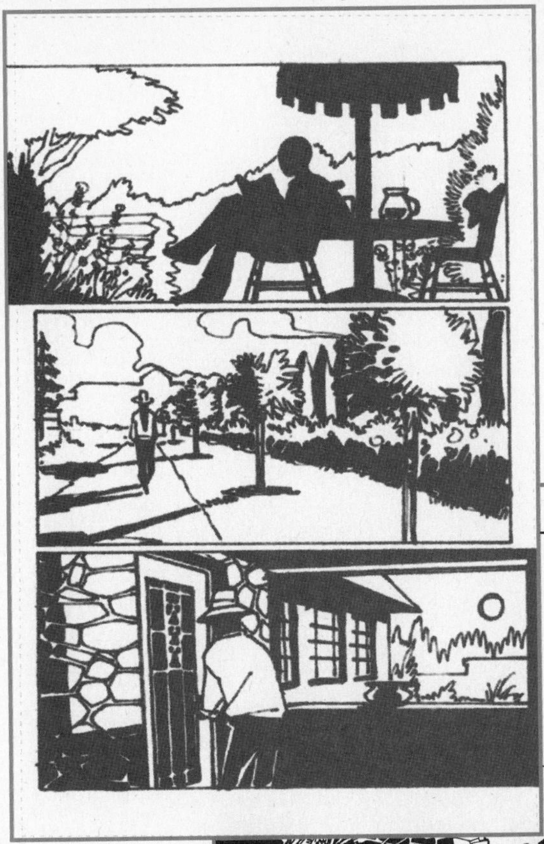

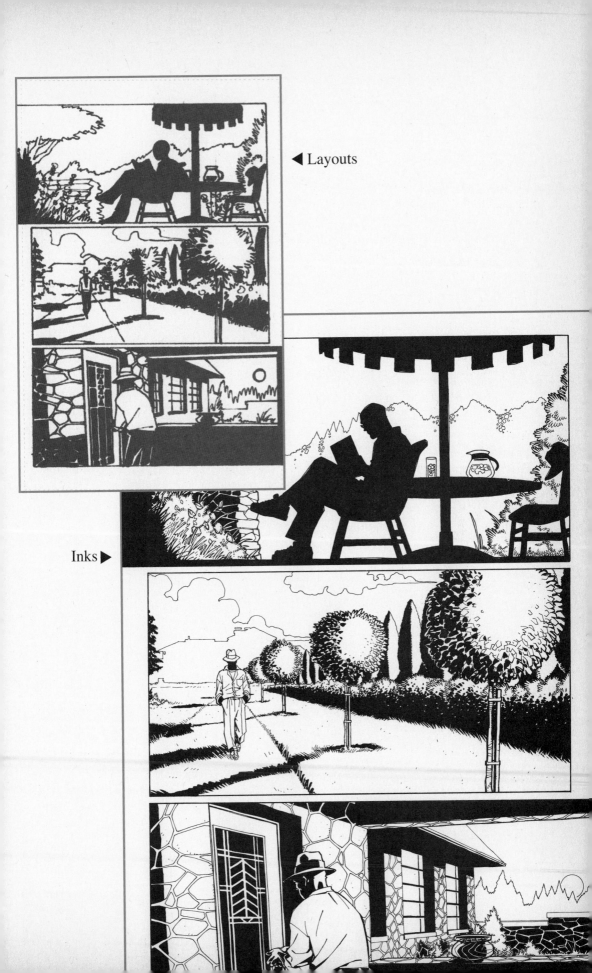

◀ Layouts

Inks ▶

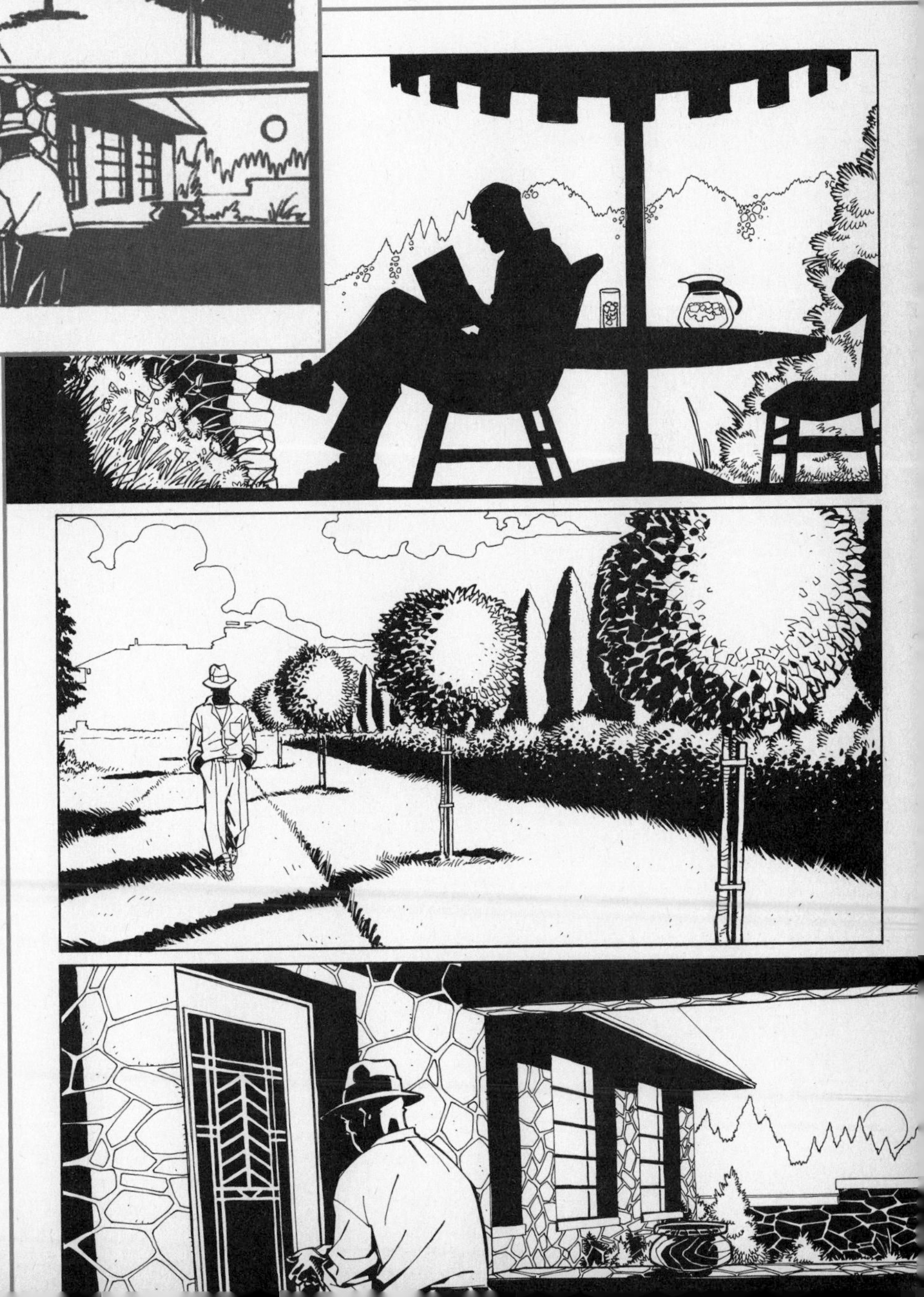

PAGE THIRTEEN

Pic 1;
From the hallway: The house is dark, as Paul pushes the front door open.

(no dialogue)

Pic 2;
He steps indoors, flicks the light switch on the wall.

(no dialogue)

Pic 3;
And nothing happens.

(no dialogue)

Pic 4;
Paul pauses. In the low light, his eyes glitter sharply.

(no dialogue)

Pic 5;
And then frowns, takes a couple of steps forward, past the entrance to the living room…

PAUL: DAMN LIGHTBULBS.

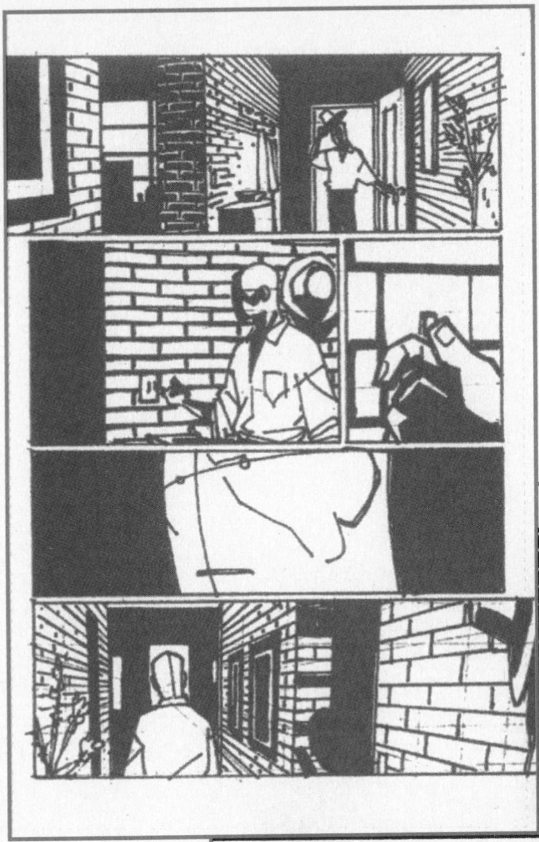

◀ Layouts

Inks ▶

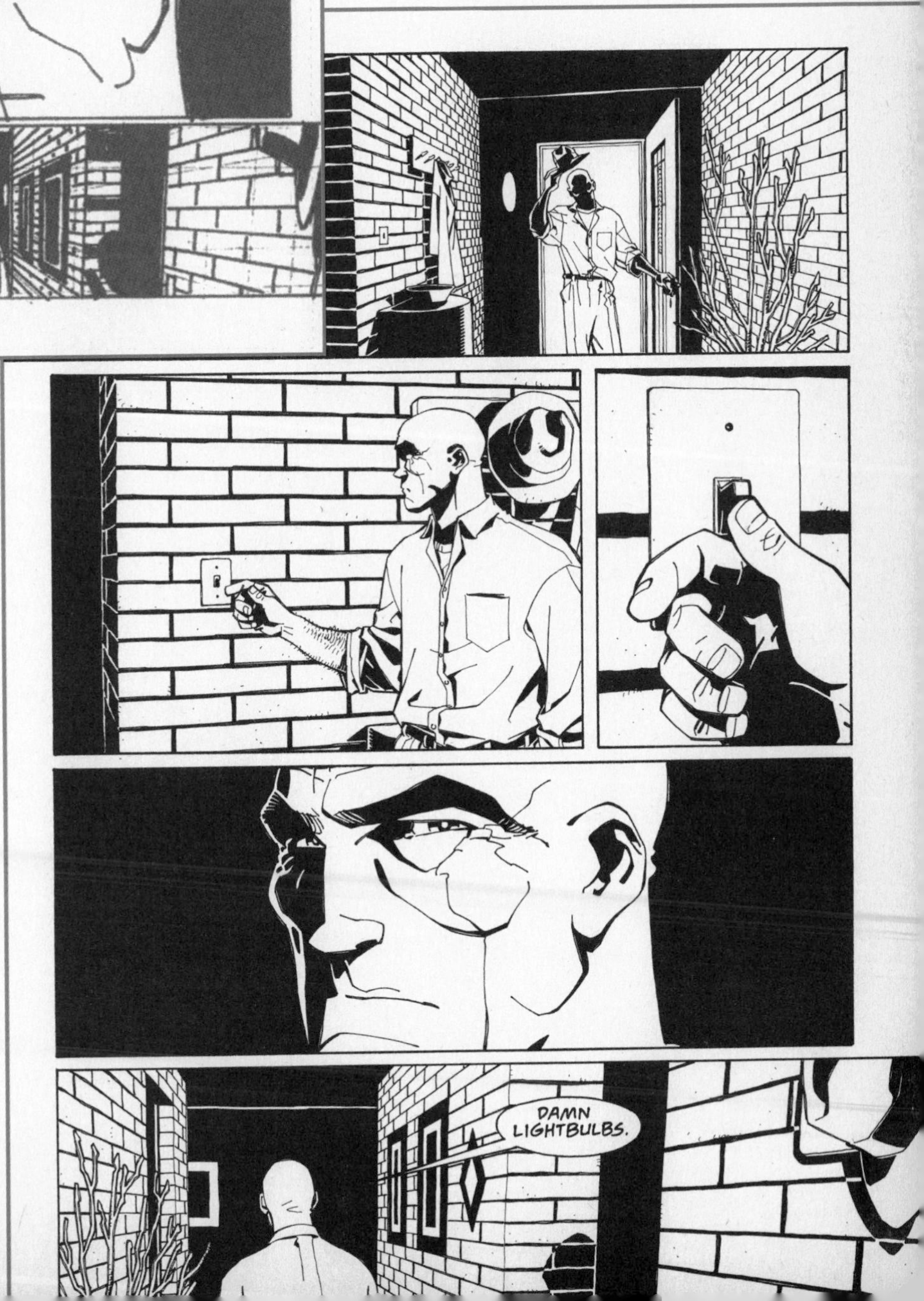
DAMN LIGHTBULBS.

PAGE FOURTEEN

Pic 1;
…and a man in black, inclusive of black gloves and a black hood,
steps from the living room into the entrance, a silenced gun in his
hand. Paul has just stepped past him, probably can't see him,
certainly couldn't react before the man in black pulls his trigger.

PAUL: GOT TO GET AN ELECTRICIAN IN HERE, CHECK
                               OUT THE

Pic 2;
And Paul's hand jabs back and to the side, first two fingers spread
and tensed in a V thrust forward --

PAUL: WIRING

Pic 3;
-- bursting the man's eyes.

(no dialogue)

Pic 4;
Paul rips the gun out of the man's hand.

MAN IN BLACK: EEEEEEEEEEE

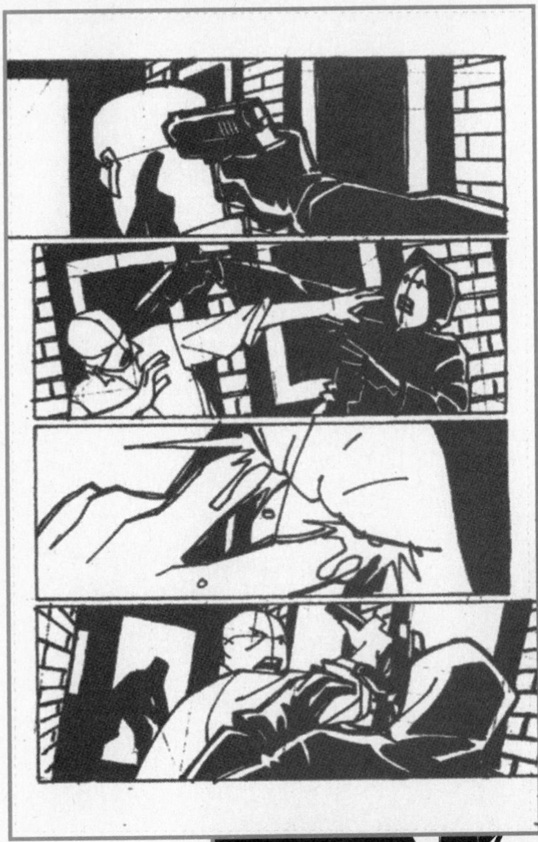

◀ Layouts

Inks ▶

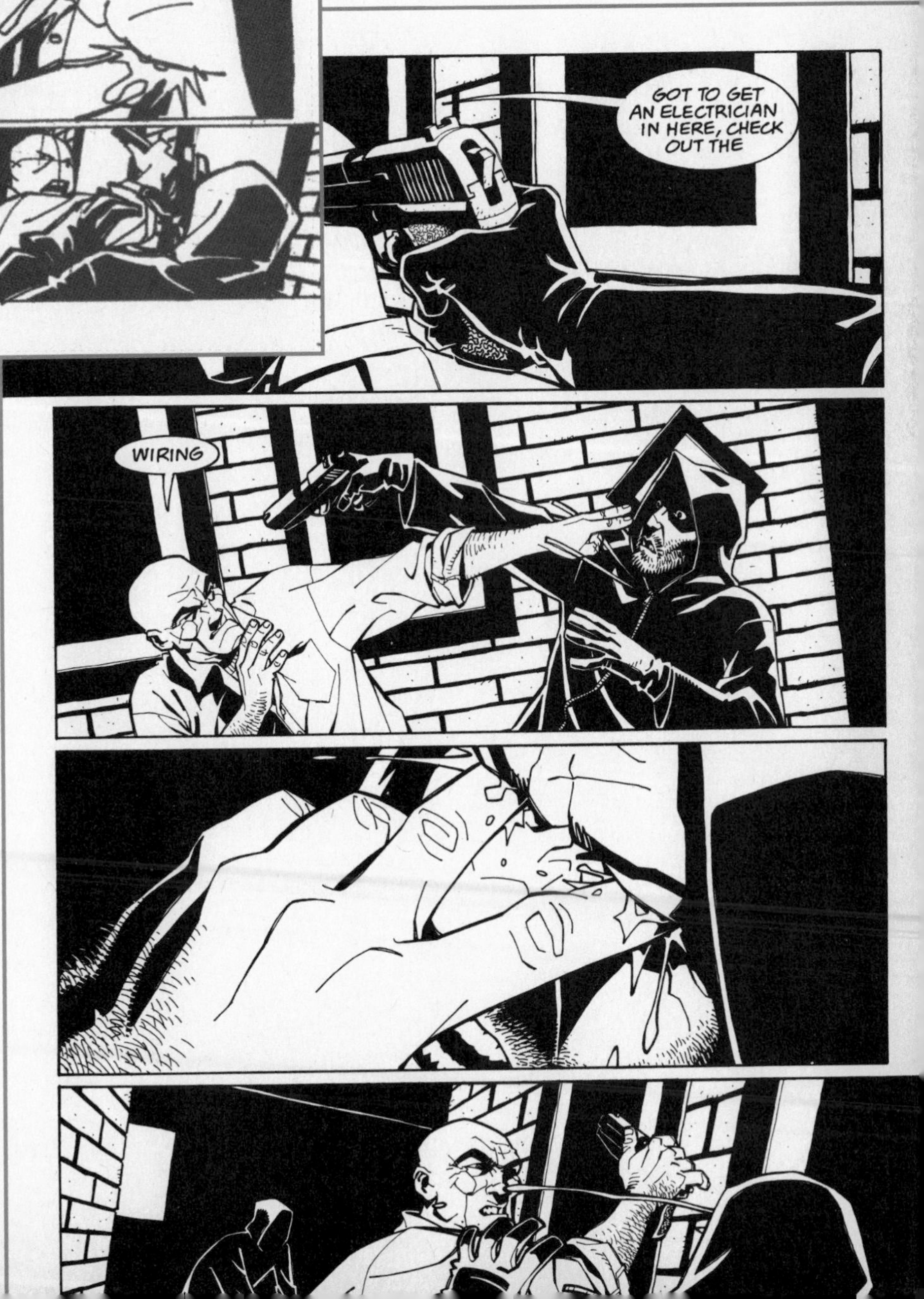
GOT TO GET AN ELECTRICIAN IN HERE, CHECK OUT THE
WIRING

PAGE FIFTEEN

Pic 1;
Down the corridor, probably emerging from the kitchen, a SECOND MAN in black appears, armed.

MAN IN BLACK (off):   EEEEEEEEEEE

Pic 2;
Paul's guy is doubled over, clutching at his exploded eyes. Paul grabs the top of his hood, holding his head steady. Paul is a professional, and his moves are economical and assured.

MAN IN BLACK: EEEEEEEEEEE

Pic 3;
And fires the gun twice into the base of the man's skull at pointblank range, two shells jerking out of the breech, bullets making bloody arcs in the air as they exit his face and rush towards the floor.

(no dialogue)

Pic 4;
The second man is moving down the corridor.

(no dialogue)

Pic 5;
Paul shoves his dead assailant out into the hallway as he himself moves into the lounge, shouting --

PAUL: NO, PLEASE--

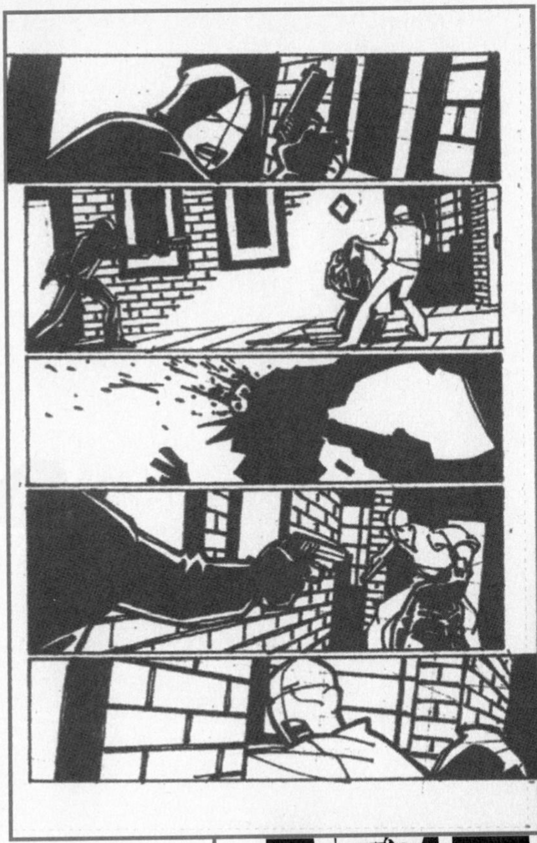

◀ Layouts

Inks ▶

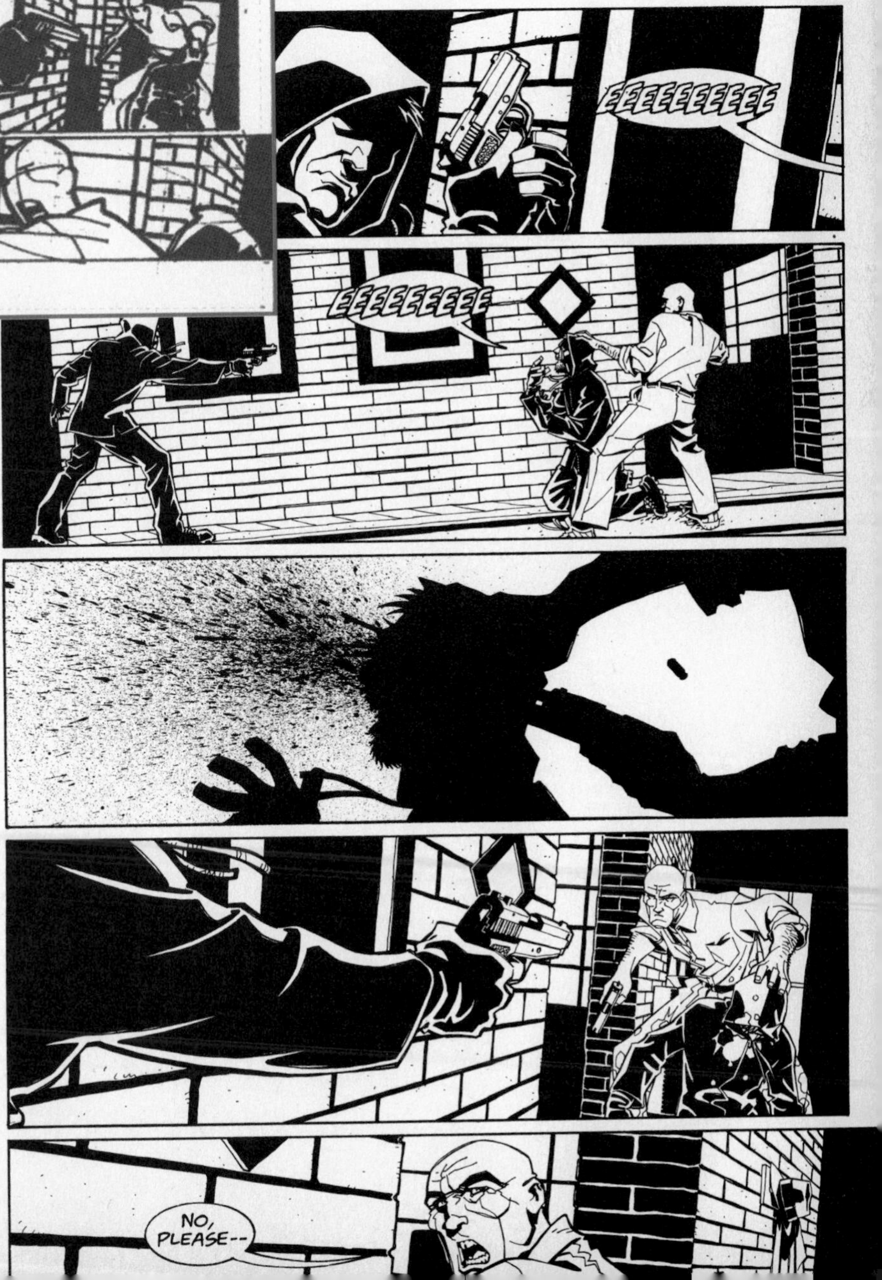
EEEEEEEEEE
EEEEEEEEE
NO, PLEASE--

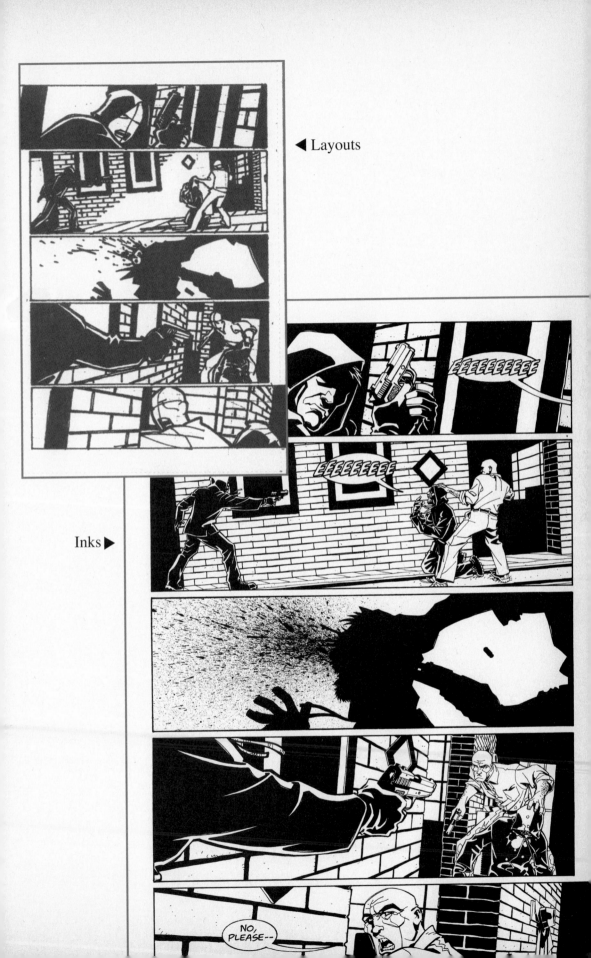

PAGE SIXTEEN

Pic 1;
The second man fires at the low-moving silhouette in front of him diving from the living room into the hallway.

(no dialogue)

Pic 2;
Bullets impact in the dead man's side.

(no dialogue)

Pic 3;
And Paul whips around the corner to fire twice.

(no dialogue)

Pic 4;
The second man in black has his gun pointing in the wrong direction, and squeezes off another shot even as Paul's two shots plough into the front of his brain.

(no dialogue)

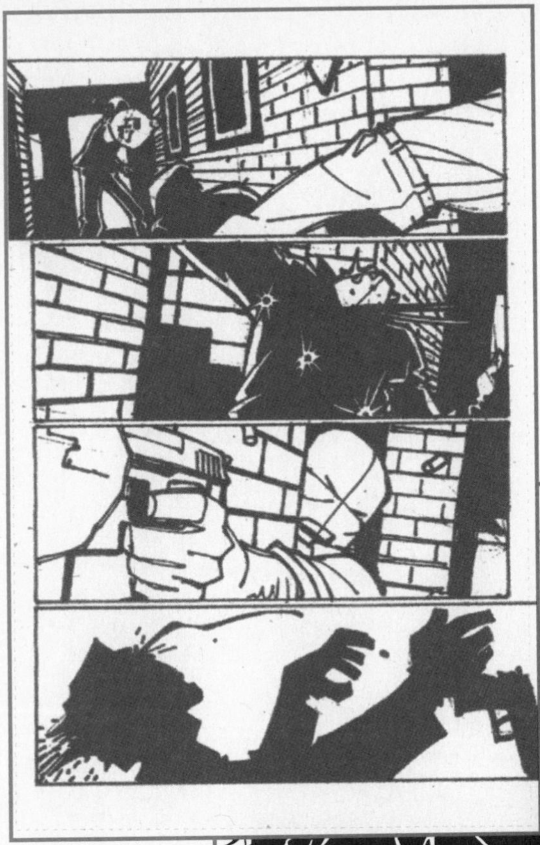

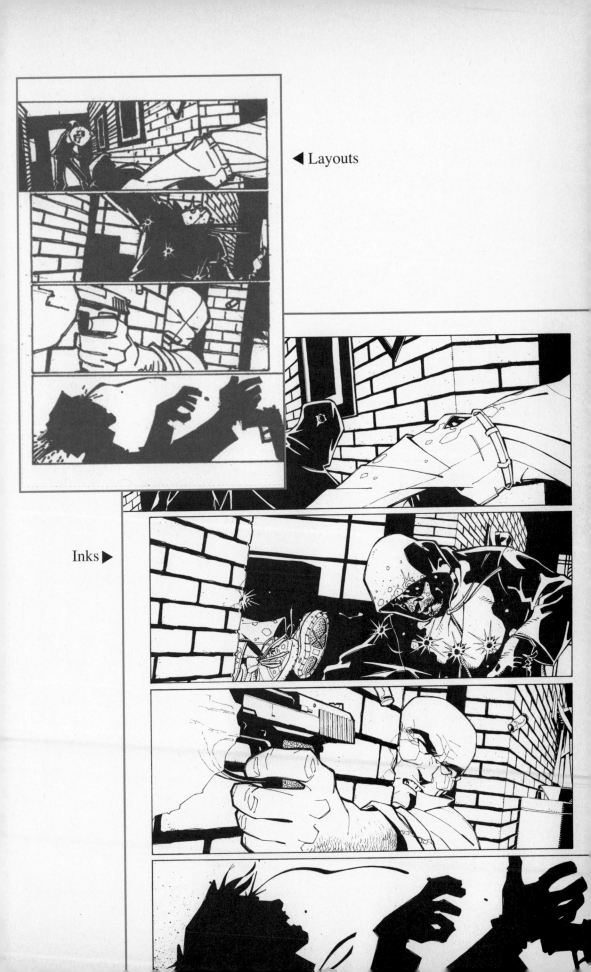

◀ Layouts

Inks ▶

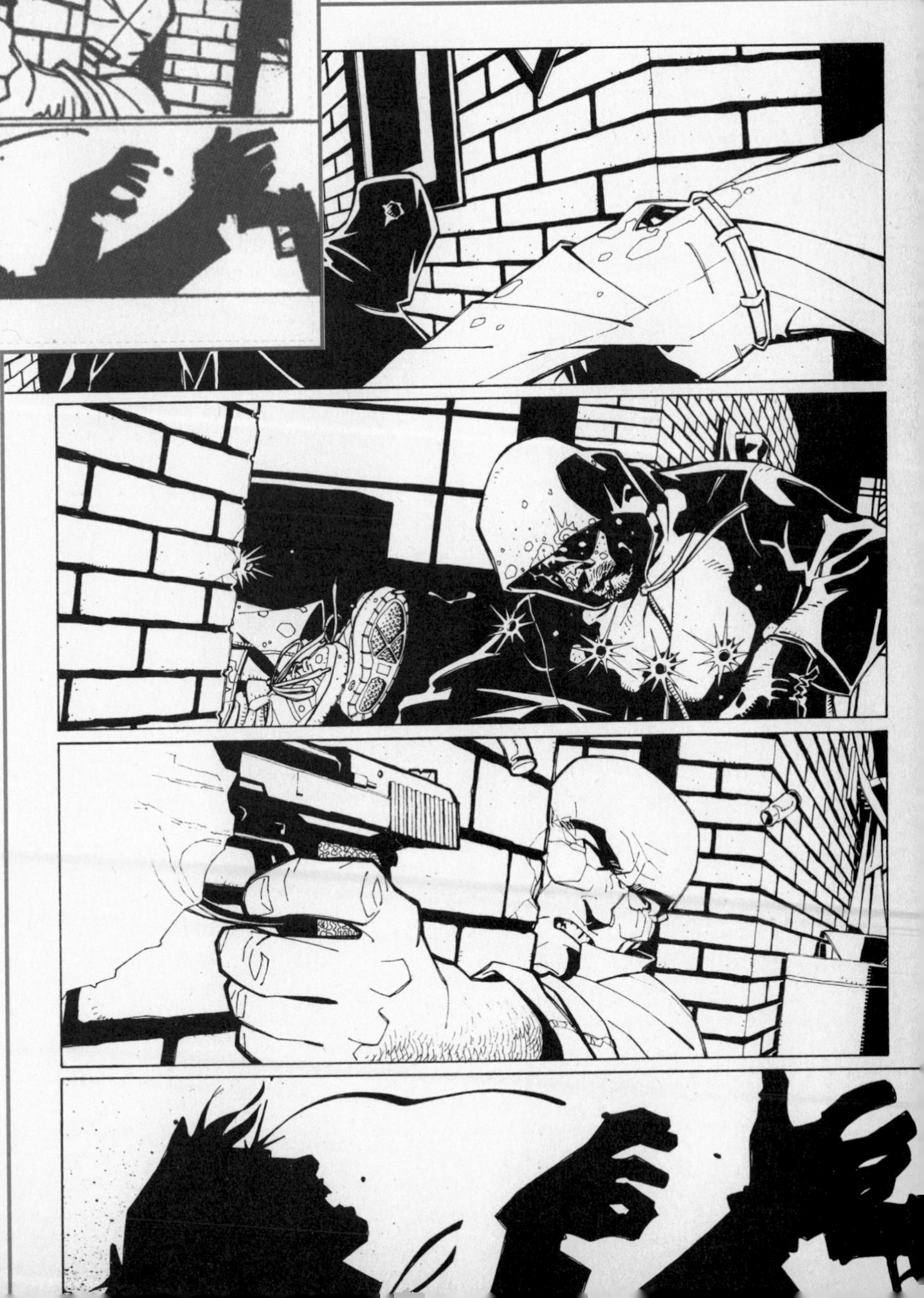

PAGE SEVENTEEN

Pic 1;
Paul squats and freezes. The two are dead, but he's still very tense.

(no dialogue)

Pic 2;
Against a window, in another part of the house; a black figure momentarily caught against the red sunset light suffusing the window.

(no dialogue)

Pic 3;
And we realise, in a wide pic, that he is behind Paul. And raising his gun.

(no dialogue)

Pic 4;
He squeezes his trigger.

(no dialogue)

Pic 5;
The gun begins to cycle.

(no dialogue)

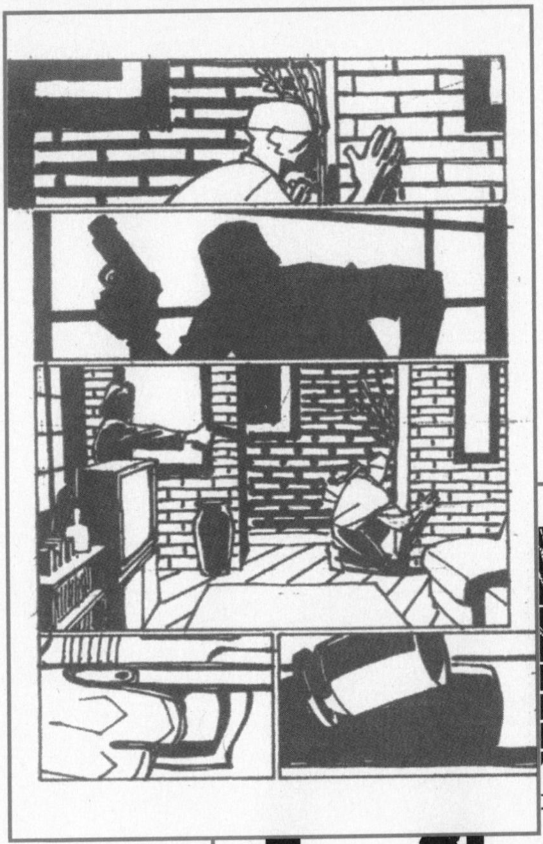

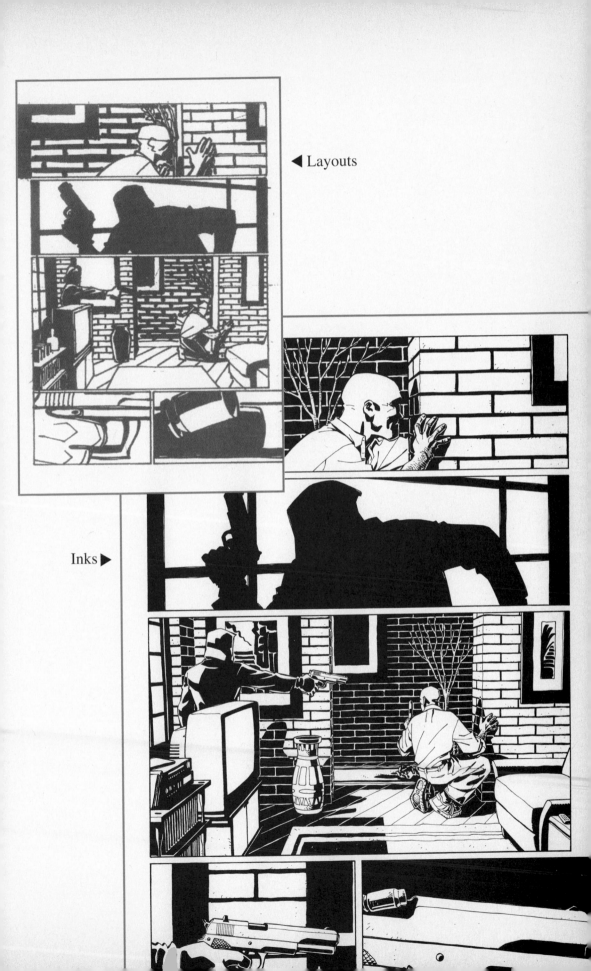

◀ Layouts

Inks ▶

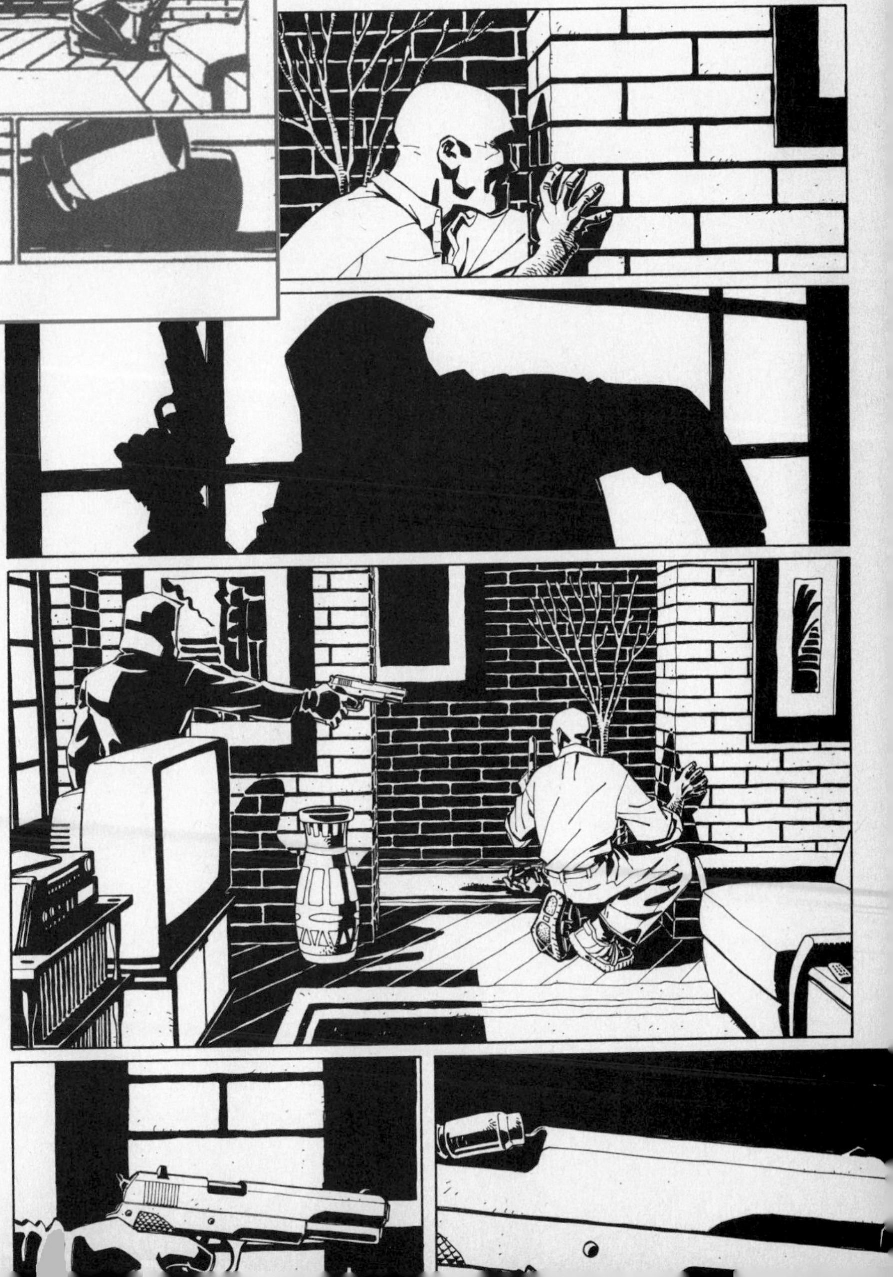

PAGE EIGHTEEN

Pic 1;
And Paul hears it. Side profile shot, centering on his ear.

(no dialogue)

Pic 2;
He flings himself to the side, towards the space behind an armchair,
squeezing off two shots wildly as he goes.

(no dialogue)

Pic 3;
The third man moves in, stood up straight and aiming his gun down
with both hands, scanning across laterally for the killshot.

(no dialogue)

Pic 4;
Two shots burst out of the armchair's back, from behind it, sparks
and stuffing flying from the exit points.

(no dialogue)

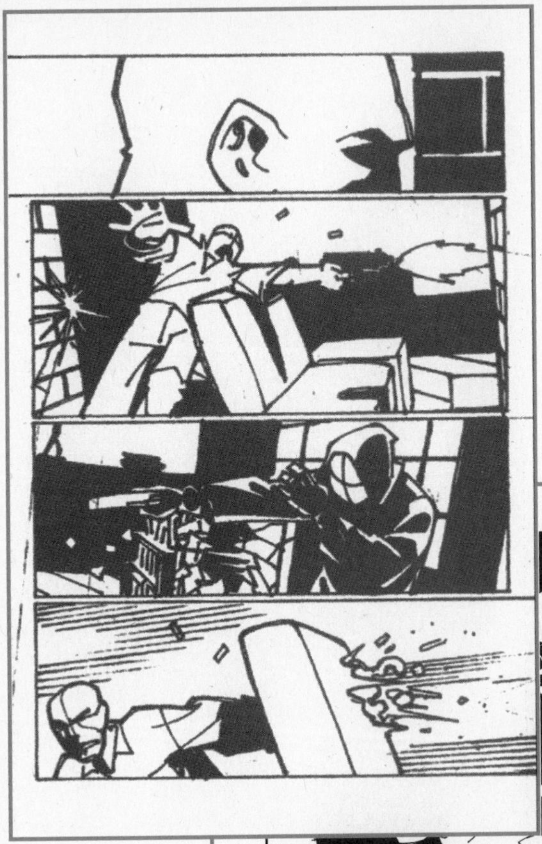

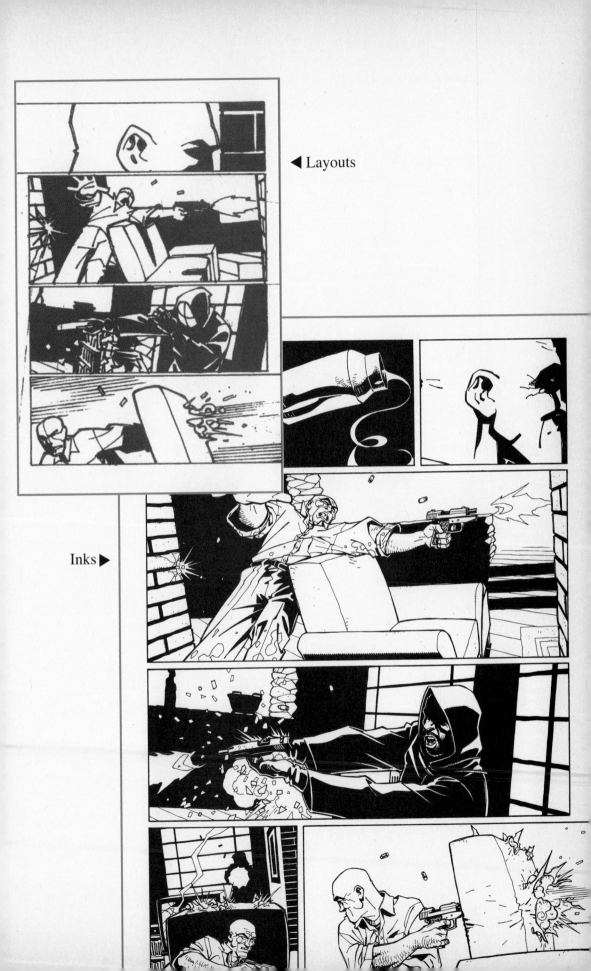

◀ Layouts

Inks ▶

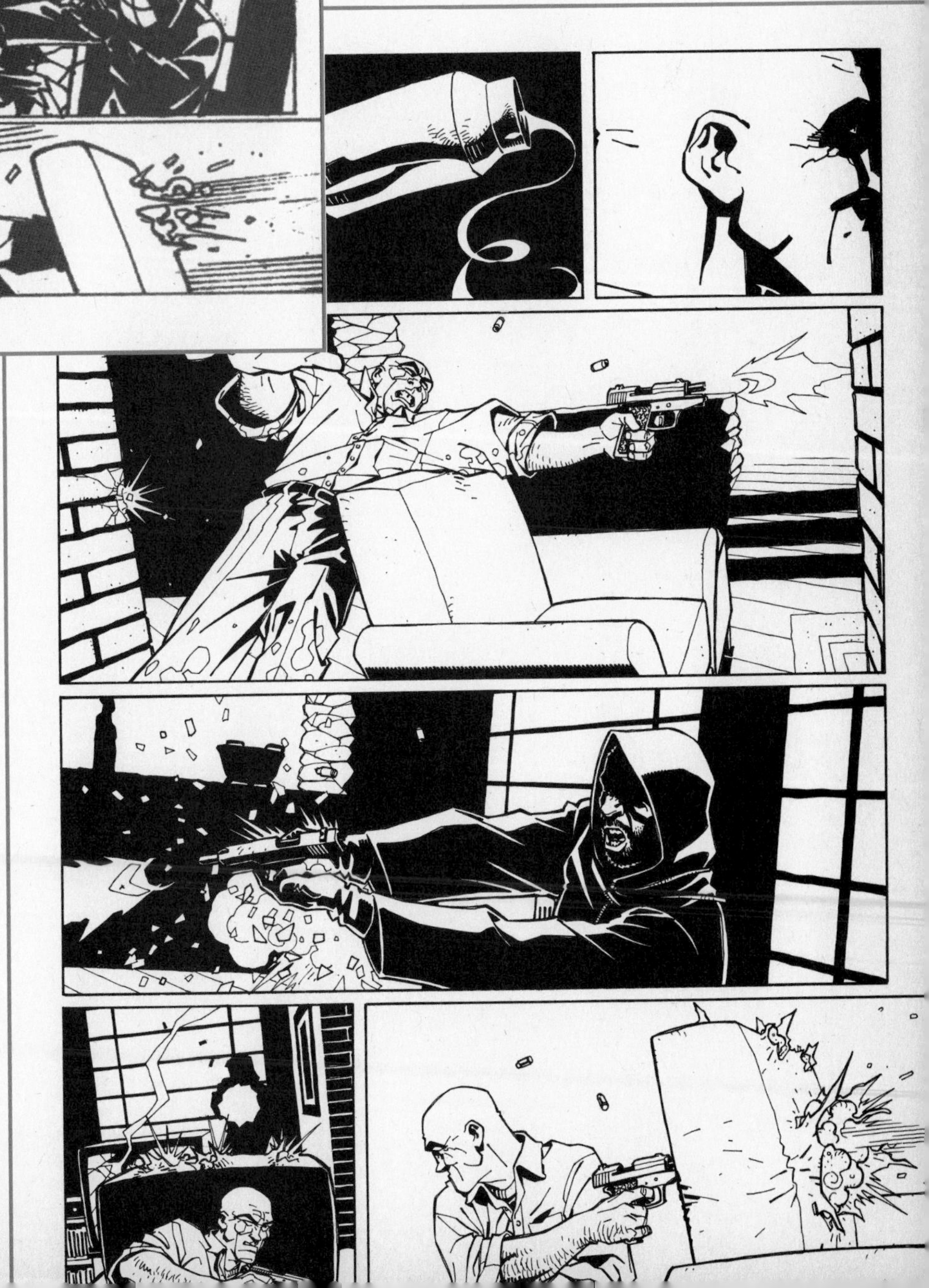

PAGE NINETEEN

Pic 1;
The two shots hit the third man in his gun hand and forearm – fabric and flesh rend, and bone gleaming in the twilight –

(no dialogue)

Pic 2;
The armchair lurches forward hard towards the gunman, tipping over –

(no dialogue)

Pic 3;
-- the top of the chair-back catching him hard across the chest and driving him down to the floor --

(no dialogue)

Pic 4;
-- where he lands on his back, the chair pinning him --

(no dialogue)

Pic 5;
-- and Paul Moses' gun is pressed between his eyes.

PAUL: LOUSY WEAPONS. THEY PULL TO THE RIGHT. MUST BE NEW.

PAUL: YOU'RE AGENCY. DO NOT TRY TO DENY IT.

PAUL: I WANT TO KNOW WHY.

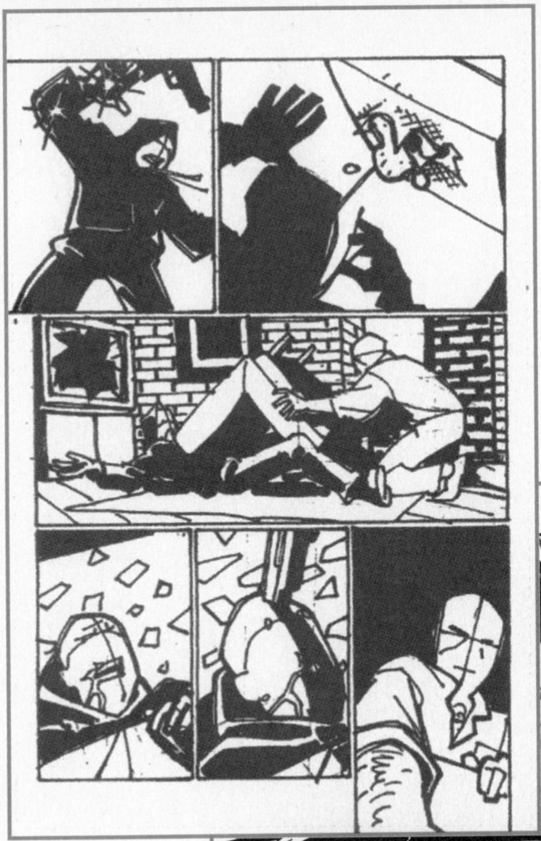

◀ Layouts

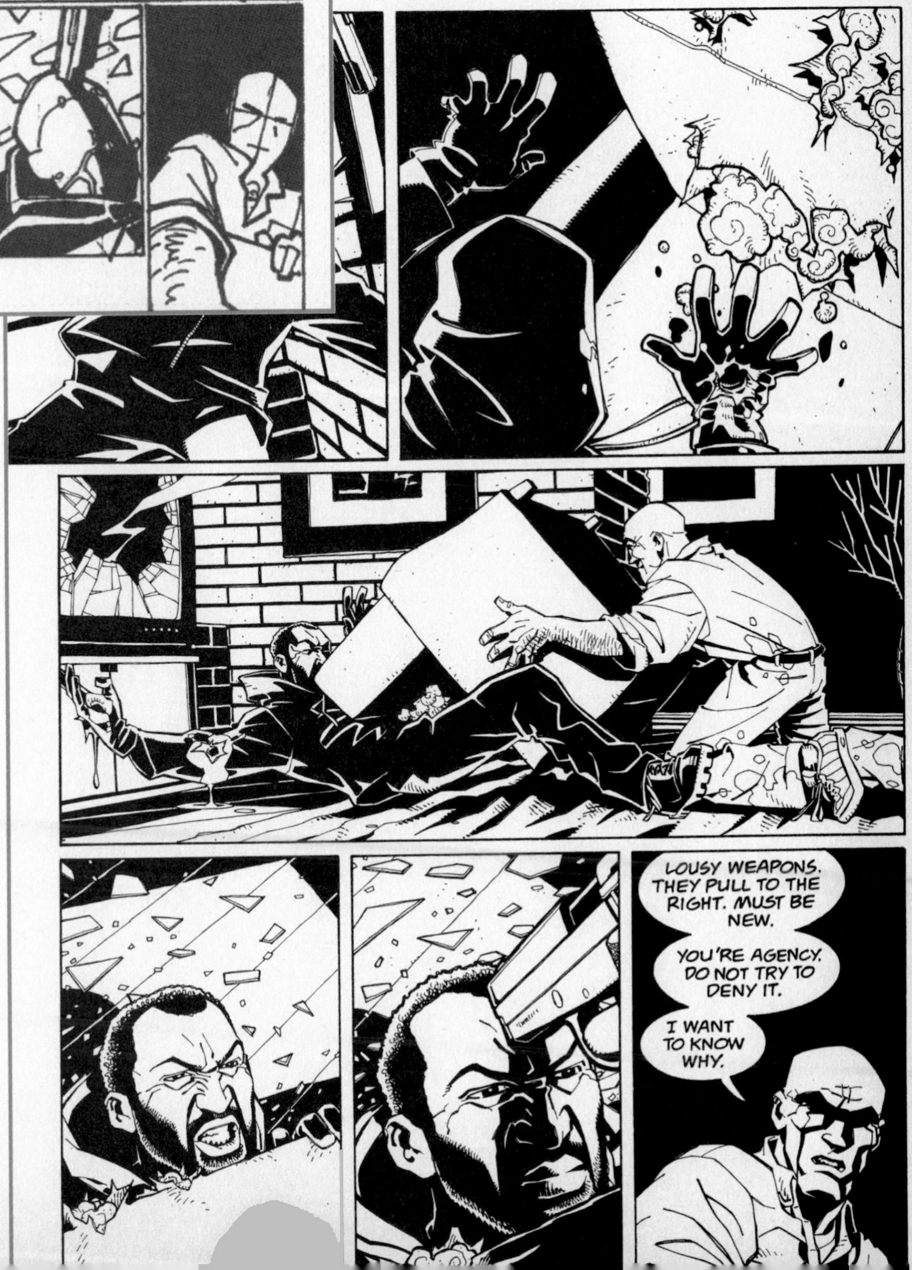
LOUSY WEAPONS. THEY PULL TO THE RIGHT. MUST BE NEW.
YOU'RE AGENCY. DO NOT TRY TO DENY IT.
I WANT TO KNOW WHY.

Inks ▶

PAGE TWENTY

Pic 1;
The man stares at the gun pointed at him.

(no dialogue)

Pic 2;
Moses studies him. Not angry. Professional.

MOSES: THREE-MAN KILL TEAM. BRAND NEW WEAPONS WITH NO IDENTIFICATION. SIGNATURE SILENCER.

MOSES: I KNOW AGENCY ATTACK PATTERNING LIKE NO MAN ALIVE. DENYING IT IS WORSE THAN USELESS.

MOSES: I AM RETIRED AND SILENT. I WANT TO KNOW WHY YOU'RE HERE.

Pic 3;
The gunman just closes his eyes.

(no dialogue)

Pic 4;
Moses shoots him in the brain.

(no dialogue)

Pic 5;
He gets up, walking straight to his phone.

(no dialogue)

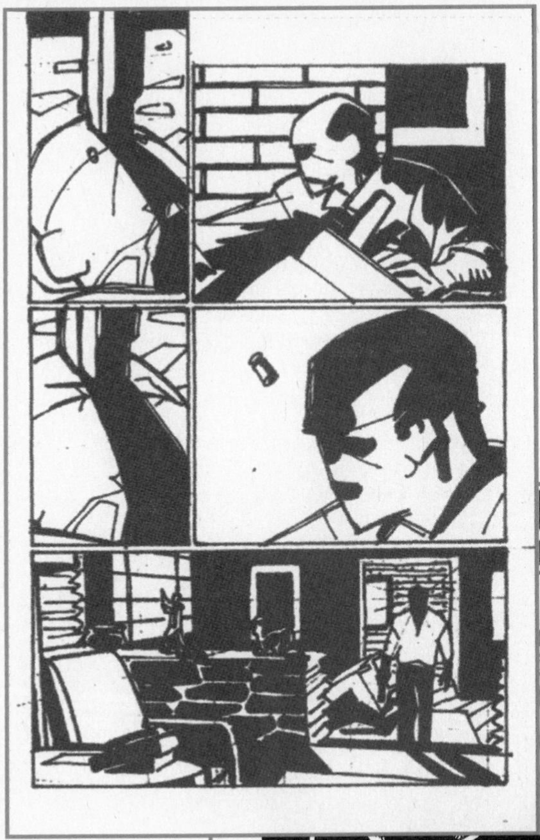

◀ Layouts

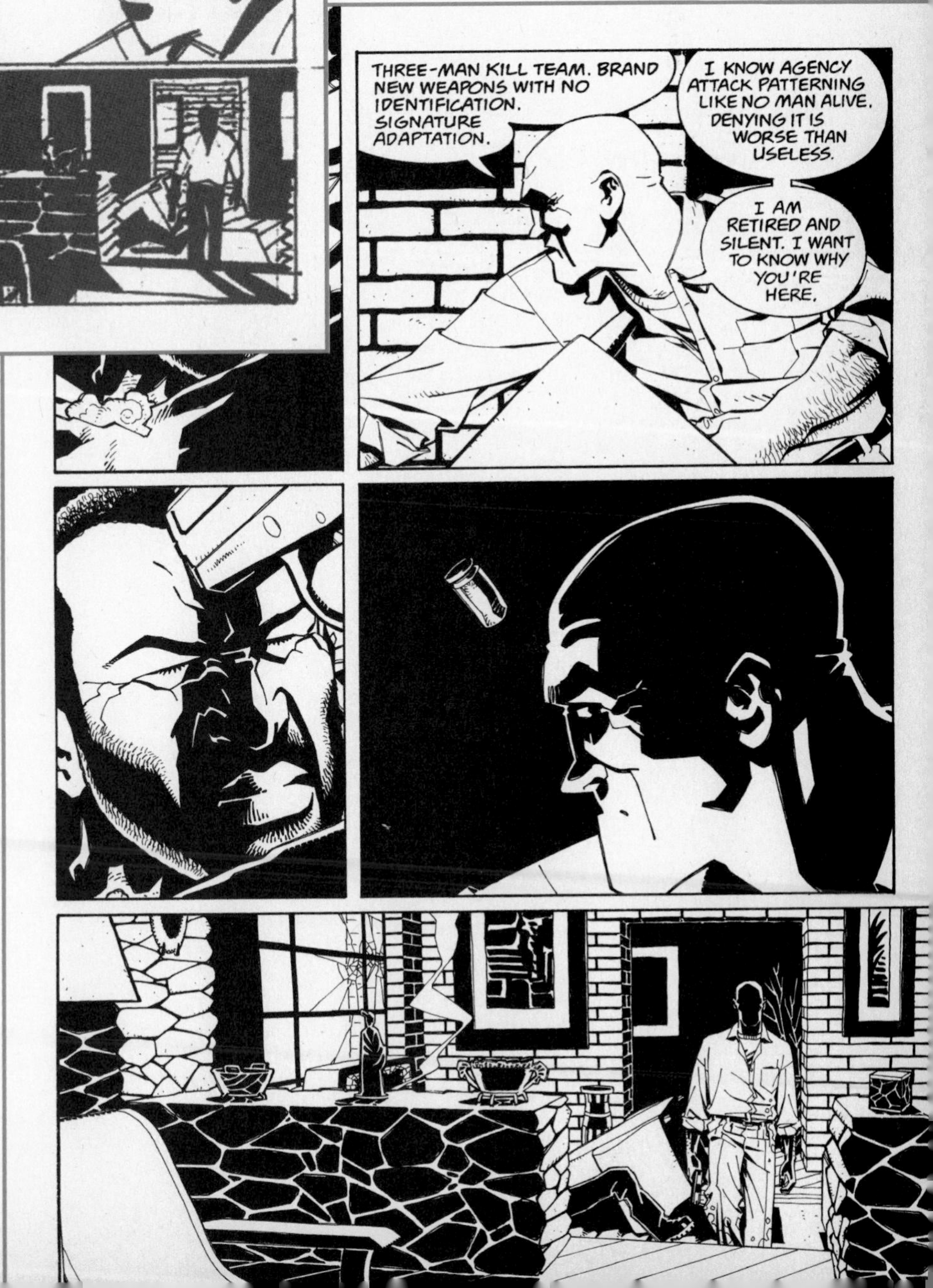
THREE-MAN KILL TEAM. BRAND NEW WEAPONS WITH NO IDENTIFICATION. SIGNATURE ADAPTATION.
I KNOW AGENCY ATTACK PATTERNING LIKE NO MAN ALIVE. DENYING IT IS WORSE THAN USELESS.
I AM RETIRED AND SILENT. I WANT TO KNOW WHY YOU'RE HERE.

Inks ▶

PAGE TWENTY-ONE

Pic 1;
Switching the lamp on, he dials. Gun on the table.

FROM PHONE: OPERATOR. STATUS, PLEASE.

PAUL: GREEN, BUT I'M REPORTING AN EMERGENCY SITUATION. I NEED MY CASE HANDLER IMMEDIATELY.

Pic 2:
Paul looks up towards us; freezes.

FROM PHONE: YOUR HANDLER HAS BEEN TRANSFERRED.

FROM PHONE: PLEASE STAY AT YOUR LOCATION AND AWAIT FURTHER INSTRUCTION.

Pic 3;
He hangs up. And picks up the gun again.

(no dialogue)

Pic 4;
CUT TO: Paul opening a cellar door, pulling a lightswitch.

(no dialogue)

Pic 5;
Lighting up a cellar full of guns, bombs, gasoline cans, knives…

(no dialogue)

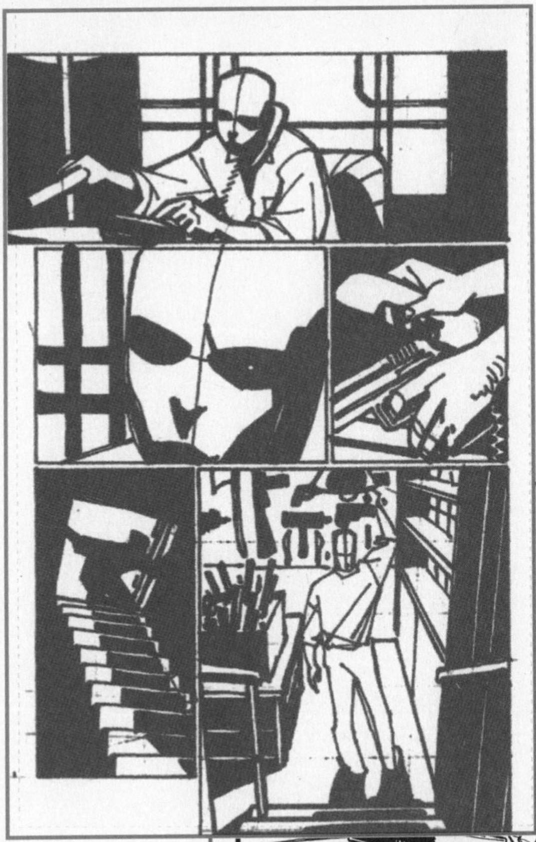

◀ Layouts

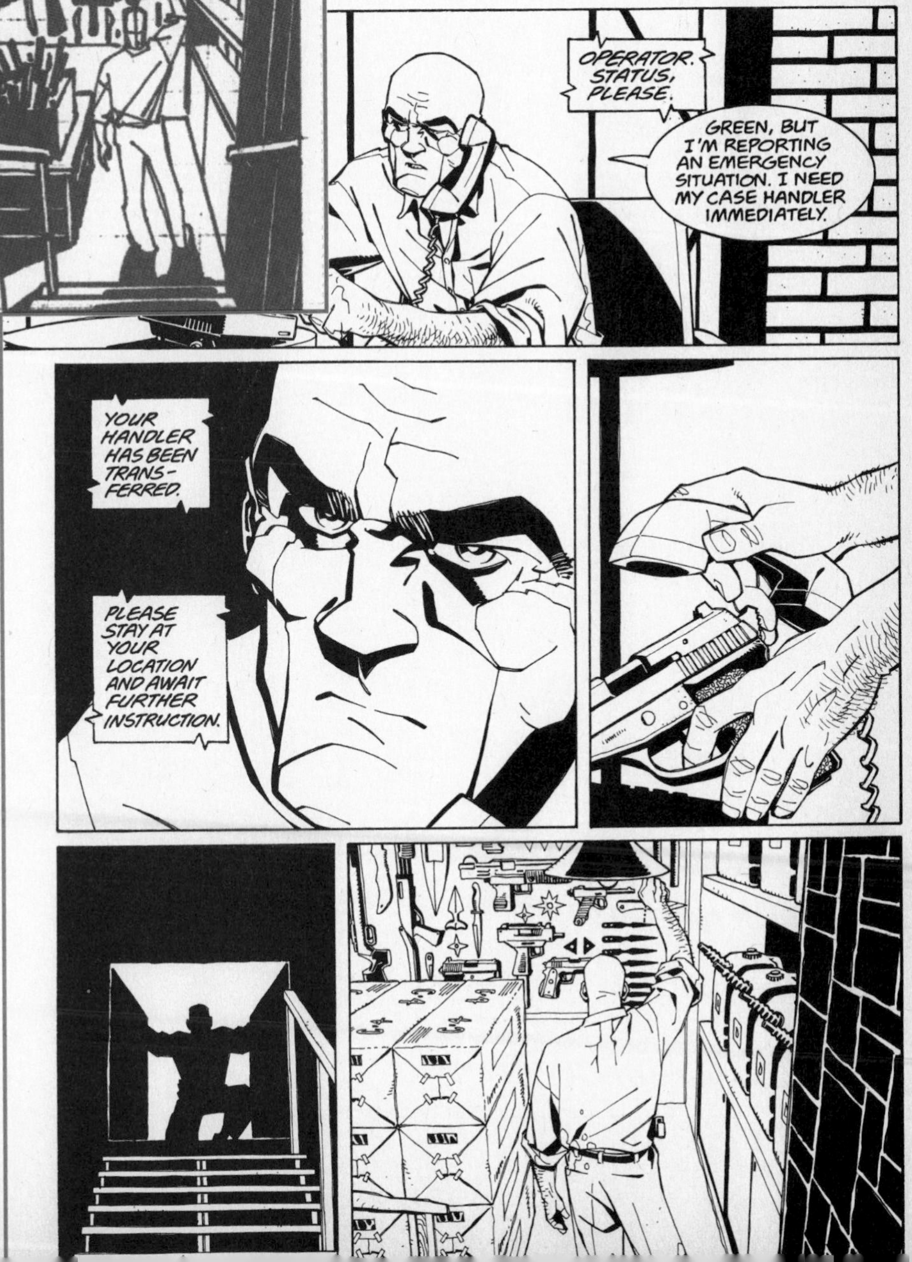
OPERATOR. STATUS, PLEASE.
GREEN, BUT I'M REPORTING AN EMERGENCY SITUATION. I NEED MY CASE HANDLER IMMEDIATELY.
YOUR HANDLER HAS BEEN TRANS-FERRED.
PLEASE STAY AT YOUR LOCATION AND AWAIT FURTHER INSTRUCTION.

Inks ▶

PAGE TWENTY TWO

Pic 1;
CUT TO: Paul's finger resting lightly on the second number on his index card under lamplight.

FROM PHONE (OFF):   CENTRAL OPERATOR. STATUS, PLEASE.

Pic 2;
Reveal; Paul in a black jacket, a black bag slung over his shoulder, speaking carefully into the phone, eyes like ice:

PAUL: THIS IS PAUL MOSES.

PAUL: RED.

Pic 3;
CUT TO; the phone dangling down.

FROM PHONE: STAND BY WHILE I BRING UP YOUR FILE…

FROM PHONE: OH. OH GOD.

FROM PHONE: **HELLO**? ARE YOU THERE? OH GOD, OH CHRIST…

Pic 4;
CUT TO; Paul Moses as a silhouette walking away from us down a road, just as the last red embers of the setting sun die away…

(no dialogue)

to be continued

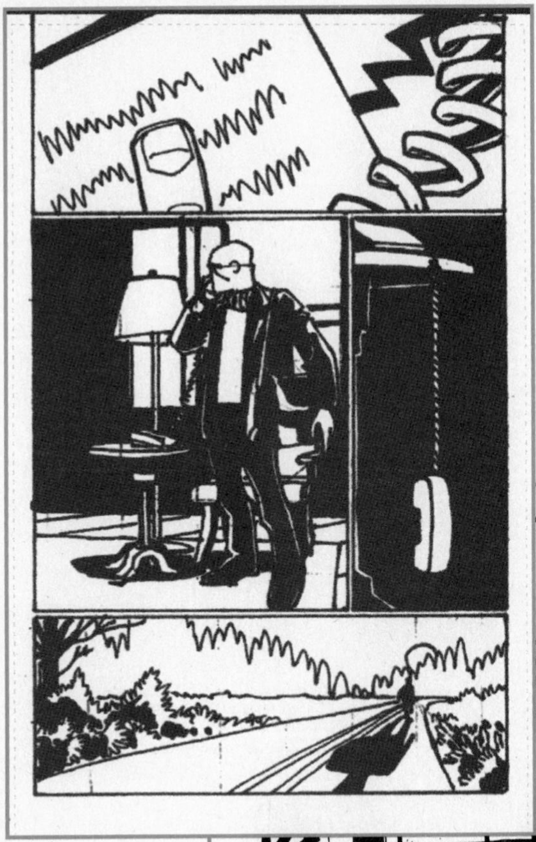

◀ Layouts

Inks ▶

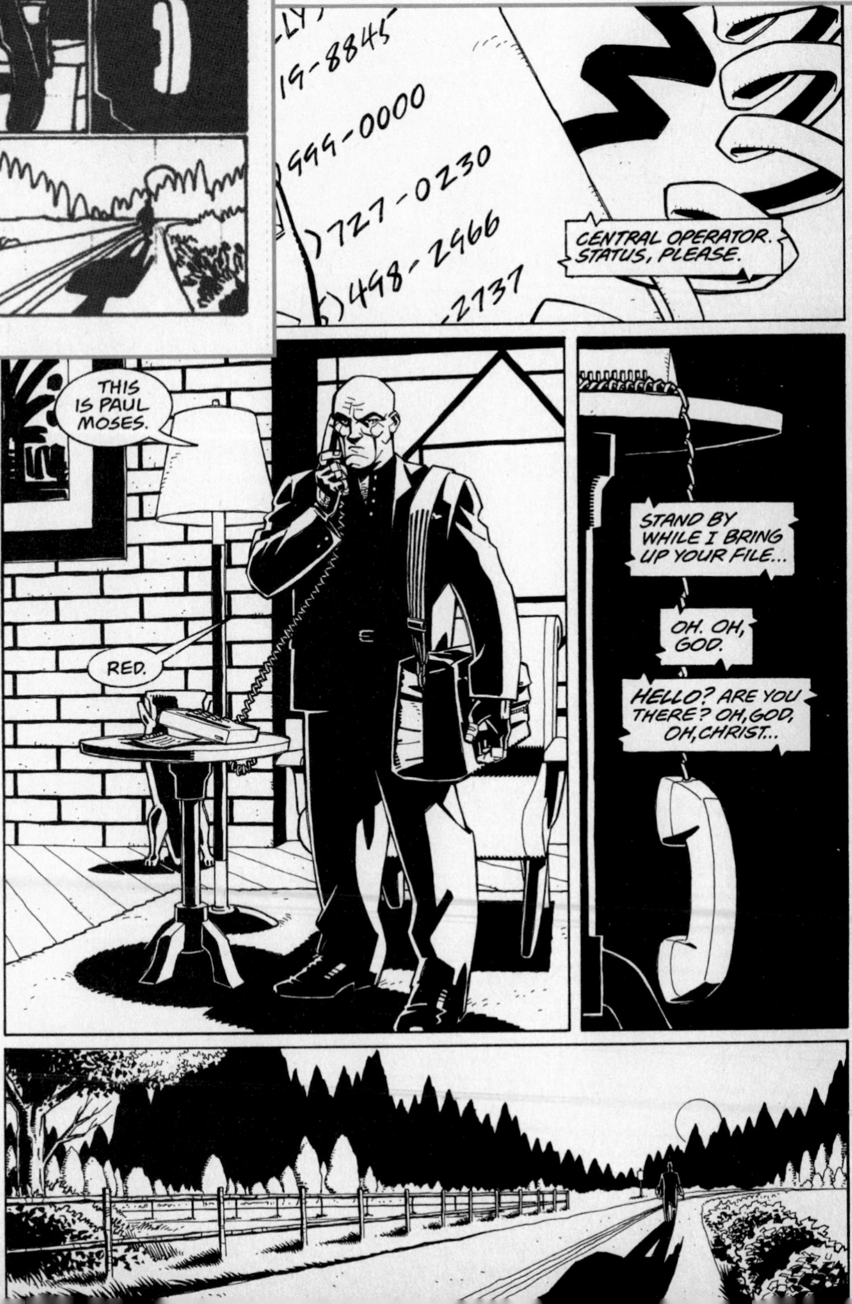
CENTRAL OPERATOR. STATUS, PLEASE.
THIS IS PAUL MOSES.
RED.
STAND BY WHILE I BRING UP YOUR FILE...
OH. OH, GOD.
HELLO? ARE YOU THERE? OH, GOD, OH, CHRIST...

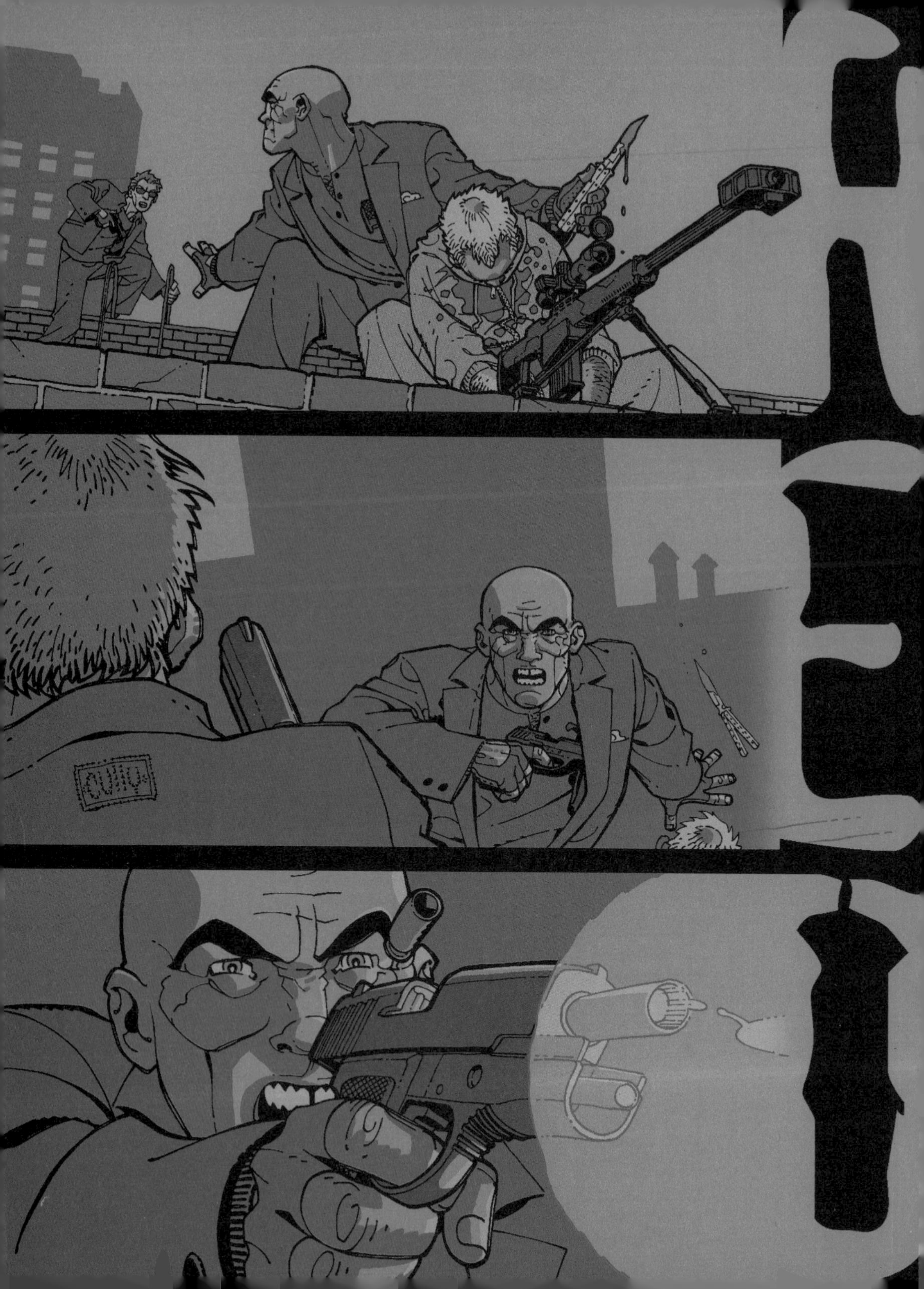